Haunted by Combat

HAUNTED BY COMBAT

UNDERSTANDING PTSD IN WAR
VETERANS INCLUDING WOMEN,
RESERVISTS, AND THOSE COMING
BACK FROM IRAQ

Daryl S. Paulson and Stanley Krippner

Introduction by Jeffrey Kirkwood

PRAEGER SECURITY INTERNATIONAL
Westport, Connecticut • London

Library of Congress Cataloging-in-Publication Data is available at www.loc.gov

British Library Cataloguing in Publication Data is available.

ISBN-13: 978–0–275–99187–6
ISBN-10: 0–275–99187–3

First published in 2007

Praeger Security International, 88 Post Road West, Westport, CT 06881
An imprint of Greenwood Publishing Group, Inc.
www.praeger.com

Printed in the United States of America

The paper used in this book complies with the
Permanent Paper Standard issued by the National
Information Standards Organization (Z39.48–1984).

10 9 8 7 6 5 4 3 2 1

Daryl S. Paulson dedicates this book to Edward E. Shubat, his psychotherapist following his participation in the Vietnam War, and Tammy Anderson, for her unfailing service as his personal assistant.

Stanley Krippner dedicates this book to his cousin, the heroic Bataan nurse Marcia Lou Gates.

Both authors express their gratitude to the Chair for the Study of Consciousness, Saybrook Graduate School and Research Center, and the Leir Charitable Trusts for their support in the preparation of this book, to Tammy Anderson, Jeffrey Kirkwood, and Steve Hart for their editing services, and to Tom Greening and D. Michael Schmidt for their original poetry used throughout this book.

History is a nightmare from which I am trying to awake.

—James Joyce, *Ulysses*

Contents

Preface

Nearly every day spent writing this book was accompanied by a new report of U.S. casualties in Iraq. By the beginning of 2007, more U.S. combat troops had been killed in Operation Iraqi Freedom than had died in the September 11 attacks on both the World Trade Center and the Pentagon. Ten times that many U.S. military personnel had either died or been incapacitated by combat wounds, accidents, injuries, or illnesses (Munk, 2007). Floundering support for the war with no apparent end goal and popular scrutiny of its increasing economic and human toll recalled the uncomfortable memory of the Vietnam War and its taxing effect on a generation of soldiers and citizens (Hiro, 2007).

Certainly, the political and social backdrop for any war has profound consequences for its legacy in collective memory, the homecoming of its soldiers, and the otherwise very personal experience of combat. Yet this book does not have political aspirations, nor should it be read with the expectation of better understanding war as a political, social, or conceptual phenomenon. Rather, our focus is on the postcombat experiences of veterans from their own perceptions, especially those suffering from what is often labeled "post-traumatic stress disorder" (PTSD). We were not hesitant about including our own perspectives along with the subjective experiences of combat veterans we have interviewed or known over the years, and for this reason it is a very personal book.

Wartime accounts by members of the armed forces have become ever more immediate and available through access to Weblogs (commonly referred to as "blogs") as well as multimedia sites. Books such as this, unlike Weblogs and online video sites, are final once published and, therefore, serve a different purpose than online resources. What this book can do, however, is lay a foundation to facilitate a deeper and more complete understanding of PTSD among combat veterans.

STANLEY KRIPPNER'S STORY

Before proceeding, we should explain our interest in the lived experience of combat. Because we use terms such as "we" and "us" to relate our interviews, comments, and conclusions, it is important to describe what motivated us to write this book.

Stanley Krippner recalls:

I grew up during the Second World War. After the Japanese attack on Pearl Harbor, my family was extremely concerned with the safety of my second cousin, Marcia Lou Gates, who was serving as a member of the Army Nurse Corps in the Philippines (Norman, 1999). After the Japanese invasion, Marcia was sent to a hospital in the Melinta Tunnel in Corregidor, where she and her fellow nurses were taken prisoner in May 1942. They were sent to the Santo Tomas Internment Camp in Manila where Marcia continued to care for the ill, doing her best with limited supplies and few medications, and, toward the end of the war, subsisting on a diet of rice mush and pigweed. After the Philippines were liberated, Marcia returned to the United States where she received the Bronze Star and a Presidential Citation.

However, Marcia was never quite the same. The prewar joy and flamboyance that were so characteristic of her personality seemed to have faded. She kept speaking of her search for "Mr. Right" and for "a bluebird of happiness," as she kept working in Wisconsin as a staff member of the Janesville Health Department. I last saw Marcia when she attended a lecture I gave in Janesville, and was touched when she gave me some Filipino souvenirs. Marcia died in 1970, and in retrospect I suspect that she never completely recovered from the horrors of her internment.

I also knew several combat veterans of both the European and Pacific theaters of World War II and, later (using the official U.S. governmental names), of the Korean Police Action, the Vietnam Conflict, and Operation Desert Storm (or the Gulf War). An acquaintance of mine was one of the 33,741 U.S. fatalities in the "police action" in Korea. As a teenager I knew several World War II veterans, one of them my scoutmaster, and what struck me was their reluctance to discuss their experiences in the line of fire, even though they probably sensed that I would have been a sympathetic and interested listener. Much later, I spoke about PTSD in Moscow at a 1981 USSR-USA health symposium and served as a consultant with two groups of Vietnam veterans, where the hot topic of discussion was not combat but the politics of that conflict. Later, I made three trips to Vietnam, visiting every war site and war museum I could find (where the "conflict" was referred to as "The American War"). Because half the population of that country had been born after the war ended, it was difficult to hear about the conflict from the official Vietnamese viewpoint.

However, I had greater success when interacting with refugees of the three dozen wars that were raging around the planet at the end of the twentieth century. I met several refugees as well as the therapists and relief workers who were attempting to assist them, most notably at the International Conferences on Conflict Resolution held in St. Petersburg, Russia, each May. In 2003 a Portuguese colleague and I edited a book on the impact of war trauma on civilians (Krippner & McIntyre, 2003), obtaining firsthand accounts from five continents.

I had taken an active role in discussion groups on warfare as an undergraduate at the University of Wisconsin, where I organized the first forum on the politics of the Middle East in 1952 (the student participant from Israel had to speak from the audience because he and the students from the Arab countries could not agree on a mutually acceptable topic). I organized another forum on the topic at Northwestern University, where I did my graduate work, and spoke at a 1968 conference on the emotional stress of war at the Carnegie Endowment for International Peace in New York City (Krippner, 1972), when I worked for a decade at Brooklyn's Maimonides Medical Center. Moving to San Francisco to teach at Saybrook Graduate School, I met Daryl Paulson, who applied my concept of "personal mythology" (Feinstein & Krippner, 1988, 2006) to his Vietnam experience. This led to our collaboration on a chapter (Krippner & Paulson, 2006) on combat veterans in the anthology *Mental Disorders of the New Millennium* and, later, to this book. So, six decades after my family and I welcomed Cousin Marcia back from the Philippines I was still attempting to understand the ravages of war on those combatants and civilians who survived the conflict, but who still found themselves entrapped in its deadly grip.

DARYL PAULSON'S STORY

The origins of co-author Daryl Paulson's interest in this book are also personal in nature. He explains the long road that led him to the project:

Four months before my high school graduation, in the late 1960s, I enlisted in the U.S. Marine Corps. I was bored with high school, I had no desire to attend college, and I did not have any practical skills, such as carpentry or auto mechanics, that could help me secure a job. I was also consumed with patriotism, wanting to do my duty for America. I felt I could make a positive contribution by fighting Communism, that evil threat to my free capitalistic society, and have an adventure as well. I had grown up with firearms. I enjoyed hunting and had attained a certain physical ruggedness by tramping through the mountains of Montana. So an infantry route seemed only natural. I got my chance to fight in South Vietnam in 1968 and 1969, the period of the Vietnam War's heaviest fighting. I was assigned to the First Marine Division's Fifth Regiment, located at An Hoa. I participated in combat operations in the dreaded A Shau Valley and Sherwood Forest in the Antenna Valley, where so many of my comrades were killed, as well as the much feared Arizona Territory, where anything that moved became a target.

Combat was vastly different than I had imagined. It was exhilarating and exciting but also physically taxing, emotionally draining, morally disturbing, and, worst of all, spiritually deadening. Ironically, the most damage to me occurred after my return from the war, when I reentered civilian life by attending college. There I was called a warmonger and a baby-killer. I became pretty much a reject from the larger community of my noncombat peers. I found myself in complete and utter despair, unable to reintegrate into my culture. I had killed, I had killed with passion, and I had enjoyed the suffering that I brought to my enemies, for it was payback for what they did to us. Combat memories loomed over me during the day, and the faces of those I had killed haunted me at night. My life became a cycle of suffering—and drinking to relieve the suffering. The cycle focused around drinking, and drinking, and more drinking. My life was not just a heap of broken images but a living hell many times worse than anything I had experienced in Vietnam. I was an alcoholic by my 24th birthday and dangerously on the verge of suicide. Unknown to me at the time, I was not alone in this dilemma. Years later, I discovered that every other person I knew in my unit also had descended into his own version of hell. It took me years of hard work to recover and to enter the social mainstream.

OUR GOALS

The objective of this endeavor is to offer a penetrating look into the embodied experience of combat and the life that follows it, particularly among those diagnosed with either subclinical or overt PTSD, as well as those at risk for PTSD later in their lives. We proceed towards this end by considering the firsthand descriptions of veterans along with an examination of the existing body of literature on the subject.

This is not an antiwar book. We recognize that extraordinary circumstances sometimes demand that a society fend for its autonomy or way of life. However, just causes, too, entail suffering on the part of their participants, suffering that is often overlooked or ignored. It is incumbent on the leaders who guide soldiers to the battlefield to bear the political, ethical, and moral responsibility of rehabilitating those who return haunted by combat.

No matter the high-level political and diplomatic jousting that establishes the reasons for war, the combatants in the field face the same immanent possibility of death, disabilities, postcombat trauma, or any number of combined conditions. Soldiers fighting in Vietnam, Afghanistan, and Iraq have all faced similar stressors: a constant threat of ambush, difficulty distinguishing friend from foe, and high casualty rates among both soldiers and civilians.

In response to this situation, the U.S. Department of Defense has instituted a universal screening program to monitor the physical and mental health of troops returning from combat. Within two weeks after returning home, every service member must complete a three-page questionnaire that includes half a page on mental health status. Those who screen positive for a mental health problem receive an interview with a physician. The assessment is repeated at three and six month intervals. Miller (2006) reported that this development is seen as a "sign of progress," despite objections by detractors who question the effectiveness of such screening based on similar approaches in the past. Critics of the program have cited the soldier-to-soldier warning, "Don't tell them you have symptoms or you'll have to see a shrink," as one of the major setbacks to the program, as well as veterans' concerns about the treatment's possible ramifications for their careers. In addition, critics are troubled by how few referrals are written for those who take the survey. Fewer than 8 percent of veterans seeking help one year after their return were referred by the screening program, and fewer than 20 percent of those who did report mental health problems on the survey were referred to a mental health professional.

Stanley Krippner is a member of the American Counseling Association, which tracks mental health services for combat veterans. In 2006, the organization's newsletter cited an investigative report alleging that the U.S. military was sending troops to combat in Iraq and keeping them there despite established signs of mental illness. The investigation was based on interviews with some 100 families and military personnel, as well as on records obtained under the Freedom of Information Act. The report observed, "Some unstable troops are kept on the front lines while on potent antidepressants and anti-anxiety drugs, with little or no counseling or medical monitoring" (Military, 2006, p. 3). Additionally, some troops suffering from post-traumatic stress disorder were sent back to the war zone, and "these practices...have helped to fuel an increase in the suicide rate among troops serving in Iraq" (Military, 2006, p. 3). According to the television show *60 Minutes*, there had been over 6,000 desertions by the end of 2004; additionally, some men attempted to immigrate to Canada (Eisenberg, 2005; Goodman, 2004). The suicide and desertion rates were especially puzzling because the all-volunteer force had been screened for emotional stability, briefed on combat stress, and trained to counter suicidal feelings (Beaumont, 2004).

The same newsletter reported that, in May 2006, the U.S. Government Accountability Office found that of troops returning from Iraq and Afghanistan, only 22 percent of those identified as at risk for PTSD on a post-deployment questionnaire were referred for a mental health examination (Military, 2006, p. 3). In turn, the Office chastised the Department of Defense for failing to get veterans mental health support when they needed it (Miller, 2006). During the same year, a descriptive study of nearly 240,000 returning soldiers and Marines concluded that 19 percent of Iraq veterans reported mental health problems, compared with 11 percent of those returning from Afghanistan and 8.5 percent of those returning from other combat arenas. One year after their return, less than half had accessed mental health care services (Hoge, Auchterionie, & Milliken, 2006).

In an attempt to fill this gap and encourage greater utilization of mental health care, organizations such as Swords Into Plowshares provide counseling, training, housing, and legal assistances to veterans. Blacker and

Fairweather (2006) have claimed that the U.S. Department of Veterans' Affairs failed to anticipate the increased demand for mental health services for veterans returning from Operation Enduring Freedom in Afghanistan and Operation Iraqi Freedom. The Veterans' Administration (VA) expected to treat fewer than 3,000 war veterans for PTSD; however, by mid-2006 VA specialists had seen over 34,000 men and women in need of assistance. According to the U.S. General Accountability Office (GAO), the VA failed to spend the $53 million budgeted for mental health services and never notified medical officials of its availability (Blacker & Fairweather, 2006). Earlier on, GAO claimed that six out of seven VA centers they visited said that they might not be able to meet the increased demand for PTSD treatments (Cook, 2005).

Claims for VA disability benefits have increased 36 percent since 2000, and the backlog has never been greater, taking several months for disabled veterans to secure due benefits. To make matters worse, veterans suffer not only from PTSD, traumatic brain injury, and other disorders, but also from extreme financial hardship and readjustment problems. In 2005, the "Comprehensive Assistance for Veterans Exposed to Traumatic Stressors Act" was introduced in the U.S. Congress, only to languish and die. The bill laid out a proactive strategy for the VA and the Department of Defense to identify and respond to mental health needs. But instead, Congress reduced funding for the Defense and Veterans' Injury Center by half in the 2007 Defense Appropriations Bill. This dismal situation for veterans was further confirmed by the Government Accountability Office's report that, in 2006, the military only referred one in five service members at risk for PTSD to mental health providers (Blacker & Fairweather, 2006). Moreover, Houppert (2005) estimated that half a million veterans never received the benefits from the U.S. Department of Veterans' Affairs to which they were entitled.

Responding to a growing cultural consciousness about the affliction, Congress in 1989 created the National Center for PTSD to address the needs of veterans diagnosed with military-related PTSD. Of course, information is no substitute for treatment, but the effort is better than nothing. As more recent data demonstrates, the intergenerational crisis of PTSD persists among veterans. For instance, the California Nurses Association reported that, in the first quarter of 2006, the U.S. Department of Veterans' Affairs treated 20,638 Iraq veterans for post-traumatic stress disorder, and they had a backlog of 400,000 cases (Roland, 2007). At the end of 2006, Operation Iraqi Freedom's Mental Health Advisory Team admitted that "there is no standardized joint reporting system for monitoring mental health status and suicide surveillance of service members in a combat deployed environment" (p. 4). Readers of this book can easily fathom why we needed to address this topic.

Introduction: Private Traumas, Personal Mythologies: Post-Traumatic Stress Disorder Among Combat Veterans

Jeffrey Kirkwood

The long fought and incremental battle to better establish the uniqueness and clinical legitimacy of post-traumatic stress disorder (PTSD), especially in the military, has come at a price. Institutional recognition of the condition, which is endemic among veterans returning from combat, is coupled with inflexible formalization and a subsequent ossification of perspective that limits approaches to understanding and healing people afflicted with PTSD. In order to treat the disorder, one is compelled to define its origins, symptoms, morphology, and various manifestations. While this is not by itself a negative impulse, the quest for comprehension quickly transforms into an obstinacy of knowing. Soldiers now returning from war with PTSD have the benefit of a medical community that acknowledges the realities of the condition and a vast body of research that identifies avenues for healing, something not available to their "shell-shocked" predecessors. However, as men and women continue to bring the infernal torments of battle home with them, the military and medical institutions continue to access the same diagnostic and treatment resources. In this sense, the acceptance of the condition into the medical mainstream aggravates the tendency to simplify something that is not simple at all.

To be sure, just as there is no single answer for PTSD, there is no single institutional problem that must be remedied. Paulson and Krippner detail a broad array of contemporary obstacles to both identifying and helping veterans with PTSD, extending from the realm of personal responsibilities for one's own health, to the crisis in veteran care, to the canopy of prevailing social attitudes that determines the light in which veterans are seen. The point is that both the practical and theoretical anchors for understanding and treating PTSD rest on deep, foundational social, psychological, philosophical, and existential questions that are not easily satisfied. The dangers associated with the increased clinical attention to the condition are that these difficult, fundamental issues are overlooked in favor of approaches that ignore important nuances and deal merely with symptoms, approaches that offer respite from bad dreams, or tranquilize a veteran who has been overrun by paranoia, without fully restoring a person. That kind of profound recovery relies on an equally profound awareness of the circumstances involved in a person's life, as well as the nature of trauma.

PTSD is a complex and multidimensional latticework of symptoms, memories, events, responses, and beliefs, and treatment hinges on these complex intersections. During and soon after World War I, symptoms of PTSD were treated as "shell shock," which as the moniker suggests, was the result of the concussive force of ubiquitous shelling during the war. As such it was a purely somatic concern, and therefore governed by existing norms of manhood, which deemed the general anxiety, hypervigilance, night terrors, and other symptoms of PTSD warrant for punishment and scorn. A man was expected to bear his wounds with stolid conviction, and if mental wounds were like bodily wounds, they were to be dealt with in the same way. W.H.R. Rivers, who was instrumental in revising this conception, conducted psychotherapy with veterans and resituated the disorder as one of a psychological character. Later still, Abram Kardiner's work helped to again invert the framework for analyzing troubled veterans and served as a portent for the current psychiatric emphasis on neurophysiology (Talbott, 1997). This kind of wholesale reversal is indicative of the bifurcating style of investigation that many times propels the clinical treatment of PTSD. With the ascent of each new theory comes a set of new pronouncements about how to and how not to treat patients, at the expense of whatever wisdom remained from the old framework.

Paulson and Krippner are cautious about dismissing modes of treatment and their corresponding paradigms. The book uncovers the intense interreliance of disparate approaches to PTSD and in the process reveals a more involved and messy reality than Rivers or Kardiner might have wanted to admit. The causal chain that gives researchers clues about how to deal with other ailments is not as clear in the case of trauma. Positron emission tomography and other tools for mapping physiological reactions to stressors in PTSD patients are useful mines of insight, but insufficient to the task of

understanding PTSD as a complete and lived experien
abilities for which there is a site of injury, or a visible p
in pain, immobility, or impairment, the site of injury fo
itself. The connection between a trauma and its symp
obscured. Difficulties of method traditionally asse
research and treatment have their provenance in the inc
mal research objectives with psychological trauma, v
phenomenological, physical, and social factors. Both sides in the contention
about whether trauma is more a physical or a psychological condition
embark from the shared belief that there is a fact of the matter and that it
will elucidate an appropriate and universal approach to treatment. Where
perceptions, and especially those skewed from the collective reality by
trauma, are concerned, it is less a matter of truth and more a matter of suspended, fragmentary memory that warps the experience of the present (Talbott, 1997). Whether or not the factual content of a veteran's war memories
match a journalist's videotape of the same moment is of little consequence
to the impact of the memory.

What is baffling, and that which demands the kind of diverse account
the book offers, is that for trauma victims fact is often modeled after fallacy.
The traumatic memory fragment that overwhelms the present for a veteran
acts like a supermassive psychic object whose gravitational field changes
the way all other nearby systems behave. So, for instance, a gruesome
memory from combat can permanently alter brain chemistry or prompt
the body to respond as if the event were recurring, even when none of
the original stressors are present. These reenactments of past memories,
and their far-reaching consequences for behavior, suggest that treating PTSD requires more than an understanding of the symptoms and
physical processes by which they occur. Even though the *Diagnostic and
Statistical Manual* offers a definition for PTSD, the number of different possible instantiations and symptoms renders it only partially useful. Paulson
and Krippner emphasize throughout that no single approach is adequate
for all cases, and that some individuals need to use several approaches
simultaneously.

The devastating experience of PTSD is partly due to the invisibility of the
problem's roots and the loss of synchronicity with the immediate world. The
moment that becomes memorialized as the source of distress is not necessarily evident or located as that which is causing the problem. Combatants
who come home to PTSD are hobbled by a psychic fragment that is the
psychological equivalent of shrapnel, less important as a remnant of the
event, which he or she may or may not remember, than it is as a presence
in every moment. Ernst Bloch, during the time the term "trauma" was being
popularized and the European continent was overwhelmed by legions of
shattered veterans, wrote a vignette that strikes to the heart of this idea that
trauma insinuates itself into every banality:

the same thing was experienced by someone even more directly, and drove him even further from himself. He had injured himself somewhat during a solitary excursion, while washing his hands. A piece of rusty metal went quite deeply into his skin. But the wound didn't bleed, or rather just neatly and inwardly, so that no bandage was needed, and his afternoon was completely uninterrupted. (Bloch, 2006, pp. 95–96)

Expectations that the disruption or the pain index against the magnitude of the original event are irrelevant for PTSD. Paulson and Krippner make clear that much of what is hard for veterans is a need to justify their plight. Sometimes there is a distinct moment of horror that generates the later symptoms, while other times it is the discontinuity between the psychological scarring beget by the trauma and the demands of civilian life.

The chasm between social pressures and a veteran's connection to the world further ruptures the streamlined experience of reality. This complicates the level of analysis for any work that seeks to deal with PTSD comprehensively. Does one address the social stresses such as media representation, family demands, and basic social conventions first? Or rather, is it more important to understand with some degree of detail how a veteran, irrespective of the social factors, sees her or his world? Rather than privileging one or the other of these possible accounts, the book looks at how the social universe and a veteran's inner world interact. Extensive excerpts from interviews with returning soldiers from Iraq, along with Paulson's own trials as a soldier and civilian seek depth to the phenomenology of PTSD. Because PTSD is fundamentally a matter of an individual's experience, the sum effect of the interviews demonstrates both a collective character to the disorder and the extreme degree to which each person's account is inimitable.

Through extrapolation from firsthand accounts, and general social analysis, the highly subjective material from the interviews is placed in contrast to a larger social setting. The disjunction between these two spheres is what accounts for much of the hardship endured by veterans. Because the fragment lodged in a veteran's memory is recalled in the present, his or her experience and according behavior is very often not like that of his or her peers. The seamless integration of past, present, and future with an individual's experience and that of shared perception is denied to veterans with PTSD. At one time these rudimentary elements of experience were synchronized and invisible, but the arrival of a traumatic event, which remains invisible to others, makes these relationships jarring and unnatural. In turn, it is not enough to focus exclusively on the one or the other factor. PTSD is as much a social affliction as a psychiatric and neurochemical one. If one were to follow the questions entangled in PTSD to their natural conclusion, there would no doubt be significant philosophical fallout.

Identity, which acts like an interpretive sieve and a stable point of contact with the outside reality, is a fragile balance. Not only does PTSD affect the social feedback that a veteran receives from his or her social network, but it also causes what R. J. McNally (1997) calls overgeneral autobiographical recall. In addition to creating chaos in the external connections a person has to society, traumatic experiences can delete or obfuscate memories that are essential to one's sense of identity. This adduces Paulson and Krippner's take on PTSD, which underscores the overall disruption to very primary notions of self, family, and society that the disorder can cause, and why the consequences of leaving it untreated are so bleak.

PTSD is just as damaging to the social side of veterans' experience, which compounds the negative feedback loop of personal disorientation and estrangement. Without the external affirmation that a veteran is who she or he thinks she or he is, the project of maintaining a stable identity is even harder. Radical upheavals in a person's social life on account of odd, violent, or reclusive behavior can lead to spousal abuse, failed relationships, lost careers, isolation, or worse. Instances of a disintegrating social life after a wartime experience are well documented. Some research goes as far as to associate PTSD with the level of a person's integration into social networks (Hodson & Kunovich, 1999). But the role of society in determining such outcomes may not be as simple as whether or not one attends a bridge club or has a strong relationship with his or her family.

The convolution of PTSD and its potential treatments extends well beyond the pale of a veteran's immediate social clime, however important it may be. Paulson and Krippner consider whether the solution and the dilemma are both partially bound to the transformation of larger mythical structures that are repositories and determinants for larger meanings and values. Mythical superstructures are inherited, preconfigured, semistatic frameworks that govern an individual's relationship to the rest of society, his or her role, and the value to be derived from participation in the larger social world. When they change or disintegrate, as they have in the past hundred years for soldiers, individuals have to reorient themselves.

Increasing gender equality has translated in the military into a shared space for men and women in uniform, even if there are still partitions that separate the roles that are available for them. While this has been an overdue revision of outmoded biases, it, and other large changes discussed in the book, undermines one of the primary myths that offered meaning for the carnage of war. Men, who still do most of the fighting, had long reconciled traumatic experience within a belief in the soldier as warrior, which ennobled the brotherhood and camaraderie of war. Even in the grimmest accounts of combat from the Greeks through the Crimean War, as well as World War I and the virtually endless firsthand descriptions of the battlefield, the narrative used male warriorhood as an axis to make sense of the experience. As women have gained their just place as equals with men, these old narratives and myths have to be rewritten, and in the meantime leave many men, and women as well, to grope for meaning on their own.

The complications of gender equality enter the traditional norms of the home as well. Whereas men who went to war could go away before believing that they were performing an honorable service, providing for their family, and returning to the stability of their family (albeit through heavy social constraints on their wives), that is no longer the case. Now it is almost as likely that a soldier's wife has her own career, makes as much or more money than her husband, and no longer feels as tied to a family life that may be unhappy and punctuated by long periods of absence and a trimmed set of benefits from the military. As a result, the support systems and belief structures that linked family to the individual combatant have increasingly evaporated.

Even more than changes in gender status, Paulson and Krippner countenance changing public perceptions and attitudes toward the military that impact mythical structures. War's new image as a sanitary, exact, efficient, and even economical enterprise in the public eye manufactures the impression that the carnage and despair of combat is fast becoming an anachronism. There is no longer a collective national war effort, as there have been tax cuts during wartime for the first time ever. Casualties are unacceptable, and combat is thought to be conducted at a distance with remote controls and precision strikes. In total, war is more often than not seen as a professional endeavor. Since there is no longer outright conscription, combatants are viewed as willing, professional participants, whose job, according to the contract they signed, is to fight upon command. However, death and gore look the same in modern warfare, even if the medicine and prosthetics are more sophisticated. Starting with the unpopularity of Vietnam, the nobility accorded to the warring class was replaced with opprobrium. When one tries to makes sense of one's experience of war he or she often looks out to look in. If the resounding message is that war and all of its participants are ignoble professionals, then the suffering and brutality one witnesses, or in which one engages, cannot be rationalized, and it is left as a painful wound from a shameful past.

In addition, Paulson and Krippner pay close attention to the new reality of reservists who have the opposite version of the problem enlisted combatants have. The shortage of recruits to fight in Iraq caused the military to send tens of thousands of reservists into combat. While the enlisted men and women may have relied on the warrior myth and are now professionals, reservists were professionals turned into unwitting warriors. Most of the reservists prior to being sent to Iraq performed their monthly weekend duties as a source of supplemental income. Once the job became a life, and they were subjected to the hardships of combat, they were marooned away from familiar belief structures that functioned to justify their actions.

The interviews with soldiers who have suffered from PTSD peer into the vertiginous feeling of being a combatant in contemporary wars. They offer a way to fuse multiple levels of inquiry and better understand how the frayed tapestry of existential and social factors conspire to leave some very shocking experiences from war unexplained and therefore alive as psychic fragments. One of the basic precepts for treatment that undergirds much of the book is a desperate need to help veterans with PTSD reinvent or create anew belief structures and myths that are positive frameworks for dealing with their experiences. Without them traumas never become integrated, dominating all encounters with the living world. Paulson and Krippner realize that these needs cannot be met by waiting on society at large to reinvest war with its outdated trappings of glory and conquest, making space for the honor of a warrior class. Instead, they suggest that a vital part of any of the numerous types of treatment available for PTSD is a rejuvenated mythical structure, engineered to identify the positive aspects to the trauma and process caustic memories.

It is unrealistic to expect that the social milieu will change in order to aid returning combatants with their difficult experiences. More likely veterans will have to find help and ultimately, with guidance, rely on their own strengths to build an interpretive framework and values sturdy enough to give their experiences meaning. This is no small order, and the litany of military, political, and public obstacles makes the work of each veteran even more difficult. However, the book acknowledges that the condition's complexity does not make it impossible to conquer, and offers as comprehensive a survey of combat PTSD as is available. Considering the current geopolitical tumult, disappearing material support for veterans, and a new and strange social setting to which veterans must return, there is no fail-safe or panacea. But Krippner and Paulson give powerful assurance that there is light and that the road is not impassable.

References

Bloch, E. (2006). *Traces*. (A.A. Nassar, Trans). Palo Alto, CA: Stanford University Press.

Hodson, R., & Kunovich, R. (1999). Civil war, social integration, and mental health in Croatia. *Journal of Health and Social Behavior, 40,* 323–343.

McNally, R.J. (1997). Memory and anxiety disorders. *Philosophical Transactions: Biological Sciences, 352,* 1755–1759.

Talbott, J. (1997). Soldiers, psychiatrists, and combat trauma. *Journal of Interdisciplinary History, 27*(3), 437–454.

Vengeance

Hatred like a high velocity bullet
pierced my skin, gathered my organs
(heart, brain, the rest)
came out the other side
and splattered all over the world.
Thus I got my vengeance.
I slumped to the ground,
a righteous martyr,
a fool, lying in a puddle
of mud, blood,
and, from the gods,
ridicule.

—Tom Greening

1

An Overview of Trauma and the Mind/Body

Traumas are assaults on the human mind/body system that affect numerous subsystems, such as physiological, psychoneurological, social-emotional, and/or spiritual functions. A trauma often leads to lasting psychiatric disorders—anxiety that will not subside, depression that will not heal, or psychosomatic injuries that will not mend (Paulson, 1994). The multiplicity of conditions that inhabit the broad term "post-traumatic stress disorder" (PTSD) share a distinction as adverse conditions resulting from trauma. In the American Psychiatric Association's *Diagnostic and Statistical Manual, 4th Edition Text Revision* (*DSM-IV-TR*), PTSD is generally defined as a condition that results from experiencing (or witnessing) life-threatening events that extend beyond one's coping capacity, emotional resources, and/or existential world view (Beck & Emery, 1985). And it is important to note the critical role of belief structures in the appearance of PTSD and its treatment (Foa et al., 2000).

Although evolutionary psychologists often view war as an essential strategy for organizing human efforts through aggressive group activity (Buss, 2004), PTSD is not a necessary consequence of war, nor is it a purely biological/evolutionary matter. Over thousands of generations, the human species has evolved to better interact with the environment. Anxiety is a valuable evolutionary adaptation that allows creatures to assess threats. But the tools we need in any moment are not necessarily the evolutionary tools that are available (Buss, 2004). In some ways, we are hardwired with

Stone Age temperaments and required to deal with contemporary problems that demand postmodern skills (Dawkins, 1982). Quick reactions to violent threats were crucial in the Paleolithic Era but can lead to harassment, arrest, and even imprisonment in the twenty-first century.

Along with chimpanzees, and perhaps mandrills and baboons, humans share the capacity to cooperate for the sake of combat (Buss, 2004). Thousands of generations ago, the behaviors that founded warring practices were probably oriented towards hunting endeavors. Military combat, then, is a companion to the increasing sophistication of society, whereby warring for food is transformed into warring for wealth, property, and slaves (Buss, 2004). During the fourth millennium BCE, warring groups from the Middle East and Central Asia began to spread out, attacking peaceful surrounding Neolithic cultures. Male warrior gods replaced fertility goddesses; scenes of warfare replaced peaceful motifs in artwork; villages became fortified; and weapons began to appear in gravesites. The hypothesized reasons vary: the decline of hunting, environmental disasters that introduced scarcity, or the rise of patriarchy. For whatever reason, war became commonplace and even noble (DeMeo, 1998; Ferguson, 2000; Wilson, 1985). In any case, the emergence of war-related PTSD hinges as much on a person's or culture's philosophical stance towards war as it does on the existence of war itself.

Some individuals and groups understand suffering as an inevitable consequence of combat and not one to be glorified (Aurobindo, 1997; Napper, 1989; Radhakrishnan, 1948). For example, Nagarjuna and Chandrakirti, in developing the Mādhyamka (Middle Way) system of Buddhism, argue that attachment to conditions, concepts, or specific outcomes in life are the seeds of suffering (Chandrakirti, 2002; Huntington & WangChen, 1989). The First Noble Truth of the Buddha is that temporal, human life is inseparable from suffering (Murti, 1956). Kleinman (1989) pointed out that serious illnesses "embody a dialectic between shared intersubjective cultural meaning and values that always provides a particular meaning of illness for suffering patients, their families and friends, and their professional caregivers" (p. 8). In other words, shared cultural myths, values, goals, beliefs, and meanings help shape the lived experiences and perceptions of wellness and sickness.

PTSD among modern western societies is identifiable by changes in behavior, attitude, and/or values following armed combat, accidents, natural disasters, rape, torture, or abuse (Friedman, 1994). The putative traumatic event can be momentary (as in the case of sniper fire or an automobile crash) or span several years (where, for instance, civilians endure threats and attacks by insurgents) (Jong, 2002). When a person who has suffered trauma fails to recover, regain equilibrium, or "get on with life," psychotherapists typically employ the diagnostic category PTSD. Because the conditions involved ostensibly stem from some original traumatic locus, the disorder itself is considered "post-traumatic" (Greening, 1997).

The "stress" of PTSD describes the residual strain on the mind/body system caused by the initial catastrophic "stressor." Unlike psychic or physical wounds that are resolved, eased, or healed but may be stored as vivid memories, traumas responsible for PTSD remain a source of distress. This means that the original trauma, rather than being relegated to the past, is still a powerful influence on a person's behavior in such a way that her or his responses may be dictated by it. Many times, the problem is evident in the disjunction between the expectations of certain social settings and the behaviors spawned by trauma. For instance, in a combat situation, learned responses to environmental dangers (such as ducking when fired upon) are vital for survival, while in civilian life, these responses are inappropriate. Technically, these symptoms are termed contingency and rule-governed behaviors, because they are produced in response to a very specific set of circumstances (like the dangers associated with certain noises during wartime) that are not universally useful or acceptable. *DSM-IV-TR* (2000) states:

> The essential feature of post traumatic stress disorder is the development of characteristic symptoms following exposure to an extreme traumatic stressor involving direct personal experience of an event that involves actual or threatened death or serious injury, or other threat to one's physical integrity; or witnessing an event that involves death, injury, or a threat to the physical integrity of another person, or learning about unexpected or violent death, serious harm, a threat of death or injury experienced by a family member or a close associate. (p. 424)

As if the trauma were not enough, the harsh personal judgment and self-rebuke of the sufferer exacerbates the condition. Dysfunctional moods lead to negative self-talk, which increases symptoms, which initiates the cycle anew. Many times, the conflict between prevailing social mores and behaviors educated by trauma (such as throwing oneself to the ground to avoid enemy fire) is internalized. A veteran with PTSD can lapse into destructive internal discourse that weighs heavily on his or her mood. In turn, he or she may avoid experiences that consciously recall the war experience and withdraw entirely. The "faraway stare" noted in much of the literature (Reitman, 2005, p. 85) results from both negativity and evasion. However, if behaviors such as the automated response to loud noises occur in a safe environment, they can be unlearned or extinguished through a variety of treatments, including cognitive-behavior therapy and biofeedback (Hayes et al., 1999). Newer treatments, such as energy psychology, are reported to be unexpectedly effective in treating PTSD by "neutralizing the emotional impact of traumatic memories, as well as of *anticipated* distress" (Feinstein, in press).

Rule-governed behavior presents more of a challenge. Here, the person judges responses, actions, fears, and defense mechanisms according to personal myths or life rules. If someone was anxious at home after returning from combat, rule-bound self-talk might cause him or her to dismiss the anxiety as simply bad or stupid. As a result, the veteran might begin to deny and suppress subsequent anxiety, further obscuring the root of the problem and complicating treatment. For these reasons, rule-governed behavior is exceptionally rigid and hard to modify (Germer et al., 2005; Hayes et al., 1999; Roemer & Orsillo, 2002).

One of the most challenging aspects of a traumatic emotional disturbance involves the loss of one's individual perspective or personal myth that ensures the security and safety of the world. This loss is not easily remedied with drugs, catharsis, deconditioning, or social support. If these interventions do produce long-term positive change, it is largely because they imbue patients' lives with new mythologies that revitalize meaning.

Signs of PTSD are indicated by reduced plasma beta-endorphin concentrations in PTSD-affected individuals. Because the hypothalamic endorphin is at least partially mediated by the corticotrophin-releasing factor (CFRRF), these reduced concentrations may occur via a mechanism similar to that of lowered adrenocorticotropin (ACTH) release in response to CRF challenge. Although plasma concentrations of metenkephalin among PTSD research participants are similar to those of controls, the in-vitro half-life degradation is reduced, suggesting decreased secretion. Despite reduced pain thresholds, combat veterans with PTSD also demonstrate a maloxone-reversible analgesic response to combat-related stimuli, raising the probability of opioral system hyperregulation (Pitman et al., 1991).

Increased concentrations of dopamine in plasma and urine have been reported in PTSD patients, and several lines of evidence point to dysfunction in the hypothalamic-pituitary adrenal axis, as well as possible increased levels of extrahypothalamic CFR. Studies have shown low levels of free cortisol in plasma and urine. There is much preclinical evidence that implicates hippocampal glucocorticoid receptors in the negative feedback regulation of CFR and argenine vasopression synthesis. Cerebrospinal fluid concentrations of CFR are higher in PTSD patients than in controls, consistent with the hypothesis of increased secretions of neuronal CFR in PTSD patients. Finally, the hypothalamic-pituitary-thyroid complex typically is involved in PTSD. Average total triiodothyronine (T3) levels are significantly higher in veterans with PTSD than in controls (Pitman et al., 1991).

For example, the stressor is reexperienced through memory recollection when a car backfires, sending the veteran face down on the street, waiting for incoming rounds to hit (Paulson, 1994). Sometimes the traumatic experience may be a horrific event that has been witnessed. Clancy was with the troops who liberated Buchenwald, a Nazi concentration camp, in April 1945. He told us, "That was six decades ago and I'm still having nightmares about the rotting corpses and twisted, emaciated bodies that I saw." Clancy's report is an example of a stressor that may be reexperienced during nighttime dreams and nightmares, during naps, or during periods of dissociation in which the stressor seems to recur, breaking into the ordinary flow of the veteran's conscious awareness, behavior repertoire, or self-identity (Krippner, 1997a).

Using PTSD as a label or construct enables therapists and patients alike to work with it fluidly across varying personal and social arrangements (Kegan, 1994). When, through psychotherapy, counseling, or other life-changing experiences (or merely the passage of time) people suffering from PTSD find relief from their symptoms, several psychoneurological mechanisms appear to be at work. The brain's hippocampus, despite its function in helping to remember a traumatic event through specific cues, no longer activates the brain's amygdala. A function of the amygdala is hyperarousal, which involves the command to release norepinephrine and other brain chemicals (Wisneski & Anderson, 2005). Rossi and Cheek (1988) have suggested that this disconnection between the hippocampus and the amygdala is a form of traumatic dissociation. This dissociation (or separation) of a person from the event and its loss from hippocampal memory is similar to the phenomenon of state-dependent learning, where a task learned in one situation or "state" is generally better remembered later in a similar situation or "state."

One combatant in the Battle of Fallujah in Iraq told a reporter, "Looking back on it, it never seemed like it was 'me' that was there, like I was watching it from the outside. But the fear was there, so it must have been real" (Reitman, 2005, p. 88). This statement demonstrates another use of dissociation, primarily as a defense mechanism during combat; this soldier separated himself from the actual event, "watching it from the outside." But whether they have dissociated or not, many veterans will experience fear, or some other emotion, in another context—and that feeling will remind them of their combat experience. This phenomenon is due to state-dependent learning, which plays an important role in "flashback" reactions.

Pole and his associates (2005) found that dissociation following a traumatic experience was accompanied by lower cardiovascular activity and higher emotionality, especially when the trauma was acute. When discussing the traumatic episode, this peculiar antinomy between blood pressure and heightened emotion made it "one of the best predictors" of an oncoming PTSD condition. This type of dissociation is a plausible explanation for reports of time distortion, depersonalization, and other disturbances of cognition and perception that accompany PTSD (Pole et al., 2005).

Another aspect of the physiological pattern of PTSD involves the endorphins that are released into a person's bloodstream during "fight or flight" emergencies. This is an adaptive response; endorphins have a tranquilizing effect as they release one from the feelings of anxiety, depression, and inadequacy that often accompany trauma and subsequent PTSD (van der Kolk,

1994). Some people even show signs of addiction to these endorphins and the memories that release them; long intervals between exposures may produce symptoms that resemble withdrawal from opiates and other addictive drugs. Repeated reexposures may evolve into permanent neural pathways, consolidating behaviors and memory structures that may become functionally independent of the original stimuli (Greer, 2005).

Brown (1994) noted that PTSD is characterized by physiological hyperarousal originating from interactions among the amygdala, hippocampus, and prefrontal cortex through disturbances of such neurotransmitters as norepinephrine, epinephrine, dopamine, and serotonin. Relief, therefore, occurs when arousal is curbed, and when the traumatic experiences are reformulated, reframed, and integrated into one's ordinary behavioral and experiential repertoire (Wisneski & Anderson, 2005). Indeed, a study of cognitive-behavior therapy involving five women with PTSD following car accidents showed a connection between symptom reduction and reduced amygdala activity (Felmingham et al., forthcoming).

From a neuroscience perspective, PTSD is the result of hyperarousal, which destabilizes the amygdala and autonomic nervous system, resulting in exaggerated anxiety, inhibitions, and agitation. Flashbacks are particularly problematic, because there is no sense of distance between the traumatic event in time or place. The cortico-hippocampal networks have not been able to contextualize the somatic, sensory, and emotional memories within the networks of the autobiographical memory (Cozolino, 2002). Additionally, during flashbacks, the amygdalic fear networks are activated. The amygdala's dense connectivity with the visual system of the brain likely accounts for the visual hallucinations experienced during flashbacks. Finally, a decrease in regional cerebral blood flow in the left inferior frontal and middle temporal cortex, "Broca's area," during speechless terror is often reported. PTSD victims may have this neurobiological component at its core (Rauch et al., 1998).

The treatment procedures described in this book represent an attempt to incorporate what is known about the physiology of PTSD, even when medication is not part of the treatment regimen. Optimally, one would hope that many veterans would move "beyond trauma" to higher levels of personality integration and development, an outcome that will be a recurring theme in this book.

Death's Rainbow

I walked upon the battlefield
and saw a grotesque scene revealed:
the corpses there, both friend and foe,
all formed a sort of weird rainbow.
The enemy and our men too—
some bled dark red and some bled blue.
The blood of others was bright green—
a stranger sight I've never seen.
When bullets mowed doomed soldiers down
blood sometimes came out rusty brown,
and who would in their right mind think
the blood of many would be pink?
Oh what a gross, macabre sight—
to see men bleeding black and white,
and on the ground where bodies lay
I saw big blotches of dark gray.
Around this place of pain and woe
some sprawled in pools of indigo,
and where brave fighters their ends met
were yellow stains and violet.
How sad that young lads had to lose
their lives in puddles of chartreuse.
I thought it simply could not be
that orange blood would flow so free.
In places there was purple blood—
at first a stream, and then a flood,
and youths shot down in life too soon
bled for their nations dark maroon.
Although they many colors bled
they share one fate: they all are dead.

—Tom Greening

2

History of the Diagnosis and Treatment of PTSD

Exposure to potential traumatic stressors is concomitant with the human condition (Buss, 2004), and human attempts to heal each other predate such contemporary etiologically defined concepts as "illness," "sickness," "disease," and "disorder" (Cozolino, 2002). Prior to the definition of PTSD by the mental health care establishment, the emotionally toxic effects of trauma were well documented in mythological, historical, and literary sources (Campbell, 1968, 1972). For example, accounts of Isaac, after he was bound and nearly sacrificed by his father, Abraham (Genesis: 20–28, *The Holy Bible,* 1952), include an arranged marriage at the age of 40, a dispute over the ownership of local wells, and the deception by his son Jacob, who stole his brother's birthright. These incidents imply a passivity and tendency for social altercation in Isaac, which are two hallmarks of what today is called PTSD. Likewise, Samuel Pepys's description of insomnia, nightmares, anxiety, and anger after the 1666 Great Fire of London are all symptoms of unresolved exposure to trauma. Shakespeare's characters underwent dramatic behavioral changes following trauma. In *Henry IV,* Lady Percy's husband, Hotspur, became melancholy, became socially withdrawn, and began talking in his sleep following a bloody battle in which he lost his kinsman.

In the nineteenth century, a few physicians on both sides of the Atlantic posited causal relationships between traumatic experience and psychiatric disabilities. In Europe, this was known as the "Swiss disease," because adverse reactions to combat were noted among Swiss soldiers. DaCosta observed cardiac and respiratory problems coupled with anxiety among Civil War veterans, while Janet noticed that people who survived natural disasters and accidents often experienced arousal of the autonomic nervous system and emotional numbing (Carr, 2002). During the U.S. Civil War, the condition was referred to as "irritable heart" and later as "soldier's heart." According to data culled from 15,000 Union Army veterans' records, soldiers who witnessed death in battle had higher rates of postwar illness (Pizarro, Silver, & Prause, 2006).

During the First World War, the condition now known as PTSD was referred to as "combat neurosis" or "shell shock," and during the Second World War as "battle fatigue" or "operational fatigue" (Carson et al., 2000; Greer, 2005). Identification of these symptoms among veterans coincided with a revival of interest in hypnosis, which became a common treatment. Freudians used the term "war neurosis" and denied an organic basis to the condition, hypothesizing that it was the consequence of adult trauma, and recommending psychoanalytic treatment. Military physicians, rarely aware of Freud's hypothesis, simply told the veteran to "Go home and get over it."

THE INTERNAL STRUCTURE OF PTSD AMONG COMBAT VETERANS

For the purposes of this book, PTSD will be treated as the most apparent or extreme instantiation of post-traumatic conditions. Detectable damage and physiological disruption of normal amygdala-hippocampus functioning may be present but clinically indeterminable (i.e., the typical symptoms of PTSD are not present). Yet this damage may erode a person's ability to function, casting a grim shadow on life and its ultimate value. This condition is even disruptive for nondiagnosed, subclinical PTSD trauma victims—those individuals who have not been hospitalized for their condition, who have not been referred for psychotherapy or counseling, and who have not sought help of any kind. The full continuum may include from 30 to 90 percent of those veterans who have experienced combat, depending on who is reporting the data and what diagnostic criteria are used. This continuum needs to be kept in mind; what is traumatic for one person need not be traumatic for another person, and there are many life experiences that can evoke as many symptoms of PTSD as there are unexpected traumas. In addition, there are life experiences that can shift a person's position on this continuum; a case of subclinical PTSD suddenly may manifest serious PTSD symptoms. In other words, PTS (post-traumatic stress) over time can become PTSD (post-traumatic stress disorder). One must remember that PTSD is a social construct, and like similar diagnostic constructs it can be problematic if applied too liberally (Baldwin et al., 2004; Young, 1995). The judicious use of our continuum could prevent both the overdiagnosis and the misdiagnosis of PTSD.

At the far end of the continuum are those who show symptoms of PTSD after events that are not generally considered traumatic. Mol and his associates (2005) collected data from over 800 adults who had filled out a number of questionnaires and checklists. When events from the past three decades were examined, Mol et al. discovered that PTSD scores were higher after difficult life events (such as divorce) than after traumatic events (such as accidents). Their findings could not be explained by differences in family background, history of stressful events, or individual scores on the questionnaire and checklists. Hence, for many people, difficult life events can generate as many PTSD symptoms as events that are considered traumatic by psychotherapists. These people manifest PTSD despite lack of obvious trauma; hence, they fall at the far end of our continuum. Because PTSD is the only psychiatric condition that requires a specific event to have occurred for its diagnosis, this latter group cannot be placed in the PTSD category. Our continuum emphasizes symptoms, behaviors, and verbal reports rather than diagnoses.

Furthermore, both predictive and retrospective epidemiological studies indicate that the majority of people in the United States will experience some type of major traumatic stressor in their lifetime. However, only about 10 percent of these will develop pronounced clinical manifestations of PTSD as a result (Miller & Keane, 2004). Our continuum model is useful for the placement of these individuals.

These studies also demonstrate a wide range of individual differences. For example, clinically diagnosed PTSD is twice as common among U.S. women as among men (Kimerling et al., 2002). This may be due to women's tendency to seek help more often than men, the latter being more aware and abiding of the stigma surrounding professional care (Gist & Devilly, 2002). The documented discrepancy between genders may also be due to increasing use of the classic PTSD diagnosis for victims of sexual assault. The fact that war-related PTSD diagnoses are more common among females may be due to the inclusion of rape in this category (Goldstein, 2001). However, it is plausible to attribute the difference to what some social scientists call the "male warrior effect," which is the unique proclivity of men to form mutual unions to safeguard their interests (Researchers, 2006).

In any discussion of PTSD, the presence of diverse predisposing factors in peoples' biological, psychoneurological, socioemotional, and spiritual makeup must be taken into account (Bryant & Guthrie, 2005). When a person is subjected to a traumatic stressor, her or his initial reaction involves an activation of the sympathetic component of the autonomic nervous system, as evidenced in both physical symptoms (e.g., tachycardia, hyperventilation, increased muscle tension, sweating, hyperactivity) and subjective reactions (e.g., anxiety, hypervigilance). In addition, there is some evidence that psychoneurological markers (e.g., such neurotransmitters as serotonin, dopamine, norepinephrine, epinephrine) are noticeably elevated in PTSD patients' temporal-limbic brain structures (Brown, 1994).

Krippner and Winkler's (1996) three-stage model encourages identification of the predisposing, activating, and maintaining factors in the establishment of a belief or behavior. That is, individuals may be predisposed to accept a belief or worldview for a number of reasons. Two major ones are the acceptance of beliefs or worldviews of their family of origin or culture and those that are genetically based. Activation is through hippocampus memory of a threat linked to a belief or overstimulation of the nervous system. Maintenance occurs through self-talk as in cognitive reinforcement or preanalytical response to activation with rationalization reinforcement. Greening (1997) has furnished a case history that illustrates Krippner and Winkler's model. Greening observed that his client's character structure (having an active talent for manipulation), family background (replete with alcoholic and depressive relatives), and social background (a business career with questionable ethical practices) predisposed him to PTSD during his deployment in Vietnam. In other words, he arrived in Vietnam with a history of life experiences that poorly suited the demands of military discipline.

He performed well in combat, but PTSD was activated when he witnessed an atrocity, became involved with illegal drugs, and became cynical about the way the U.S. military was conducting the war. His personal history of manipulation, his family history of alcoholism, and his career history devoid of strong ethics was repeated, albeit magnified to a much grander scale, in Vietnam. Upon returning home, his PTSD was maintained, as he had a constellation of PTSD symptoms: flashbacks in which he had difficulty differentiating his own appearance from that of a soldier's corpse he remembered, and a social life filled with manipulative women, one of whom had an unannounced abortion. His PTSD was coupled with depression and distrust, but it led him into a successful period of psychotherapy and a worthwhile job as a hospital fund-raiser (Greening, 1997). He was able to transcend the family history of depression and his own history of ethical transgressions, as well as the specific symptomatology of PTSD.

For people predisposed to PTSD, war trauma often reactivates a repressed or suppressed trauma. Dave, a veteran of the Gulf War, came upon a group of Iraq police who had just shot two children for stripping a car for parts. He drove right by the bodies because he had been instructed not to interfere in "internal affairs." However, experiences of this nature came back to haunt him when he returned home, and he began having recurrent nightmares, not only about his time in Kuwait and Iraq, but about his earlier service in Vietnam and his abusive childhood. His sex life suffered, he bought a pistol, and he drank too much whiskey (Frosch, 2004, p. 17). Had it not been for his pattern of physical abuse as a child, he might have been able to assimilate his war experiences more easily.

Predisposing socioemotional factors are influenced by one's developmental stage and place in a community. Those who experience greater vulnerability to stress often "score thin" on tests that measure the psychological boundaries that individuals erect between themselves and the outside world; those with "thin boundaries" also report more nightmares than those who "score thick" (Hartmann, 1999). Maturity, defensive coping style, personal and family mythology, and a social support system are part of a complex socioemotional lattice work that can insulate an individual from the effects of trauma or, conversely, increase his or her vulnerability (Hudgins, 2002). If one's family myths emphasize threat, danger, suffering, and fear, that person will be predisposed to PTSD. Family myths may be accompanied by a social environment that evokes shame, guilt, stigmatization, or self-hatred —additional precursors to PTSD. When trauma occurs, people from these backgrounds have difficulty integrating their experiences and are likely to connect the trauma with an expectation of danger or to blame themselves for the occurrence.

Arguably, resilient individuals have more flexible self-concepts that allow them to better deal with trauma as they can assimilate new experiences more easily than someone with a rigid worldview and self-concept (Seligman, 2005). Even the media's portrayal of events has the dispositional effect of either reinforcing or undermining a person's resilience. During World War II, the U.S. media were completely supportive of troops and their mission and trumpeted each military success, especially in dozens of films that extolled the bravery of the U.S. military. The Korean Police Action and the Vietnam Conflict, ending in a draw and a loss, produced much less support; most of the films dealing with the Vietnam Conflict took a dark view of the war (e.g., *The Deer Hunter, Apocalypse Now, Platoon,* with *Hotel Hanoi* and *The Green Berets* being the most notable exceptions). The role of media coverage in Iraq and Afghanistan has been labeled "postmodern" by Serlin (2006) because, for the first time, "it mixes the roles of spectator and participant" (p. 147). Reporters have been "embedded" with troops; Internet blogs have countered official governmental "spins"; public relations experts have been employed by those who "mouth" the official line, as well as those who represent other voices. Depending on which film one sees, which blog one reads, or what television commentator one hears, the onset of PTSD can be hastened, delayed, or directed in unexpected ways.

In addition, social attitudes such as familial support are integral predisposing factors that impact the activation of PTSD. Many of these variables were addressed in the 2004 documentary, *Final Letters Home,* which featured grieving relatives reading letters from troops who had died in Iraq. In one of the letters, Michelle Witmer, who was killed ten months later, told her family that their company needed to prepare themselves for what lay ahead, events like children running out in front of vehicles to try to get them to stop. She wrote, "We have to prepare ourselves to hit people because stopping is not an option....These things, as you can imagine, are a lot to take in. I'm trying my best. I've been a little depressed lately but I'm trying to keep my chin up. I really miss home. Tomorrow will be exactly three months since I got deployed" (Schwartz, 2004).

Variables in the greater societal milieu can be powerful predisposing factors as well. A cross-cultural study of conflict-related mortality among civilians revealed that, at the beginning of the twenty-first century, some 38 countries were engaged in or recovering from a civil conflict. Close study of four of these countries, Afghanistan, Somalia, Sudan, and the Democratic Republic of the Congo, concluded that factors such as malnutrition, lack of sanitation, inadequate water supplies, poor public health services, illness, and death played a more significant part in predisposing civilians to PTSD than the intensity of the conflict (Guha-Sapir & van Panhuis, 2003).

Active membership in organized religion and one's internal spiritual belief system can give an individual an interpretive scaffolding to guide his or her reaction to trauma (Maldonado & Spiegel, 1994). Personal myths, the imaginative narratives that address life meanings, and thus an individual's day-by-day decisions, often determine how traumatic experiences will be framed (Krippner, 1997a). Lifton (1979) found that, if death imagery interrupts the perception of a traumatic incident, it could jeopardize one's core belief in her or his own general safety. This intrusion of an impeding catastrophe undermines a soldier's security and, hence, his or her ability to perform well. It confirms the work of Janoff-Bulman (1992), who argued that PTSD arises from a general violation of deeply held beliefs and expectations about the world and one's place in it. Solomon, Greenberg, and Pyszczynski (2003) have found that introducing thoughts of one's own death into an otherwise innocuous task dramatically changes a participant's response. They conjectured that if humans were able to accept the reality of death and divest themselves of the illusion that their culture or religion affords them a "protection" against demise, there would be a decrease in genocides, doctrinal warfare, and wanton destruction by fanatics (p. 307).

As mentioned earlier, each person faces potential traumatic stressors with a different set of predispositions that are activated by a traumatic event (MacNair, 2002). Whether or not the stressor (or series of stressors) will trigger classic PTSD depends not only on its severity but also on its dispositional factors (at the time of the experience), the environmental factors (many of them seemingly mundane at the time), and the interaction with one's predisposing factors.

For example, about one out of four individuals exposed to traumatic threats to life or physical integrity (e.g., combat, rape) develops PTSD, a much higher figure than the 10 percent estimated for all types of potential trauma (Miller & Keane, 2004). In 2005, the U.S. National Center for

PTSD reported that some 30 percent of combat veterans suffer from the condition at some point in their lives (Adam, 2005), a phenomenon that many explain as a consequence of killing another human being (MacNair, 2002). In fact, a 1994 study of PTSD of veterans of World War II, the Korean Police Action, and the Vietnam Conflict found the "responsibility for killing another human being is the single most pervasive, traumatic experience of war" (Hayes, 2006, p. 27).

However, these figures overlook subclinical instances of PTSD that represent another dimension to the disorder. Scaer (2005), for one, has described traumas suffered by virtually everyone in the course of a lifetime, in order to demonstrate the idea of a "trauma continuum." Throughout our consideration of PTSD, it will be useful to reflect on our proposed continuum or spectrum rather than a definite categorical boundary.

Incidents later in one's life that summon traumatic memories often serve to reinforce and even aggravate classic PTSD (Miller & Keane, 2004). Generally, a war veteran working in a noisy factory will be at greater risk for recall of combat memory than one filling orders for organic foods. Yet, some individuals feel, even in times of low stress stimuli, that a threat is imminent (Cozolino, 2002). Paulson (1994) has described this sensation as "waiting for the other shoe to fall." Individuals become aroused and anxiety-ridden awaiting a threat to which they can attach their free-floating anxiety. From a physiological perspective, it stems from hippocampal memory that activates the amygdala's "fight or flight" response, inducing the release of norepinephrine from the adrenal glands that hyperarouse the entire mind/body system.

Physical combat is a massive, potential traumatic stressor, because it exposes the combatant to situations that involve killing, as well as the constant possibility of being killed. It is not theoretical, nor can it be deferred into the future; the threat is now—a long, continuing, and seemingly endless "now" (Paulson, 1994). Kaye Baron, a psychologist with a private practice near the Fort Carson Army Base in Colorado, learned this quickly after working with returning military personnel:

> I've seen a lot of PTSD symptoms, if not full-blown PTSD....The social withdrawal, the nightmares, the sleep disturbances, the memory and concentration problems, the anger, the lack of trust—I'm seeing all this within the troops coming back from Iraq. (Greer, 2005, p. 38)

When investigating phenomena that maintain the high levels of anxiety in PTSD victims, one must remember that military action does not occur in a vacuum, but within a web of complicated cultural interactions. They include one's own immediate culture (i.e., the military), as well as the political climate at home, cultural attitudes in the host country, the host country's government, and the larger international setting (Paulson, 2003a).

According to Krippner and Colodzin (1989), Vietnam veterans' flashbacks "might represent unsuccessful attempts to make sense of an experience that many of the veterans' fellow Americans considered to be pointless or wrong" (p. 81). Besides flashbacks, common symptoms of PTSD among veterans include hypervigilance, dejection, panic attacks, substance abuse, inappropriate acting out, unpredictable episodes of rage, depression, and cycles of anxiety and guilt (Rotter & Bovega, 1999). Oftentimes, guilt and anxiety form a feedback loop, which plays out in self-talk that stimulates or even conditions a hippocampal memory response. This, in turn, activates the amygdala, releasing norepinephrine, thereby galvanizing feelings of hypervigilance and the valuations of self-talk. Ultimately, these perceptions exaggerate danger, which further stimulates the amygdala, causing the cycle to repeat (Goleman, 1995). Seemingly innocuous comments like, "You're not the same any more," by noncombatant peers sometimes compound these symptoms producing increased feelings of worthlessness in the individual (Paulson, 2004). Some veterans may feel like they have lost everything of value and suffer a total alienation from friends, lovers, family, and themselves. As Mabel, the daughter of a Korean War veteran confided to us:

> My father served honorably as an officer in Korea and was distressed that the war ended in a stalemate instead of in a victory. As an adult, I am aware that he had been traumatized for the rest of his life by what he had seen and experienced, especially the death of the soldiers serving under him. I don't think he ever forgave himself for losing those gallant troops.

Anxiety is often generalized to areas that were not associated with the actual trauma (Maldonado & Spiegel, 1994). The stressor finds many ways to intrude into the patient's stream of consciousness, particularly from recall; but whether the stressor is reexperienced or avoided, it brings about some type of arousal (Nutt et al., 2000).

Stressors may be reexperienced through conditioned responses and, sometimes, as hallucinatory episodes during which a veteran "sees" the enemy upon awakening, "hears" a bomb explode during a television drama, or "feels" shrapnel entering his or her body when getting jostled unexpectedly on a streetcar or subway train (Pitman et al., 1991). Similarly, reactions to stressors can reemerge in nighttime dreams and nightmares, naps, or periods of dissociation in which the stressor seems to recur, breaking into the ordinary flow of the veteran's awareness, behavior repertoire, or self-identity (Krippner, 1997a). In each of these ways, the stressor comes to dominate the veteran's waking life, usually unexpectedly and in ways that are maladaptive and dysfunctional (Rothschild, 2003).

Veterans try to avoid reexperiencing the stressor in a number of ways. They try to forget anniversaries of the traumatic event, they attempt to stay away from activities or feelings that arouse recollection of the event, and they engage in "emotional numbing" so that they will not have to share feelings about the event with anyone (Brown, 1994). This "numbing" often is carried to extremes, leading one to avoid responsibilities, even important ones relating to marriage, children, long-term employment, and close friendship (Pitman et al., 1991; Tedeschi & Calhoun, 1995; Zoroya, 2006b). It may also lead to "detaching" emotionally from others if the emotional involvement becomes sufficiently anxiety-producing (Maldonado & Spiegel, 1994). Veterans may even forget key elements of the traumatic event, engaging in defensive repression, suppression, or denial (Paulson, 1995; Peterson & Nisenholz, 1999). The situation is serious enough that the U.S. military has organized "marriage enrichment" sessions and "romantic getaways" to reduce the divorce rate among veterans (Hefling, 2005).

Because of increased arousal, a veteran may also experience persistent anxiety not present before the traumatic experience (Nutt et al., 2000). Sleep disturbances and nightmares pose special challenges for the field of sleep medicine. Joshua, an Iraq veteran with PTSD, was beset with irregular sleep patterns, and one night hit his wife in the face, muttering about having to kill the person coming after him (Frosch, 2004). Several useful approaches for dealing with nightmares have been developed over the years (e.g., desensitization, ventilating, expressive arts therapy, sandplay, confrontation during the nightmare, altering the dream scenario (Carey, 2006; Halliday, 1987; Kramer, 2007), although most mental health professionals are unaware of them and prescribe medication instead.

The evolutionary benefit of the survival behaviors learned in wartime is apparent (Buss, 2004). What makes behaviors maladaptive is the geographic and temporal change from a war zone to a nonwar zone or from an era of war to an era of peace. And because the combatants cannot easily drop their war time behaviors, many returning from combat judge themselves negatively, which inspires inner conflict between "what is" and "what should be" (Paulson, 1994). Society's adoration of the warrior has paled in recent years because of changing gender roles. Hence, stereotypical "macho" reactions are looked upon with disdain by many men and women, leading to further negative self-concepts on the part of veterans.

SOCIAL CONSTRUCTS AND PTSD

Certain roles and responsibilities within cultures, including our own, are gender-specific (Paulson, 1994). The breadwinner and the warrior were prevailing American models of maleness just a few decades ago. Likewise, being a homemaker, stable and family-oriented, was a traditional American female role. We, as a culture, have witnessed the blurring of many male and female roles and responsibilities over the past several decades, as both men and women step into each other's stereotypical arenas (Taylor, 1989). As a result, the acknowledgment of male superiority has eroded (Gilligan,

1982). While not yet achieving complete equality, more and more women have claimed their right to choose their roles, independent of males. In contemporary society, women have successfully challenged men in most professions, and now, hardly any endeavor is purely a male one.

Although many women serving in various military capacities have been killed, U.S. infantry troops are still primarily men. Even so, after their successful and impressive combat participation in both the Gulf War and Operation Iraqi Freedom, frontline U.S. combatants of the future are sure to include women (Goldstein, 2001). By the end of 2006, some 70 female soldiers had been killed in Iraq, more than the total from the Korean, Vietnam, and Gulf wars combined (Scarborough, 2007). Women have already excelled in military service in Israel and have been key elements in various insurgent, militant, and paramilitary groups. Gender differences in PTSD have not been thoroughly studied but need to be seen in a cultural, social, and psychological context (Kimerling, Ouimette, & Wolfe, 2002). For example, Operation Iraqi Freedom's Mental Health Advisory Team (2006) found no evidence that female soldiers were less able than male soldiers to cope with combat stressors. In fact, the more intense the combat, the greater the impact was on male soldiers in comparison with females (p. 79). The Team identified some 30 types of combat experiences (p. 13); the impact of each of them upon women has yet to be explored.

Current male and female Iraq combat veterans are in a unique situation. At the outbreak of the war, the military was deployed as a volunteer force. Yet, many believe that reservists shouldered the burden of combat missions interminably because of a "back-door" policy (Webel, 2005). Relatively few Americans endured the onerous multiple combat tours in Iraq, though it was very stressful for the soldiers involved (Carbonell, 2004). To compound matters, the images of Iraq and foreign Arab fighters held at Abu Ghraib prison, forced to wear underwear on their heads, stacked in naked human pyramids, and led on leashes with dog collars were repulsive to viewers around the world and demoralizing for many U.S. combat troops (Dorsey, 2005).

The purported reason combat and support troops were sent to Iraq was to protect the world from Saddam Hussein's nuclear and biological weapons programs. Little more than a year later, it was discovered that reports of both programs were greatly exaggerated. As a result, many U.S. soldiers became disillusioned about their involvement in the war, leaving them no goal except duty and survival. Upon returning home many tried to "put the experience out of their heads" and not think about their involvement in the conflict (Nelson, 2004). Ray was one of many soldiers subject to the personal political gravity of the Iraq War. He was given a medical discharge for PTSD and gained some relief from his symptoms by ritually donning his Marine uniform two or three times a week, walking around his hometown carrying a sign reading, "I killed innocent civilians for our government" (Goodman, 2004, p. 82).

If the history of U.S. wars has taught us anything, it is that all too often veterans are unable to let go of their war experiences—instead, denying, suppressing, or displacing their traumas (Shay, 2002). However, there is no unanimity on the topic. Keith, an infantry officer, told a reporter that there was nothing wrong with the morale of his men. "When time comes to re-enlist, you hear them standing in front of the company...saying they're ready to go back there because they want to make a difference" (Babbin, 2004, p. 13).

Personal myths and cultural myths interact, often in surprising ways. Many of the veterans we interviewed seemed as if they had been saddled with outdated beliefs out of childhood storybooks and World War II movies: myths about doing one's duty, displaying one's patriotism, protecting the homeland, and "confronting the enemy there" so "we won't have to fight them here." These sentiments were noble and even admirable. However, they clashed with the emerging cultural mythology of many ordinary citizens of the homeland they hoped to defend: the decision to invade Iraq was misguided, the weapons of mass destruction were an illusion, and the war seemed to increase rather than decrease the number and the resourcefulness of terrorists.

These mythological discontinuities associated with the Iraq War have also exacted a toll on military families (Drummet et al., 2003; Hunter, 2004). Vast and unprecedented deployment of reservists has compromised the stability of intimate relationships with their partners and children, who experience loneliness, role overloads, gender shifts, financial concerns, changes in community support, and frustration with the military bureaucracy (Baum, 2004). The reservists' return is often equally inauspicious, as they frequently find themselves referred to credit agencies by the U.S. military because of pay discrepancies or "failure to pay" for lost equipment. In 2005, the Government Accountability Office found that more that 90 percent of the soldiers in some Reserve and National Guard units incurred payroll errors during deployment (Regan, 2005).

These situations and their relevance must be kept continuously in mind, because the families of combat veterans with PTSD face challenges along with those faced by the veterans themselves (Carr, 2002; Drummet et al., 2003). To be sure, the dynamics of PTSD are best understood when they are properly contextually situated. Many combat veterans cannot sustain their marriages, especially after combat, and others commit acts of violence against their family members, including murder. In these cases, incarceration becomes a "treatment" only insofar as it protects others (Bustos, 1990). It is rare that these veterans receive any direct continuing help resolving their issues.

Historically, psychology has focused primarily on individual combatants when addressing the consequences of war and designing interventions to meet those needs (Brown et al., 2002; Carbonell, 2004; Chirot & Seligman, 2001). The literature on the impact of war stress on families is scarce, matched by a paucity of theoretical models, assessment tools, and models for large-scale intervention on behalf of civilian victims of war and their families. Consequently, many psychologists and other aid workers who attempt to address the needs of these populations lack the training and resources required to find solutions for war-shattered families and communities (Carr, 2002). This need has spurred some in various areas of psychology, in collaboration with other disciplines, to conduct research and experimentation using several different models of intervention with civilian victims of war trauma (Krippner & McIntyre, 2003).

Perhaps the single most prevalent fixture in the experience of combatants was the recognition that there were no sanctuaries in Iraq (Hoge et al., 2004). Death could come at any moment from a sniper's bullet, an improvised roadside bomb, a mine, a stray mortar round, a surgical insurgent attack, or a friendly fire accident (Fullerton & Ursano, 1997; Nutt et al., 2000). Terror and trauma bear some semantic relation, but little clinical research has focused on their interaction (Paulson, 1995). Based on 72 interviews with survivors of five decades of terrorist attacks, genocides, concentration camps, and military bombings of civilian centers, Webel (2005) has referred to political terror as "the external terrorizer," and trauma as "the internal terrifier." Both represent threats to self-identity at its very core. Once the Iraq veteran has returned, the combat landscape supervenes on the home environment, such that "there is no safe place."

PTSD is one of several war stresses and traumas. When someone, or some group, is traumatized, the rest of his or her continuity is shattered. There may be a loss of personal resources, coping skills, networks, and values (Paulson, 2003a), and resiliency and recovery may occur quickly or may never happen at all (Rotter & Bovega, 1999; Scaer, 2005). If asked to give a more complete list of psychological disorders resulting from war, then certainly one must include brain injury and loss of limbs or body function (Glasser, 2005; Gottfried, 2004). Blacker and Fairweather (2006) refer to traumatic brain injury resulting from the concussive force of improvised explosive devices, as "the signature wound" of the Afghanistan and Iraq wars (p. B11).

As was true of numerous Vietnam War veterans, many veterans of Operation Iraqi Freedom have not gained much by way of meaning from participation in the war and the subsequent occupation (Baum, 2004). Combat veterans returning from Vietnam were commonly shunned by their communities and were labeled by war protestors as "warmongers" and "baby killers." On the other hand, they were called "losers" by some members of the military community, including the American Legion and Veterans of

Foreign Wars ("In search," 2006), because they "lost the war" (Krippner & Colodzin, 1989; Paulson, 1994). There have been fewer hostile reactions regarding the status of Iraq combat veterans. One of the reasons may be that, as of 2007, there has been no real danger of a draft, so the war remains an eyesore rather than an outrage (Gerbode, 2004). Nevertheless, returning veterans cannot help but become aware of the disjoint between their personal myths and the cultural myths awaiting them. They went to war as women and men of the professional elite, as members of a warrior class. Upon their return they were not reviled, as were many Vietnam veterans, but many were hard pressed to find jobs, a place to live, and a way to cope with PTSD.

Without unified social support for the war and the emotional distance between veterans of Iraq combat, reintegration into civilian society has been particularly difficult (Shay, 2002). Most civilians cannot identify with Iraq combat veterans, know very little about them and their concerns or their fears, and find their vulnerability and fear of being in a "no-exit" redeployment situation foreign. This apathy and estrangement is rationalized by a presiding belief that soldiers should have known what to expect when they volunteered.

Vietnam veterans were forced to hide their involvement in that unpopular war and forego the much-needed support essential for adjustment and re-entry into civilian life (Paulson, 1994). But Iraq veterans have the opposite dilemma of reentering a society that is minimally concerned with them (Nelson, 2004). Civilians may wave flags as military units parade through enthusiastic crowds, but, at the same time, the debates rage as to whether the United States should have ever invaded Iraq in the first place. Young men and women and their parents, many of whom were anti–Vietnam War protestors, have not been affected personally by the war, and thus lack any passionate impetus for involvement (Wright, 2004). They nurture a vague notion that the poor, the unskilled, and those not bound for college join the military, and that this does not apply to them or their children (Serlin & Cannon, 2004; Volkman, 2004; Webel, 2005).

In moments of solitude and reflection, when they are not preoccupied with staying alive, Iraq combat veterans often find themselves without personal, positive meaning from their involvement in the Iraq occupation (Nelson, 2004; van der Veer, 1998). They did what they were told to do, killed those they were supposed to kill, but still were acutely aware of a fine distinction between "freedom fighters" and "terrorists" (Kamalipour, 1999; Kennedy, 2004).

Most in-country soldiers opt to interpret their actions as a matter of duty, but upon returning home, many try to put the experience out of their minds and avoid reflection about their involvement (Krippner & McIntyre, 2003; Paulson, 1991, 1994, 1995, 2003a, 2004). Like their Vietnam-era elders, once these veterans have left the combat theatre and reenter civilian society, they feel ashamed of themselves, battling serious existential conflicts, aliena-tion, and even homelessness (Bustos, 1990; Nelson, 2004). Unemployment for young veterans is twice the national average and has been climbing since 2000 (Zoroya, 2006b), a situation due, in part, to negative self-concepts of combat veterans.

As the anxiety-guilt cycle revolves, it is sometimes reinforced by "moraliz-ing" peers who leave veterans with a sense of profound worthlessness (MacNair, 2002), lost in a "dark night of the soul" (LeShan, 1992), and haunted by a feeling that no one really cares (Paulson, 2004). Many even feel that God no longer wants them, for they have killed God's children (Paulson, 1995).

INSTITUTIONAL RESPONSES

As Kathy Platoni, an army psychologist, observed: "They watched their beloved fellow soldiers being blown up right in front of them" (Munsey, 2006). To address this issue, various on-site programs have been instituted in Iraq. During their breaks, soldiers, sailors, Marines, and pilots have the option of talking to health professionals. Marines have adopted what is called Operational Stress Control and Readiness, which matches psycholo-gists with Marine regiments in the months before deployment, continuing during rotation in Iraq and after returning home. This promotes sturdier relationships and a more incisive evaluation of how service members are coping or preparing. Psychologists help servicemen and servicewomen deal with two types of stress: combat stress and deployment stress, the latter caused by being overseas and working in harsh conditions (Munsey, 2006).

The army's Combat Stress Control (CSC) program focuses on brevity, immediacy, centrality (treatment away from army facilities to avoid stigma-tization), expectancy (soldiers are expected to return to duty), proximity, and simplicity (a warm shower, a good meal, and a comfortable place to sleep ensures that basic needs are met) (Munsey, 2006). A combat stress reaction may or may not lead to PTSD, but it is the mission of the CSC pro-gram to assist and treat soldiers as quickly and as close to their units as pos-sible (Moore & Reger, 2006).

Most veterans assume that the military or the Veterans' Administration (VA) will "fix" those who suffer with traumatic and existential issues, but the reality is that it depends upon one's definition of "fix" (Paulson, 1994, 1995; Roberts & Yeager, 2004). Traumatic wounds generally require con-siderable individual and/or group therapy, a task that is both very expensive and time consuming (Beck & Emery, 1985; Hoge et al., 2002). The military and VA view "fixing" as providing veterans with limited treatments, with little mention of "healing" (Roberts & Yeager, 2004). Treatment also relies heavily on pharmaceuticals, because they are less expensive than psycho-therapy and provide more predictable results (Horowitz, 1998; Sheikh &

Nguyen, 2000). Hence, "fixing" for the VA centers on symptom reduction and group medication (often called "herd" medicine by veterans). To a large degree, attaining effective psychotherapy falls on the combat veteran's shoulders, with whatever support families and friends will provide (Paulson, 2003a).

It should be noted that until the early 1990s, treatment at VA hospitals was so substandard that Congress considered shutting down the entire system and giving veterans vouchers for treatment at private facilities. Twenty years later, the VA ran the largest integrated health care system in the United States, with more than 1,400 hospitals that, on the whole, scored higher than private facilities on the American Consumer Satisfaction Index. Furthermore, males 65 years of age and older receiving VA care had about a 40 percent lower risk of death than those enrolled in Medicare Advantage, and in 2006, Harvard University gave the VA its "Innovations in American Government Award" for the agency's work in computerizing patient records (Waller, 2006).

Nevertheless, many veterans complain about the red tape involved in getting an appointment, then waiting a month or more to see a health care worker. Concern was raised that the disabled servicemen and servicewomen returning from Iraq and Afghanistan could swamp the system; in 2004, a future shortfall of nearly two billion dollars was predicted (Frosch, 2004, p. 17). And enlarging the scope of veterans' health care benefits presses the alarm buttons of economic conservatives who fear that it would take business away from the private sector (Waller, 2006). Opposition comes from a different group of men and women who believe that therapy is eroding the character of those who use it. Sommers and Satel (2006), in the spirit of stoicism and extreme individualism, contend that Americans should eschew psychotherapy, use their own common sense and self-reliance, and take care of their own problems, relationships, and grief reactions. In other words, the country does not speak with a single voice when there is a call for increased mental health benefits for veterans.

Then there is the special case of those dismissed from the armed services because of conduct linked to PTSD, where a less-than-honorable discharge can warrant the denial of VA benefits. Zoroya (2006a) has described the case of Chris Packley, a top marksman on a sniper team showcased by the Marines Corps for the team's 22 "kills." When he returned to the United States, Packley had recurring flashbacks of a friend who died on the battlefield. He smoked marijuana to escape the images and left his base without permission. He remarked that he "wanted out" and was expelled from the Marine Corps, in turn losing free medication and counseling. A lawyer who supervises the legal defense of Marines in the western United States told Zoroya that scores of combat veterans like Packley were dismissed because of alcohol and drug abuse. Lieutenant Colonel Colby Vokey noted, "The

Marine Corps has created these mental health issues" and then just "kicks them out in the streets" (Hampson & Solvig, 2006, p. 1A).

In the meantime, whether from the VA hospitals or from private hospitals and clinics, specific treatments such as behavior modification, desensitization techniques, and cognitive-behavior therapy have positive value in helping veterans heal from the war (Peterson & Nisenholz, 1999; Roberts & Yeager, 2004). Cognitive-behavior therapy, as well as psychodynamic psychotherapy can assist veterans to face repressed memories, enabling them to cope with life as it presents itself in the present (Runte et al., 2004; Stolorow et al., 1987). But these approaches cannot, by themselves, empower a person to uncover positive meaning from a negative war experience. Can most U.S. combatants feel good about killing and watching others being killed? It is doubtful. However, one can view the situation from a larger perspective to find positive meaning. Perhaps one can reframe the war experience as a "rite of passage," that is, a life transition process.

Many Jungian analysts and humanistic-existential psychotherapists have used rites of passage metaphorically to describe their patient's growth toward "individuation." Most of these therapists have included the cognitive, behavioral, and existential aspects of their clients' recovery. Without them, rites of passage are simply an introduction to a complex process with little or no completion (Norcross & Goldfried, 2005). Multiple therapeutic approaches may be necessary, depending on the condition and worldview of the veteran. Many traumatized veterans require active one-on-one counseling, including cognitive, behavioral, humanistic-existential, and psychodynamic approaches (among others). With the involvement of other veterans, family members, and friends, these clients can discover positive meaning in their experience (Carson et al., 2000).

This ritualistic process does not need to be a lengthy one. Roland (2002) has employed a seven-session program to heal traumatic memories, based on the principle that most are either a real or an imagined separation from love of themselves and others. His seven steps of ritual move from "Finding the Child Within Yourself" to "Understanding your Life as a Quest," "Taking Accountability for Your Life," "Connecting to the Child Within Yourself," "Remembering Love," "Opening Your Heart," and "Listening to the Path of the Heart." Roland (2002) has taken the position that this type of therapy is a form of self-healing because his clients eventually take responsibility for accepting love instead of denying love. The use of ritual in psychotherapy may appeal to many veterans who are accustomed to orderly, sequential tasks. Furthermore, ritual underscores the need for revised personal myths if treatment for PTSD is to have long-lasting effects.

Throwing Babies on Bonfires

Throwing babies on bonfires
doesn't make sense to me.
I can't imagine that they burn well,
so what's the point?
Political change is hard enough
without wasting efforts
on mere stunts.
Still, if it keeps the soldiers happy
maybe it's a necessary evil,
at least until some saner species
evolves to govern the earth.

—Tom Greening

3

The Phenomenology of PTSD

Looking back at recent history, it seems as if nearly every generation, or at least some segment within that generation, must fight a war. Political, religious, ethical, and economic differences often prevent cultures from living side-by-side in mutual respect, understanding, and tolerance and thereby ensure a future of conflict, one in which men are tortured, women are raped, and babies are thrown on bonfires. Rather than ferreting out the material processes and factors involved in PTSD, this chapter approaches the disorder phenomenologically. In other words, we will attempt to create some window into the actual experience of combat veterans, relying on their own descriptions. In addition to illuminating what can be a highly individuated and secret recess of personal experience, we hope that the accounts of veterans will also establish a continuum for PTSD that highlights significant similarities as well as differences in their ordeal.

What made service members sign up in the first place? Some Iraq combat veterans were fueled with youthful enthusiasm about partaking in a larger purpose, perhaps even with aspirations of changing the world for the better, or at least protecting their family, friends, and country from another terrorist attack. Others were at a crossroads in their lives and simply did not know what the next career step was for them. "Do I want to go to college?" "Do I want to join the work force?" "Do I want to get married and start a family?" For many of them, military service was a way of taking a break from routine civilian life. Following initial major combat operations, the main combatants have been reservists who were not looking for an overseas adventure. Most were trying to supplement their income or find a way to pay for college.

It seemed to us that the members of the first group of Iraq War combatants were both the youngest and most idealistic. They may have joined for reasons similar to Mike's. He told us:

> I was tired of high school, didn't want to go to college, but didn't want to work construction, either. I wanted to get away [from home] and so I joined.

Then, there is an entirely different population that had jobs but needed more money and selected the Army reserve as a solution. They assumed they would never be called up unless the entire country had been mobilized. Holly told us:

> I joined the Army reserve initially to help pay for college. I did not mind the weekend drills every month, and I liked the idea of being in the motor pool because I am a mechanical engineer. I never thought seriously that I would have to go to Iraq.

These are typical responses of the military personnel we interviewed who were sent to serve in Iraq. Yet we also found this war to be different from previous conflicts, such as that of Vietnam. Speaking to civilians, we found great superficial support for the military, but when questioning them more deeply, we found that few had any personal stake besides the distant fear of a draft.

Although the military has gained considerable experience in dealing with combat trauma since the Vietnam War and has made some effort to respond passively, the effects of war trauma are very difficult to treat, particularly in that they are multidimensional in both etiology and robustness to treatment. It seems that the simple moniker, PTSD, prompts the military establishment to think that the cause and treatment are just as simple. But, for those who experience it, it is torment. Billy told us:

> I am actually afraid to go to sleep at night. The nightmares are unbearable. My combat buddies died once in Iraq. But I have nightmares several times a week in which they are killed all over again. And I can still hear them screaming when I wake up.

One needs to remember that PTSD is a complex response by humans to protect themselves from a systematic or prolonged threat to their well-being. Many of those combatants who did not meet the official PTSD diagnosis have been negatively affected by combat, even if they were not immediately aware of it. We have referred to them elsewhere as subclinical cases and place them at a different point of our hypothetical continuum than the clinically diagnosed cases.

The stoic resolve essential to veterans is slowly dissolved by acidic war experiences. For these veterans, death is omnipresent, and the vague but portentous knowledge of it seems to envelope their lives, often completely.

Simply stated, the quality of the combatants' lives is negatively affected by their war experiences. For those who directly experienced combat, life will never be the same. Some will employ defense mechanisms to blot it from their minds, while others will be disabled immediately. Although the long-range plans of getting married, raising a family, and eventually enjoying retirement are still consciously present for many veterans, the ever-present memory and realization of war, forever operating on both conscious and unconscious levels, has taken the joy and sparkle from many lives. Many of those lives become "stalled." Abbie Pickett of the Wisconsin National Guard is an example of a woman who returned from Iraq with shattered plans. She had hoped to become a physician's assistant but recurrent symptoms of PTSD made it difficult for her to concentrate, and her plans were put on "hold" while she tried to get her life back on track (Shapiro, 2005).

Because most combatants have lost friends to snipers or improvised explosive devices (IEDs), seen secure areas in Iraq transformed into civilian killing fields by insurgents, and experienced other calamities, the combatants become extremely vigilant, even when there is no actual threat. Many veterans told us that initially they thought this was just an overreaction, but as time went on, it was interpreted as a threat looming somewhere very close to them. While most civilians seek to accomplish various goals in life, former combatants, all too often, channel their energies into an ill-advised protection strategy against nonexistent threats.

This process of protecting oneself from perceived threats is fueled by anxiety, and, in due course, the anxiety is generalized to additional perceived threats, resulting in yet another kind of vicious cycle. Such anxiety is not always classifiable by way of PTSD symptomatology—that is, conscious subjective anxiety, usually with a feared object easily identified by the veteran. The anxiety we are discussing is a vague sense of uneasiness or of feeling rushed, an inner restlessness, a feeling of strain and muscle tension, and an underlying feeling of danger. This danger is sensed, but it cannot be clearly perceived. Usually, it is displaced or projected onto an object or person. It might be the person who delivers mail, the check-out clerk at the supermarket, a spouse or sibling, a winding road, or even an unusual animal, and it tends to leave the veteran with an isolation that estranges her or him from her or himself and others. For many observers, this isolation is mere detachment, but the veteran experiences it as the dulled luster of life and an escape from anxiety-producing situations. Once the veteran begins actively to protect himself or herself from perceived threats, feelings of isolation become ever more prominent. Eventually, the balance between protection and engagement with the environment is grossly skewed toward protection. Over time, the original stressor (war combat) is but one of many multiplying triggers, until combat may not even be recognized as the original stressor.

If the veteran was affected only by memories of past combat episodes, the condition would probably not be as damaging to his or her quality of life. However, the condition seems to expand into other areas of life (Hayes et al., 1999). That is, threats of combat are extended to extremely mundane situations. It is not just that firecrackers become gunfire and thunder becomes explosions, but that the entire world seems to change. It becomes a world of looming violence, a very threatening place, where terrorists run rampant, and one's life is in constant danger. Although there is some truth to the view that most Americans, even those without PTSD, are more cautious since the attacks of September 11, 2001, it is the degree of wariness that differentiates the PTSD sufferer from others. Individuals who are not dangerous are perceived as hostile, close friends can become suspect, and finally one's own body may be suspected of betraying the veteran. One can point out that they are overreacting, and often they will agree. But, at the same time, they just cannot seem to find equanimity. Juan, an active duty Marine infantry officer, back from a year in Iraq, stated:

> Boy, I was glad to get back from Iraq. I didn't think I would ever see home again. All I could think about was getting home in one piece and back to my job. When I finally did get home, I was overjoyed. I felt everything had been worth it. But as the weeks went by, I felt like shit. I should be glad I survived, but I just didn't know it would be this tough to adapt.

Ann, an active Army logistics personnel and truck driver, stated:

> Yeah, when we got back, all I could think about was how happy I was that we made it. Yet, as the weeks passed, I felt sad. I was not sure why. I even felt edgy a lot of the time. At first I thought it was jet lag, but now I don't know.

We should point out that these two individuals were frontline support for Marine Infantry Units in Anbar Province. Like their Vietnam elders, some began to feel inadequate in living their lives after combat in Iraq. We originally uncovered this phenomenon with Vietnam veterans a number of years ago. Decades after their initial Vietnam experiences, some Vietnam veterans felt that their symptoms merely reinforced the conviction that they were weak and inadequate. Ironically, many of those who could successfully function in their work and environment had trouble getting close to others emotionally for fear that they would be viewed weak and inadequate.

Others in the Vietnam era initially perceived themselves as heroes. However, the unpopularity of the war soon drove them to hide their experiences. As time passed, many claimed to feel unworthy of love due to their involvement in Vietnam. The following is an excerpt from an interview detailing the return from Vietnam (Paulson, 1994):

> I sensed the overt damage within myself. I remember fantasizing about how warm and caring I would be when I got back from Vietnam. I would find that special woman and devote my life to our relationship. The entire time I was in Vietnam, I thought to myself how nice it would be to be held by a warm, loving

woman, to watch her laugh and smile as I teased her. I would fantasize over and over what it would be like.

When I did return, things were different. I found that I did not really like to be with women; they made me nervous. To be held by a woman made me feel very vulnerable. Instead of feeling good, I would feel terribly sad and afraid in her arms. It was almost like being a little boy again, in need of a mother to hug away my pain. But I was 21 years old; I was too old to need a mother figure. Because these vulnerable feelings were, I thought, a sign of my weak character, I began avoiding any closeness with women.

I did find that I could get close to a woman when I drank. Drinking made relationships with women much easier; I did not feel vulnerable and could use them for sexual gratification. After all, what was a woman for, except to fuck? (p. 30–31)

Looking critically at the era and the sensationalized freedom of sexuality, such a personal mythology is understandable. Yet that stance did not work when trying to establish a relationship with an actual woman. The same Vietnam veteran continues:

We had to distance ourselves from any meaningful [emotional] encounter with women because we felt that we could not share with them what we had experienced. How could you tell your girlfriend what it was like for you to shoot another human being? How could you tell her how vulnerable and scared you had felt, never knowing if you would live another hour the whole time you were in Vietnam? How could you tell her what it was like to kick dead [Viet Cong] soldiers because you were so angry at them for killing your friends? I was afraid to tell any women what it was like.

How could I tell her about the horror I felt watching a dump truck taking the corpses of 17 of my friends to be embalmed? How could I tell her what I felt when I watched their blood drip and flow from the tailgate onto the ground? How could I tell her how deeply I hurt, of the agony I was in, and how gnawing my suffering was? How could I tell her that the pain and guilt followed me like a beast tracking its prey? How could I tell her that the pain hounded me at night, during the day, and even while making love? What would she think of me if I told her? I feared that if any woman knew this about me, she would freak out, go into convulsions, vomit, and totally reject me for being such a disgusting human being. What was I to do? I did what seemed best: I drank and drank and drank. (p. 31)

While this kind of guilt did not appear in any of our interviews with active duty veterans in Iraq, we intuited that it may have been there; perhaps there had not been enough time between the combat theatre and civilian reintegration for it to appear. In the meantime, there is a subtle cue that continues to alert researchers to deeper psychological disturbances among Iraq combat veterans. They may not have experienced the intense levels of combat found in Vietnam, nor are they consciously aware how they feel about it. However, every male we interviewed claimed to avoid emotional engagements with women that would require discussions about combat.

Additionally, the emotional availability of each combatant seems to have been seriously diminished. Their emotional relationships demand energy, care, and concern, yet none of them had the vitality to provide it. From our perspective, this has become one of the major aspects of failed post-Iraq relationships.

A pattern among these Iraq veterans now living civilian lives also emerged. They felt as if they were not part of any group other than the military, something also common among Vietnam War veterans (Paulson, 1994). Yet, they knew that they no longer were a part of the military. These feelings seem to have been linked to combat experiences that could not be reconciled with civilian roles. Symptoms of this sort are not limited to combatants but are also found in civilians coping with disabilities, "recovering" alcoholics, and immigrants for whom English is a rarely spoken second language.

Apparently, low-level anxiety is at the core of this phenomenon. Instead of avoiding overt danger, many Iraq veterans compensate through potentially dangerous behaviors. This may not be obvious to a casual observer, in that many veterans on the surface live passive lives, albeit somewhat outside the customary social standards. For example, many do not wear seat belts and drive dangerously. Others participate in high-risk sports, such as hang gliding and parachute jumping. Safety, in this case, does not coincide with any conventional notion, although it becomes more salient in its distorted form. One way to achieve this new kind of safety might be to store guns in the car or under the beds or to maintain control of situations in inappropriate ways, such as leaving a social gathering at awkward times. Many take their own vehicles to events, instead of riding with others, so that they can decide when they want to take their leave.

Safety is experienced when one feels in control, either by avoiding perceived dangers or by using drugs and alcohol to soften perceptions. As Juan said, "Yeah, the one thing I learned was the value of having a drink, not to get drunk but just to take the edge off." This sounds quite familiar when compared to our previous work with Vietnam veterans.

Many of the veterans who would not be classified as clinical PTSD cases claimed to worry about a myriad topics—being capable of finding and keeping a job, being able to experience happiness, and not having to return to military service. They reported experiencing less anxiety when worrying about something specific than when not worrying. Researchers who evaluated clients with a generalized anxiety disorder also made this interesting discovery. Borkovec et al. (2004) proposed that this type of worry is actually a form of avoidance that reduces internal distress in individuals. While worriers find the experience of worrying unpleasant, their own internal experiences are even more unpleasant without some specific object of worry on which to focus. They also found that worriers did not experience increased heart rates as did those who used general relaxation strategies prior to a negative exposure task. Additionally, another group of researchers reported that chronic worry is not associated with increased activation of the sympathetic nervous system; however, it reduces the autonomic nervous system's flexibility (Connor et al., 2003).

This inability of the autonomic nervous system to cope with emotional reactions may lead to substance abuse. One veteran said, "Things were different [after the return from Vietnam]. To protect myself...I found a friend that night. It was a friend that would keep me calm and mellow. That friend was Budweiser" (Paulson, 1994, p. 29). Substance abuse has also been reported from Operation Iraqi Freedom:

> Part of the problem is boredom....In Iraq the Americans don't leave the base unless they're on a mission. [Some troops use amphetamines to keep awake.] Imagine driving around on patrol for 24 hours in 130-degree heat with no air conditioning. (Hampson & Solvig, 2006, 7A)

There also seems to be a flattened sense of real life fulfillment or success after returning from Iraq. Specifically, Ann recalled that she felt a definite letdown after her return from Iraq, the end of her active duty, and reentry into civilian life.

> I used to enjoy dinner in nice restaurants on Saturday nights. I would slowly drink a bottle of wine with friends and enjoy an after-dinner snifter of brandy. I don't really like doing that any more. There's just no deep pleasure...in anything.

Another indication of trouble with subclinical PTSD is the difficulty the Iraq veterans we spoke to had in staying focused on the present. Their lives tended to vacillate between the past and the future without focusing in the here and now. Combatants described what they enjoyed prior to going to Iraq, what they did in Iraq, and what they planned to do in the future. Future plans, however, tended to be vague and general, with little emphasis on enjoying daily life.

Vietnam veterans' descriptions of their experiences sometimes seemed so exaggerated that they took on the tone of mythological storytelling. The combatants clearly endured horrific experiences that were undoubtedly magnified to equal their perception of the danger but were difficult to describe without certain mythic devices. Combat veterans encounter immense danger but not all of the time. Boredom and endless monotony is as much a part of a combat routine as violence but is rarely recalled. Hence, a veteran's narrative tends to be almost a nonstop combat story. Hernando put it this way:

> The best way I can describe my duty in Vietnam is like it was the most terrifying horror movie you have ever seen. Villagers we thought were friends would transform themselves into enemies, just like the shape-shifters in a Hollywood thriller.

Part of this, of course, is that an event like a roadside bomb explosion happens and is experienced at Time 1. Later, at Time 2, the veteran recalls the experience through writing a report, engaging in dialogue with others, and through self-talk. Although these are perceived as Time 1, they actually occur at Time 2, with all of the coloring allowed by the confusion of the two. In addition to the conflation, audience expectations and emotional biases creep in. When these interviews occurred at Time 2, many internal memory adjustments had taken place, unconsciously distorting the events of Time 1. Nevertheless, these interviews represent veterans' past experiences as accurately as they can relate them. In some ways, the process resembles dream recall. When people report their dreams, they tend to forget details and "smooth out" what may have been a disjointed narrative.

Other veterans, of course, might do the opposite. Some might demythologize their experiences, not admitting to themselves or their audience the real horrors that attended the event. This low-key approach was far more common among the Iraq veterans than among the Vietnam veterans. Kim told us:

> Being in Baghdad was like a job. We had signed up to do our duty. We went out every day, did our best to complete our assignment and protect ourselves. We came back, relaxed, got some sleep, and woke up ready for the next day of duty.

Finally, Iraq active duty combat veterans have a distinct advantage over their Vietnam compatriots in that they went to war as a unit and came back as a unit. They have a built-in support system, with access to others who experienced the same phenomena. Hence, they are less likely to view their combat participation in Iraq as negative. This was not the case for returning Vietnam veterans who lacked unit member support. Iraq-era combat troops were well aware of the dissension back home, the absence of a draft, and the problems of being redeployed multiple times. However, most continued to resonate with their fellow combatants about the positive work they did and not with the dissension back home. Lucia told us:

> Sure, we were able to watch the downbeat newscasts. But television news shows rarely interviewed the men and women who privately thanked us for their freedom or showed the coffee shops where people can talk freely for the first time in decades. We hung in there, and it was worth it.

In his gripping book of poems, *Here, Bullet,* Brian Turner (2005) who served in Iraq as an infantry team leader, described day-by-day violence from both the combatants' and the civilians' perspectives, demonstrating the permeability of these categories. Wistfully, in referring to Iraq, he noted that "They say the Garden of Eden blossomed here" (p. 51). This book of short poems is one of the most phenomenologically gripping accounts of twenty-first century warfare.

To Recruits

You are pawns—
don't you understand that?
It's a game
and you aren't worth much,
but you can be used
strategically.
Presidents and generals need
obedient pawns.
You will get deployed, maneuvered,
maybe sacrificed
on a dusty foreign chess board.
If that makes you feel good—
patriotic, macho, or whatever—
go for it.
You'll come back with some honors,
souvenirs, ghosts,
or maybe in a box.

—Tom Greening

4

The Experiences of Reserve Soldiers

For the most part, Army reservists did not participate in company or battalion strength combat operations, such as the Marine assault in Fallujah. However, after the initial 2003 invasion, the operations were mainly conducted by reserve troops who, not long before, were full-time civilians working only part-time for the military. Once called up, they had to resign from their civilian jobs to fight in Iraq, where they would assume a police function, patrolling Baghdad in armed personnel carriers, and providing escorts for convoys that made them constantly vulnerable to roadside bombs and sniper attacks.

So what were their common experiences?

Ben, an army infantry reservist, was working in home construction in Virginia. His unit was activated in 2004 for combat duty in Iraq, with 14 days to report. So that his wife and two children would not endure the separation alone, Ben quit his job and moved them back to Montana.

John, a carpenter working in San Diego, had a similar experience. He was shocked when he received an order to report for active duty in 14 days. When he called his parents to inform them, his father answered. John gave him the unbelievable news, "Hi, dad, you'll never guess what happened to me. I was called up for active duty." For the most part, those interviewed for this book, when asked about their experiences, described a dissociative "dream-like surreality—like watching yourself from outside yourself." There was, however, very little time to complain or reflect on the situation, because everything proceeded so rapidly.

Soldiers sent to Vietnam were already active members of the military. Their pretraining consisted of two to four weeks of advanced combat training and staging, acquiring what the military calls "battlemind" for their flight into Vietnam. This was not the situation for reservists fighting in Iraq. They needed a much longer training period to bring them up to the level of active duty personnel.

For each of the Army reservists interviewed, the first stop was Fort Bliss, Texas, for four to eight weeks. Here, activated reservists were brought to an active duty level of proficiency, both in terms of their individual occupational specialties and the collective specialty of their unit. Once they completed the necessary drills, the unit was sent to Fort Polk, Louisiana, for advanced training and simulation in an Iraq-like environment, followed by a final combat evaluation. Depending on the unit commander, units were offered a final leave before departing to the Middle East or immediately rotated to the Middle East.

Their first stop after the transcontinental flight was Kuwait, where soldiers were acclimated to the hot and dry desert environment and collected their unit's equipment, which had been shipped there prior to their departure from the United States. For most soldiers, this was not a period of deep reflection, but one of practical preparation for the task. The personal and collective ethos was, as Jeremy recalled, "We wanted to do our job and come home."

Time spent preparing for the deployment did not count towards the overall time required on tour. For example, a year's tour in Iraq could actually mean a year and half away from home, once all of the training and preparation was finished. Ronald describes the frustration and anticipation of waiting for the actual deployment:

> We waited and waited and waited. Our energy and motivation were high, but we were in a sort of limbo—not really in the war but not outside of it either.

Several combatants felt as if they would never come home and see their families again. Yet, they faced this with a certain amount of poise and stability. In the end, they finished their jobs so they could return, provided they were not killed. Noah, returning from the Gulf War, remarked, "It is all a matter of luck, with a little bit of skill that can tip the balance."

The process of actually entering Iraq entailed traveling by convoy during the day or flying to the Baghdad airport at night, which reduced the probability of insurgents shooting them down. For most of those we interviewed, their initial journey into Iraq was relatively uneventful. Even once they were assigned a task, such as patrolling Baghdad, training continued for at least a month with the unit they were replacing. According to the soldiers we interviewed, this time was not marked by heavy clashes with insurgents. But as they gained experience, they were required to go into areas not under U.S. or Iraq police control, changing the fundamental character of their situation. A knowledge of this process has important implications for treatment. Charles Figley, a professor of social work and a specialist in traumatology, has pointed out that stress is high before a battle, drops during the fighting, and rises afterwards once reflection begins (Levin, 2007).

INITIAL EXPERIENCES OF COMBAT

Once the new units were ordered into areas not under U.S. control, it did not take long for units to come under fire—the predominant threat being roadside bombs called "improvised explosive devices" (IEDs) and snipers. Martin, a California reservist whose unit was assigned to Baghdad, recalls his first day as a military escort for private contractors, entering new and unfamiliar areas of Baghdad. From his armored vehicle, he felt, heard, and saw several IED blasts explode around him, all of which missed the convoy vehicles. About an hour into the ride, he remembers:

> I was on the radio when a huge fireball exploded, shredding our vehicle. The force of the explosion was beyond all words. It was like being hit by a giant baseball, but my ears were ringing so loudly, I could not hear. When the smoke cleared, all around us was the shredded vehicle. I looked at the driver, and he looked at me. Then we looked at our arms and legs and body to see what we still had. When we saw we were not wounded, we both just laughed. I can't explain the feeling of looking into death's eyes and living to tell about it. Some of the other convoy members came to our aid but could not reach us right away, due to sniper fire. That was really scary because we were sitting ducks. But soon the snipers left, and we were medevaced [evacuated for medical reasons] to a field hospital for examination. For the next couple of days, I could not get out of bed because my body was so wracked with pain from the explosion.

The IED threat is a paramount material threat in Iraq, evidenced by the fact that virtually every Iraq veteran interviewed for this book had firsthand experience with IED detonations near his or her vehicles. Roadside bombs can be made from hand grenades, mortar rounds, artillery rounds, or highly explosive compounds, such as TNT or C4. They are generally placed under a road or at the side of a road and ignited by a pressure switch, a charge wire, or a cell phone in the case of radio detonation. Often, when a vehicle is hit, at least part of the convoy must stop or slow down, making it a convenient target for snipers armed with rifles or rocket-propelled grenades.

Dylan, an Army reservist who went from Kuwait to an area north of Baghdad, had his vehicle hit by an IED.

> We were traveling fast, as all convoys do, and [we] were shot at throughout the day by rifle and rocket-propelled grenades. Then, out of the blue, our vehicle was hit. I felt the heat and bits of metal, rock and dirt blowing all around me in the Humvee, which was now on fire. The driver and I were okay, so we grabbed our gear, blew up the Humvee [so the insurgents could not use any of it] and got the hell out of there!

During his first month in-country, Billy, with a California infantry reserve unit, was patrolling just outside the Baghdad International Airport as part of an escort patrol when the vehicles both in front of and behind his vehicle were blown up. Incredibly, he was spared.

> I could not believe what happened. All of a sudden two blasts and dirt and smoke were everywhere, but we were not hit. I still can't believe it. We were in a real bad part of town and had to get out of there as soon as we could.

Contrary to their objective, many IEDs wound or kill Iraq civilians driving or walking near the explosions, sparing U.S. military personnel protected, to a degree, by armored vehicles. However, whether wounded or unscathed, soldiers who have been near IED attacks become very nervous and apprehensive while driving the roads. The ostensible randomness of IED explosions engenders a more general anxiety about the insecurity of any environment. This can contribute to the spawning of an anxious corona, one which englobes otherwise safe situations.

Feedback from disenchanted combatants reveals that they felt their participation in the Iraq war was neither necessary for the security of the United States nor for the maintenance of the Iraq government. While this stance was shared by almost everyone we interviewed, they were adamant about the duty to serve when asked about civilian criticisms regarding the mixed motives for going to war (e.g., oil, U.S. geopolitical interests, an administrative blunder). As Drew stated, "I signed up and had to go; no one made me." But Nehemiah, an army sergeant, wryly commented, "I am disheartened and personally hurt to learn the reason I went to Iraq never existed" (Goodman, 2004, p. 55).

The initial period for these U.S. combatants was one of acquaintance with the role of military police force more than combat force. They learned the ropes from reservists who had been there before, a practice commanders used with the stated objective of limiting casualties. Most of those interviewed felt as if the real motive for this process was to prevent arousal among those members of the American public who were actively opposing the war. Yet, as time went on, some changes in the combatants' worldviews occurred.

THE NEXT PHASE OF THE COMBAT

As the combatants learned their tactical assignments and settled into their roles as "peacekeepers," most of them became paradoxically fervent about survival and fatalistic about dying, as well as ever more fiercely loyal to their comrades.

As a matter of loyalty, there was a sense of guilt about midtour periods of R&R (rest and recreation). Reservist combatants identified strongly with their units and its members, and the opposite edge of their allegiances was a sharp feeling of guilt about abandoning them, even for necessary rest. There were no replacements, and units rotated into and out of Iraq together. Each person in the unit filled a distinct position in that unit that was established prior to even being called up for active duty.

This is not to say that everyone liked each other or all were friends. Rather, everyone knew everyone else and the degree to which they could depend on each other. In the Vietnam War, soldiers did not enter as units, except during the early years of the war. Instead, they went as replacements. Replacements—usually referred to as "fresh meat"—were tested and hazed, often severely, before being accepted into the main unit group. This situation, nearly ubiquitous in Vietnam, did not occur among the Iraq reserve forces.

For the Iraq combatant, as time in-country continued, one concentrated on doing her or his job and supporting or contributing to the group's success. Thoughts about the ethics or morality of the war did not seem to creep in. As Ben stated, "We were well aware of the politics of the war [going on at home]. But that didn't concern us. We were here to do our job, and we did it."

Yet, for some, there was a growing internal conflict concerning how they viewed the Iraq people. On the one hand, they wanted to support the Iraq people whom they were in the country to liberate. On the other hand, most U.S. combatants felt that, for a price, Iraq citizens in general would shift their alliances and could not be trusted.

Matt, a 48-year-old high school history teacher and father of two, underwent just this kind of perspective shift about the Iraq people. Initially, he viewed them as desperate for liberation, but by the middle of his tour, he detested them. In his unit's sector of operation, north of Baghdad, every morning, as he and his team were out spotting and clearing IEDs, they would also recover bodies of Iraq civilians who had been murdered. They had been killed for being friendly to the Americans, or because they were from a different tribe or sect. Many civilians had been shot; others' heads had been severed. The worst scenes, he recalled, were the bodies of Iraq citizens who had been tortured before being killed.

> The things I saw I couldn't tell anyone about—the sheer evilness of it—pouring acid down the throats of [their] victims, burning their flesh with a blow torch and brutalizing them was real bad. I remember thinking that, if I fell out of the Humvee and the Iraqis got me, that would happen to me. I used to pray, "Please, God, don't let that happen to me."

Politically, Matt was against the war, but he went to Iraq out of concern for his subordinates, for his comrades, and for fulfillment of his patriotic duty. Over the course of his in-country tours, he confided that in some ways, he became complacent about his welfare and became aggressive in leading charges through buildings, shooting at concealed snipers. After his convoy was hit with an exploding IED, out of his peripheral vision he saw several Iraq soldiers shooting at them. He fired once and heard the distinct sound of the bullet hitting a living body. About a half an hour later, he and another commander went into the area and found a massive, frothy blood trail. Evidently, the person was squarely hit in the chest and was carried off by fellow insurgents. Matt knew right then he had really killed someone—a human being who had tried to kill him but a human being nonetheless. In Matt's words, "I knew I had just killed a person. There was blood and blood clots all over the ground. I felt good but dazed—but I really did it."

Matt also said during the interview that the military effect of stopping the insurgent violence was minimal at best. The reason, in his opinion, was that there were insufficient ground troops. In addition, he was ambivalent about whether the Iraq people were worth saving. He thought some of the Iraq farmers were great, but in certain towns, he could see the hatred that most Iraq citizens had for Americans. He was aware of the polls indicating general Iraq dislike for the American occupation, and he experienced it firsthand.

Tom took a mid-duty leave and went back to the United States to spend Christmas with his parents. He was not disheartened about having to go back to Iraq, but, instead, felt guilty because, while he was gone, his company had lost a member. He felt somehow responsible for his subordinates and wanted to get back to be with his unit, yet another instance of the indefatigable loyalty to one's comrades prevalent among the veterans we interviewed.

Unlike the Vietnam War, where mortar flares were continually launched in order to provide a dim light in front of the infantry or fire base perimeter so those defending the perimeter line could see the advancing enemy, no flares were launched at night by Americans. As Matt stated,

Unlike Vietnam, where most of the action took place in the night, we owned the night. The insurgents did not mess with us during the night. They did that during the day.

The main reason for this was the highly advanced night vision devices assigned to American troops, as well as the night vision devices placed on the weapons systems. Much of the helicopter air travel—both combat and logistic—was relegated to the nighttime, when the danger of being shot down by small arms and shoulder-launched antiaircraft missiles was minimized. But this was not the case for truck convoys, which operated mainly in daylight and were one of the most common targets for snipers, roadside bombs, and shoulder-fired rocket-propelled grenades.

The vast majority of official combat offensive actions, except for Marines stationed in Al Anbar province, were suspended after the Bush administration officially called an end to military operations in Iraq in 2003. Yet, this had not calmed those who served. As Juan stated:

As time went by, my primary concern remained my men and, of course, myself. I did not spend a lot of time trying to philosophize about our involvement in Iraq. It was just my job to be there. If I felt it was wrong, there was nothing I could do to change it or my situation anyway.

The majority of those service personnel we interviewed saw their combat role as military police and not actual rifle company combatants. They were in Iraq to keep the people and territories in their sectors from being taken over by the insurgents. Yet most of them witnessed, with time, more and more insurgents and fewer and fewer American troops, whose strength was spread ever more thinly throughout the country. They were waiting for the Iraq people to take over the defense of their country, but it did not happen. Juan continues:

> We were very honored to be there when the Iraqis had their election. We were able to see something very positive come out of our efforts. But things just didn't take off. The killings [of Iraqis], the strife, the anger toward Americans, and the turmoil just continued.

When asked if the servicemen and servicewomen felt there was a plan that had been put in place by the Americans, Matt replied, "I did not know of any. But then, how would a Sergeant First Class ever have that information anyway?" Matt commented further,

> I had no idea what the picture [plan] was for Iraq. They [the contractors] were going to rebuild it [Iraq], but that never happened. As soon as something would be built, they [the insurgents] would just blow it up.

This certainly does not mean there was no war plan, nor that buildings were not being repaired in Iraq, it was just not taking place in any of the sectors represented by those veterans we interviewed. According to the combatants we interviewed, not many perceptible changes occurred between the time of their first arrival in-country and the time at which they ended their tour.

Although we targeted our interviews to reveal the most subjective and personal details of combatants' experiences, the overwhelming majority of those we interviewed gave third person accounts of their experiences. It was as if they were unable to get in touch with deeper feelings or a personal sense of self. Their descriptions seemed as if they were issued without an anchored "I" of experience. Their lived experiences were replaced with events devoid of emotional involvement. Few of our respondents discussed the actual trauma and their experience of it. This was the case of war veterans of earlier U.S. wars we had interviewed as well.

In the meantime, reservists have been fighting the U.S. government bureaucracy. In 1985, Congress passed a law creating a G.I. Bill of Rights for reservists because during the Gulf War, some individuals in the National Guard and the Reserves were called up for active duty and had to discontinue their education. The law allowed eligibility deadlines to be extended for a period equal to the time they had served plus four months. However, the Department of Defense later interpreted the law to restrict benefits to those who remain on drill status. Many Iraq and Afghanistan reservists were told that they could not receive benefits, although they maintained their eligibility. Some 20 percent of reservists who served were students (Tuhus, 2007).

Opting Out

I'm growing old and prone to dodder,
thus I'm no good as cannon fodder.
The politicians' speeches bore me
and they in turn with ease ignore me.
They'll have to wage their wars without me,
and when I rant for peace they'll doubt me
because they're sure their ways are noble
and will resolve all conflicts global
While helplessly I watch and weep
blind righteousness will corpses reap,
more blood will run, more heads will roll,
humanity will lose its soul.

—Tom Greening

5

Coming Home from the War

By one observer's account, the armed forces of the United States "stumbled, dazed, defeated, and demoralized, out of the jungles of Vietnam" (Boot, 2006, p. 30). In 1970, the armed forces were beset by racial tensions, illegal drug use, and alcoholism. During their service in Vietnam, most officers refused to venture into enlisted men's barracks without a sidearm because of some recorded 800 "fragging" incidents in which soldiers attacked their own officers. When the draft was abolished in 1973, defense spending went down, and the military could not meet their own recruiting quota; half of the Marine Corps and Army were eventually composed of high school dropouts (p. 30).

As mentioned earlier, all of this changed when Major General Maxwell Thurman took over the Army's recruiting command. He compelled Congress to boost military pay and revise the G.I. Bill of Rights so that it offered college scholarships to veterans. He marketed the Army as a place to learn valuable skills and adopted a new slogan, "Be All You Can Be." Other services followed Thurman's lead, while Hollywood produced such pro-military films as *Top Gun* and *The Hunt for Red October*. The military began to rack up small victories in Grenada (1983) and Panama (1989), and the armed forces were able to turn away low-quality applicants. By 1990, 97 percent of Army recruits were high school graduates, and the soldiers using illegal drugs fell from an estimated 28 percent in 1980 to 4 percent in 1991. A conscious effort was made to give African American men and women positions of responsibility; the masthead for this accomplishment was the selection of Colin Powell to chair the Joint Chiefs of Staff in 1989.

Weapons were upgraded with an emphasis on precision-guided technology, such as the stealth aircraft and laser-guided bombs. During the Vietnam War, 93 percent of the more than 1,500 aircraft shot down were downed by ground fire, and during World War II, it took an average of 17 shots to disable one enemy tank; in the Gulf War, the Abrams tank came close to a "one shot, one kill" success ratio (Boot, 2006, pp. 34–35). Operation Desert Storm took three weeks of air attacks and 100 hours of ground war to drive Saddam Hussein's forces from Kuwait, losing just 147 men and wounding another 467 (p. 29).

By the time of the Gulf War, the armed forces had been transformed. The Navy, once concerned about its aircraft's poor showing in Vietnam, offered its pilots realistic training in dogfighting that significantly improved their combat performance. In 1975, the Air Force opened its own version of *Top Gun,* allowing pilots to fight a simulated "aggression squadron" (Boot, 2006, p. 37). In 1981, the Army organized another realistic fighting program, sending battalions to fight a simulated enemy; computers kept track of wins and losses while umpires delivered thorough postexercise evaluations. At the start of previous wars, American soldiers had been thrown into battle without much combat experience or realistic training to draw upon— and paid a steep price for their inexperience. The dusk of the industrial age gave rise to the dawn of an informational revolution that reinvented approaches to training and allowed more realistic encounters and adaptive simulations of real combat. Instead of first losing battles and then rebounding, the military shifted to a stance of initial wins, thanks to improved technology (Boot, 2006, p. 35).

There were also transformations in strategies that enhanced group solidarity. Vietnam veterans often complained of poor organization and a lack of a shared spirit among soldiers. This changed for the Gulf War, in which units left and returned from battle *together,* and from there went to Kuwait for processing. After that they were debriefed at a base in the United States prior to returning home. Vietnam veterans, were "let out on the street," so to speak, within hours of their homecoming.

Iraq combatants we interviewed were sequestered while they met with counselors and, upon request, participated in individual counseling sessions. At that point, they also started one to two weeks of demobilization from active to reserve status. The effect of counseling was debatable, entailing a long delay for soldiers who just wanted to go home. Given the usual lapse between combat and the appearance symptoms of PTSD, the counseling program, no matter how well-meaning, probably was not particularly effective.

Psychological rifts lurked just beneath the surface of the cheery family reception at the airport. The ceremony appears as an end of war duty and as a prelude to the resumption of normal life. But more often than not, this is not what actually happens. Matt detailed this phenomenon:

I am pissed and have seen too much killing. I had to go to counseling to deal with my anger. I don't know where it is coming from, but it is there. I can't tell anyone what I saw, like the [bodies of] civilians who had been killed during the night and left on the road for my group to recover during the early morning road clearings of mines.

Rich, who married a woman with two children prior to going to Iraq, found that he was withdrawing from his wife:

I told her I needed time alone [not to be involved with the relationship]. I loved her, but I was not available. I went on a trip to California, and when I returned, I found my belongings packed in boxes and left in the garage. My wife needed me, but I just could not give her [the emotional sharing] that she wanted.

Paul had a similar experience: "My parents were really supportive, and so was my girlfriend. But I needed to be away from their demands. I was not ready, and I'm still not." When asked "ready for what?" Paul could not answer. He simply did not know.

Matt's view confirms the pitfalls that await soldiers after the action is over. Sometimes the family is the best stalwart against destructive behavior:

I am really glad I have a strong wife, or I would be lost. I worry about others in the unit, for they have gone nuts with drinking and partying and womanizing. They [those in my unit] are trying to forget.

These are strong indications that the effects of trauma are present in the veterans' experiences, and that these experiences, at the time of our interviews, had not yet been owned and integrated. There was a distinct disconnection between the lived experience, reported in third-person terms, and the first-person effects of anxiety, depression, and guilt. The film, *Rough Times,* is a poignant portrayal of a U.S. Ranger who returns from Iraq to find that his job has been outsourced to India. Trying to adjust to his life in Los Angeles, he is haunted by the faces of those he was forced to slaughter, but he frankly misses the thrill of killing. To compensate, he inhales any substance he can find and drinks to excess. One reviewer commented, "There's a warning in Jim's disturbed state about the risks of training American servicemen to kill, the letting them loose with little or no debriefing or psychological counseling" (Stein, 2006).

It is our view that the psychological return from battle is not simultaneous with the physical return, a concept termed "pseudo-return" (Paulson, 1994). The actual return, we assert, will require the veterans to deal directly and consciously with what they have experienced. This will require them to return consciously to their memories and reexperience the war in first person.

In examining the Vietnam veterans' experiences, we found that combatants went through three distinct combat stages (precombat, postinitial combat, and fatalistic stages); we did not find the same pattern emerging from our interviews with Iraq War combatants. From the time prior to their arrival and a month or two in the country, there was no perceptible change in the combatants' worldviews. Nor were there dramatic changes within the combatants' psyches by the time they left Iraq. Was this due to the nature of the soldier, the nature of the war, or to the cultural climate at home?

More than likely, a combination of factors came into play. The combatants we interviewed, who ranged from 18 to 48 years old, did not appear to have experienced the war subjectively. Perhaps this is attributable to the short time between when they left combat and when they were interviewed. It is possible that what is easily explained after nontraumatic events becomes baffling after trauma. Because they radically threaten not only the physical self but the conceptual self, it makes sense that such events would produce an alternative species of experience and, therefore, personal narrative. Perhaps there was a repression and suppression of the combat experiences preventing a first-person report, something not uncommon among victims of all varieties of traumatizing encounters. The impact of the event does not fully enter awareness for some period of time. Herman's (1997) pioneering analysis of PTSD patients noted commonalities among combat veterans, adult rape victims, and children involved in incest, in particular, that some symptoms did not surface for years.

The "myth of the given" is undoubtedly at work here as well. Individuals who attempt to report their experiences in personal subjective terms simply are not able to experience pure subjectivity. Instead, the cultural frameworks and personal myths in which these individuals have been immersed do most of the interpretive work for them. Hence, perception and memory of combat are indisputably shaped by military culture, which stresses discipline, bonding, and self-control (Hayes, 2006). The principles and values with which soldiers are inculcated do not allow admissions of weakness or shock that no doubt are a part of the war experience. In turn, there may be a facile narrative acknowledgment of the trauma, but it takes place on a purely descriptive, third-person level, and is therefore removed from any implication for the soldier him or herself.

Because each individual remained a part of a larger combat group (or unit) with its own informal codes, values, and aspirations, there also seemed to be a much greater collective identity in Iraq than in Vietnam. The veterans we interviewed referred to "the group," "our unit," or "my guys" more often than did the veterans who had fought in Vietnam. In fact, the personal combat experiences reported by each person interviewed were not only similar but also expressed a single collective view. Only the postcombat relationships with noncombatant peers were expressed with a high degree of individuation. However, almost everyone we interviewed said those relationships were painful—"like being targeted at point blank range." Each person in the combat unit experienced many of the same phenomena and interpreted them similarly. But outside of this unit, each person had unique and independent relationships with the other people in combat. Outside of the unit, the combatants seemed to lose their own voices in favor of a collective interpretation presented as a firsthand account.

Vietnam veterans, on the other hand, rarely had the continued unit relationship that the Iraq combatants did and had to begin new ones both inside and beyond the combat theatre. Hence, Vietnam War veterans were less hampered in forming new or renewed relationships with lovers, spouses, and families. Of course, those veterans with classic PTSD symptoms were often unable to form or maintain these relationships.

Most of the Iraq veterans we interviewed said they could not tell their friends, families, spouses, or significant others what they actually saw or how they interpreted the war, even though many claimed that "it wasn't so bad." This is another peculiar duality within the soldiers' own accounts. Maybe combatants were imitating previous veterans they observed, or, perhaps through suppression and repression of entire blocks of experience, they just could not fully recall specific combat experiences. Only time will tell whether "it wasn't so bad" or "it was too horrible too bear," and if the truth lies somewhere in between. In other words, was the experience less mythic (as seemed to characterize Iraq War reports) or more mythic (as seemed to characterize Vietnam War reports)?

Operation Iraqi Freedom exposed a variable not encountered in the past. The Iraq situation was a much more turbid engagement than even the guerrilla warfare of Vietnam. The enemy of the United States became a group of people labeled "insurgents." No clear concept of the enemy, other than the vague and misleading term "Islamic fascists," as the U.S. government described them, was ever created. What Islamic fascists look like, what they wear, what kind of people they associate with, and what their political objectives are remain confusing at best. Obviously, they are the ones who plant IEDs and shoot at convoys, but what more solid understanding is there? One might think that the West is very naïve concerning the internal differentiations of its multifarious enemy. It may be that, in terms of their individual and shared values, meanings, aspirations, and goals, in other words, their mythology, the United States had failed to fully investigate its opposition.

Clearly, the intersubjective bond of religion, unknown to most Westerners and often marginalized, plays a huge role in this kind of war. For example, money did not convince radical Muslims to divulge the location of bin Laden. The $25 million reward on his head has been completely ineffective as a motivator in the Middle East. What motivated insurgents were the collective values of radical Islamic groups who would die for their beliefs. This is not unlike the Wolfen-SS of Hitler or the Hitler youth corps, or the Marxist dogmas held by members of the North Korean military and the Viet Cong. But this more recent group of warriors appeared to think nothing of killing fellow Muslims of a different sect to promote their radical goals.

The assumptions held by the Iraq War "coalition of the willing" in dealing with the insurgents seem flawed and simpleminded. For example, as Kim firmly put it, "The insurgents are as evil as the Nazis were." But simplistic thinking overlooks the history of Islam, its many contemporary divisions in the region, and the role of radical religion as a motivating factor in warfare. The technology that was so successful in the Gulf War did not adapt easily to hijacked airplanes, suicide bombings, and kidnappings (Boot, 2006, p. 39).

Veterans' frequent demonization of Iraq insurgents and their international supporters in a way mirrors the demonization of the West by Islamic radicals. But does this affect trauma? There is no pattern of cause and effect to normalize the experience of being under attack. There is no distinct safe or unsafe region—just a constant, but ebbing, threat. Some people eventually give in to passivity, concluding that they cannot change the situation by deliberate activity. Upon returning home, veterans are no longer subject to random attacks from radical Muslims. However, they find themselves subject to random panic attacks, random nightmares, and random startle reactions, in response to a host of random domestic activators. Many submit to passivity, finding no exit from the torment. The disjoint between the promise they would be "welcomed with flowers" and the reality of coping with kidnappings, car bombs, and suicide attacks undercuts both expectations and one's ability to cope with the unexpected.

The underlying condition is an intrapsychic conflict of unresolved issues from combat: fear, suspicion, vigilance, and the constant need to guard one's self from threats. This leads to protective strategies that prevent the successful assimilation of war experiences into the psyche. These combatants typically feel that time will resolve their problems if they stop thinking about them. When time appears not to be a healer, many veterans surrender to passivity, alcoholism, substance abuse, or asocial behavior. For some, the use of drugs started in Iraq where some troops used amphetamines to drive around on patrol, especially if they had a 24-hour shift in 130 degree Fahrenheit heat with no air conditioning. Others used drugs and alcohol out of boredom while waiting to be sent on a mission (Hampson & Solvig, 2006). The Operation Iraqi Freedom Mental Health Advisory Team (2006) reported that one-third of the soldiers and Marines in their survey reported boring or repetitive work as being a major concern when being faced with redeployment (p. 16).

Patriot

I never guessed that my friend Howard
would turn out to be a coward.
Both of us were raised to fight
whether we were wrong or right.
Mostly we were right, we knew,
and fighting is what brave men do.
"I don't trust commies," he once said,
"except the ones I'm sure are dead."
Thus it was a big surprise
when I came to realize
that Howard had begun to doubt
and wasn't always sure about
the verities that we were taught
regarding wars our country fought.
He had always served our cause,
and never took time out to pause
and ask himself if someday peace
would ever make the killing cease.
So what turned Howard's head around—
how can it be that he has found
some fault with what we both fought for
and lost his shining faith in war?
I do not know and will not ask—
I'll carry out my patriot's task.
If he won't fight at least I will.
I'll find more enemies to kill,
and rid the world of all that's bad.
The only thing that makes me sad,
the part that I'll find hard to do,
is killing off the Howards too.

—Tom Greening

6

Preparing for What Is to Come

In the September 5, 2005, issue of *Newsweek* magazine, Rachel Yehuda of the Bronx Veterans' Administration Medical Center in New York stated that her "therapy lasts for just three months and vets come back for a 'tune-up.'" She called this "the new model" of treatment for veterans with psychiatric disorders. Although we appreciate her candor, we question this model because it implies that "one size fits all." Three months and a "tune-up" might suffice for some veterans at the low end of the PTSD continuum, but it may be insufficient for serious cases of the condition. Incidentally, the word "tune-up" implies that returning soldiers can be viewed mechanically, as machines that need to be "fixed." This certainly is not the intention of health care providers at VA centers, but it does reflect the implicit view of the Western medical establishment.

On the one hand, human beings are composed of cells, organs, and organ systems that function through biochemical interactions. But, on the other hand, humans do not experience biochemical interactions; they experience fear, terror, love, hate, and contentment. Their combat experiences and reactions are, for the most part, learned behaviors shaped by their internal values, meaning, personal myths, and self-concepts. These men and women do not go into combat as biochemical machines built to fight; they go into combat and their experiences and perceived threats "rev up" biochemical reactions. Reactions that are normal under combat conditions become "abnormal" or "pathological" only when viewed from a noncombat perspective.

Combatants can be unduly influenced by their culture to think in terms of what is "normal." At home, if they feel uneasy going down a street in a car, their values of their culture judge them as "abnormal" or "sick." The combatants, of course, project that value onto themselves without even considering the underlying reasons for their discomfort.

Because it is far less expensive to administer antidepressants like selective serotonin reuptake inhibitors (SSRIs) than to deal one-on-one with combatants' learned behaviors, the core problems underlying PTSD are rarely addressed, at least not by the government that sent them in the first place. This is not a critique of the government; it is simply a statement of what is generally available. We agree with Hunter (2004), a physician who has worked with trauma victims since 1977; she advocates "minimizing" medication and "maximizing" nonpharmacological treatments in favor of psychotherapy, hypnosis, massage, yoga, meditation, and other procedures. But let us return to the medical model, examining its strengths and its weaknesses.

It could be claimed that PTSD is ignored by much of the U.S. medical establishment because of concerns with money, power, and influence. Discovering or admitting governmental malfeasance would open the door to controversy and lawsuits. The medical model, when it does focus on PTSD, views it as a fundamentally biophysical phenomenon. The view of this model is that the neurophysiological and neurochemical excitations physically responsible for the behaviors are the source and site of correction for the condition.

A "tune-up," in this model, refers to an adjusted dose of a tranquilizer or an SSRI to short-circuit the neurophysiological reaction. No doubt, much of this focus is due to the Veterans' Administration's limited budget and its search for "cost-effective" ways to treat veterans, but it is not likely the best option. On the other hand, one-on-one psychotherapy may be effective, but it is not cost-effective.

Medication is only a partial solution. Csikszentmihalyi (Bupp, 2006) remarked, "Drugs can do neat things, but I doubt any state of consciousness worthy of the label 'happiness' can be induced by them—except in temporary bursts that do not have long-lasting effects" (p. 39). With PTSD, the amygdala and hippocampus operate in opposite directions, hence are overstressed, and epinephrine and norepinephrine often bring the biophysical system into hyperawareness, but the result does not address veterans' deep-seated experience. Their experience is not the release of epinephrine into the bloodstream; it is being filled with raw feelings—feelings of rage, of hate, of despair, of pain and loneliness—and these are unique to each veteran. Hence, the boundaries of a description of PTSD might be expanded to include veterans' interior worlds, as well as their feelings about ongoing interpersonal relationships. Psychiatrists empowered to write out prescriptions for medication are not the only practitioners qualified to deal with the inner world of the PTSD client; pastoral counselors, clinical psychologists, social workers, nurses, and others often carry out this function as part of their routine function in health care settings. A number of studies have identified nondrug therapies that are as effective as medication, and last longer with fewer reports of relapse (Wampold, 2001).

Relapse following medication has been attributed to its failure to address veterans' existential issues and allow them to advance beyond the pale of the trauma (Greening, 1997; Tedeschi & Calhoun, 1995). We do not take a reductive position on the nature of psychological phenomenology. Indeed, it is possible that all psychic conditions are ultimately the result of complex electrical and chemical exchanges in the body, yet trying to directly manipulate those processes may not be the best way to achieve results. Even in the absence of an immaterial spiritual substrate or self, treatments that engage with a veteran at a more complete level tend to be more effective. It is estimated that one out of every six U.S. military men and women returning from Iraq are in need of psychotherapeutic care, if not for PTSD, then for some other disorder (Hamod, 2005), and if there is to be any solution, it will certainly not be by medicine and pills alone.

In an attempt to address these issues in a program that combined pharmacology and psychotherapy, a group of South Carolina psychiatrists obtained permission from the U.S. Food and Drug Administration to initiate the trial use of MDMA (popularly known as "Ecstasy") for Afghanistan and Iraq veterans suffering from PTSD, specifically to reduce the occurrence of flashbacks and nightmares. The head psychiatrist commented, "It's too early to draw any conclusions but in these treatment-resistant people so far the results are encouraging." He added that the 8-hour drug sessions helped people discuss traumatic situations without triggering anxiety (Adam, 2005, p. 7).

The plethora of treatment approaches for dealing with PTSD has motivated a call for "evidence-based practice" and "empirically validated interventions" (Roberts & Yeager, 2004). This quest is commendable and sorely needed. However, PTSD is a multisymptom phenomenon that operates in a context involving several potential stimuli and stressors; the longitudinal staying power of a particular treatment needs to be evaluated, as well as the specific components of an intervention.

For both reservists and other veterans, there are often opportunities to choose a mental health provider. We would suggest that several questions be asked or at least considered.

1. What formal training in assessment and treatment of PTSD does the practitioner have? Many clinicians have had no formal training in evaluating the severity or the prognosis of PTSD, much less treating it.

2. How many trauma PTSD assessments and treatments has the practitioner managed? Remember that treating the victim of a car accident or a sexual assault is considerably different from treating combat-related PTSD.

3. In what professional societies or organizations related to traumatic stress does the practitioner hold membership? He or she should be a member of a national psychological, psychiatric, medical, or social work organization, as well as the International Society for the Study of Trauma and Dissociation, the International Society for Traumatic Stress Studies, or a similar group.

Trauma survivors need to take a proactive stance in seeking and receiving treatment. They need to avoid thinking of themselves as "victims" but as women and men who are capable of regaining some control over their lives. There are many governmental agencies, professional organizations, and computer links that can be used as resources in this quest.

POST-TRAUMATIC STRENGTHS

No matter how one evaluates the causes of wars and their repercussions on those who fight them, we take the position that, no matter how bad or unjust the combat experience was, it offers the veteran an opportunity to transcend it and engage in positive growth activities. For us, this growth represents one's personal shift from conventional, conditioned behaviors to those reflecting more authentic, individual choices. Conventional behavior is the functional level at which most Americans reside. They hold jobs, take responsibility for their behaviors, and have a sense of fairness about the way their actions impact those around them. Most of their values are tied tacitly to conventional ideas and cultural myths. The combat veteran, more often than not, rarely finds these values useful simply because her or his experiences are well outside the usual cultural norms. This gives veterans an incentive to move beyond the conventional ways of living and find values, personal myths, and worldviews that more appropriately fit their experiences (Paulson, 1994). Some veterans regress to a preconventional level, where they survive but do not flourish. Other veterans, however, transform their post-traumatic stress into what we might call "post-traumatic strengths."

When considering these strengths, we give central importance to meaning, particularly the existential meaning that veterans find in their lives and for which they so desperately search. Meaning, or what is important to the veteran, entails values—ethical, moral, aesthetic, and spiritual. In establishing values that provide meaning, veterans need to make choices about how to live the rest of their lives and personally own those choices. Choices, however, evoke anxiety when the decisions or options are not clear. No choice occurs in neutral space but is influenced by motivators. It is essential that the veteran be critically aware of what these motivators are if their stresses are to be transformed into strengths. Frederick and McNeal (1998) have provided a comprehensive manual for discovering traumatized clients' strengths through hypnotically facilitated psychotherapy, guided imagery, and relaxation procedures, emphasizing the importance of a "therapeutic alliance" for confronting the pitfalls in treating PTSD.

Instead of feeling stigmatized by asking for psychological help, veterans should realize that it takes strength and courage to request assistance. Such an act is not shameful nor an act of weakness; it is a manifestation of self-love and self-respect that enables one to love others as well. Many veterans feel empowered by the sense of honor, self-respect, pride, and commitment given to them by their military service. Others are pleased with the bonding that allowed them to accomplish tasks under difficult circumstances. They can utilize this courage to face difficulties at home, whether or not their community receives them respectfully. And others appreciate the freedoms they have in the United States and the way that their spiritual beliefs assisted them during trying times (Armstrong, Best, & Domenici, 2006). This upbeat emphasis is especially common among mental health specialists using a humanistic-existential psychotherapy and positive psychology perspective, both of which focus on optimal personal functioning rather than on dysfunction and psychopathology (Seeman, 2001, p. 619; Seligman & Csikszentmihalyi, 2000; Snyder & Lopez, 2002). Research data have not answered all the questions concerning the role of religion and spirituality in recovery from PTSD, but it appears that, in cases where religious beliefs assist recovery, it is a medium for other factors such as community support, an examination of spiritual values, and dedication to personal goals (Livingston, 2006).

For veterans, the ultimate post-traumatic strength would be to learn to appreciate and enjoy themselves, their lives, and a great variety of relationships with others, instead of distancing and isolating themselves. In addition, they would learn to live in a self-determined, authentic way, based on who they are, rather than who they "should be." They would learn how to develop the neglected "shadow" sides of their lives, to increase their freedom and control by accepting responsibility for their lives, and to become more aware of both inner and outer experiences. Some U.S. soldiers have displayed these strengths during combat. For example, the infantryman, Brian Turner (2005), in his book of poetry, *Here, Bullet,* filled his verses with powerful images of death and dying but also of love and loss, passion and anger, feelings he was reluctant to share in conversation (Guthmann, 2007). Nathaniel Flick (2005) and Bing West (2005) have written eloquent accounts of their time serving in Operation Iraqi Freedom to popular acclaim. Flick's *One Bullet Away* describes his training to become a Marine officer; its apolitical perspective helps the reader appreciate Flick's criticism of his company commander who, he felt, made poor combat decisions, and the rapid shift in his battalion's duties, which made real accomplishment impossible. *No True Glory*, by West, focuses on the battle for Fallujah and the house-by-house fighting it entailed. Here, too, he levies criticism, this time against the first U.S. ambassador, who did not allocate sufficient funds for training troops deployed to Iraq. West ends his book with a quotation by the Greek poet Pindar, "Unsung, the noblest deed will die." These three books, and others like them, ensure that the noble deeds in war, despite less than noble wars, will remain venues for the demonstration of heroic capacities and courageous action.

SOME PREDICTIONS

We need to make several predictions of what the future holds in light of an unclear present. What Iraq combat veterans will require in terms of counseling, psychotherapy, and coaching is not predictably grounded solely in their present existential situations. Yet, they are not devoid of maps and clues.

We base our next set of comments on our interviews and work with other combat veterans—World War II, the Korean Police Action, the Vietnam Conflict, and the Gulf War, assuming a certain commonality with Afghanistan and Iraq. We will present what we term a holistic or an integrated approach. We will not offer a "cookbook" approach, but, instead, posit that specific problems will need specific and often unique directions.

Combatants, like noncombatants, not only present a specific set of symptoms but have established certain levels of cognitive and moral development, emotional maturity, and resilience (Scaer, 2005). To varying degrees, each person is in search of positive meaning from life, not only through their own eyes but through the eyes of their society. That is, former combatants not only want to believe that they did a service for the country, but also that the country appreciates what they did.

This is questionable at the present time. First, Iraq combat veterans, at least those we interviewed, often cannot find value in their combat service from within. As has been mentioned, most have not integrated a personal view of their involvement because they are still tied to their collective unit and the values it imparted. They went because they were called. None of the veterans we interviewed expected that to happen, and no one volunteered to go to Iraq.

As American society's view became ever more disillusioned with the Iraq War's purpose, goals, and scope, positive social portrayals of the veterans became harder to find. The combatants we interviewed know this. Fortunately, however, they were not entirely rejected by society in the same way as were veterans of the Vietnam Conflict.

Constructing positive meaning from wartime experiences among ex-combatants will require therapeutic support. This can be very difficult, particularly if the therapist sees little purpose in the war and cannot separate her or his political orientation from the personal trials of the individual soldier. Therapists need to inquire into a combatant's experiences in order to uncover valuable lessons she or he learned but have not yet come to appreciate.

In the search for positive meaning, veterans will often call into question the very significance of their lives. Much has been written on this process in the humanistic-existential work of such psychotherapists as Victor Frankl (1956), Rollo May (1981), and J.F.T. Bugental (1987). These writers have described how issues of choice, freedom, responsibility, meaning, tragedy, aloneness, and alienation are often rich resources for personal myth. The very act of questioning the meaning of one's existence offers the possibility of authentically coming to terms with life. There is usually, however, a period of turmoil and tension before the deepest levels of meaning are discovered.

The morass of negative feelings often buries positive aspects of veterans' experiences and prospects. They were caught up in a situation—often described as a "hell"—of perpetual suffering. Continued suffering is seen very often as retribution for participation in an unjust war or the enjoyment that can come from killing. It is useful to tell veterans that the therapeutic process is a metaphorical journey. A magnificent tropical shore awaits them, but to get there, they have to traverse a swamp with many pain-ful and threatening obstacles they must overcome prior to reaching their destination.

In traversing the unpleasant bogs on the way to healing, insights from Jungian analytic psychology can be very useful. Particularly, viewing war-time involvement as a mythical rite of passage provides a story through which the value of a person's experience can be rewritten (Tick, 2005). A mythical approach enables the veteran to objectify what was once subjec-tive, that is, to tell his or her story as a matter of fact rather than a muddy episode of personal history. This helps veterans think about their situations without being enmeshed in its personal fallout (i.e., negative emotion-causing avoidance, suppression, repression, and escape through alcohol and drugs). Sometimes, though, if the story becomes too distinct from the patient, the dissociation between the two actually can inhibit growth (Serlin & Cannon, 2004).

The basic procedure for investigating not just the combat experience but other aspects of one's life as a rite of passage has three basic stages: (1) the call, (2) the initiation, and (3) the return. The call is the life situation that led the combatant to join the military—those events and decisions that served as the catalyst to begin the journey. That is, it is what got her or him into a combat situation in the first place. It is important that this process elicits the veteran's story, not the therapist's. Shay (2002) compared this journey to that of the mythical hero Ulysses who left Ithaca for Troy, cap-tured the city, and (after a long sojourn) returned to Ithaca to great praise.

Tragically, too many veterans who return from combat face derision, not acclaim.

For Danielle, the call to the adventure of going into the military was not just the extra money, but the pride of being an important and valuable part of something larger than herself. She felt it was an opportunity to defend her beliefs and "a way of life that too many of us take for granted." It may have been dumb luck, or it may have been fate. However they choose to define it, recognizing the call can be empowering to veterans.

The "call" is part of the shamanistic journey as well. In traditional shamanism, a neophyte is beckoned by spirits, by elders, or by a serious illness to an odyssey into the underworld, into astral realms, or to a distant location as part of a rigorous apprenticeship, after which the neophyte returns and is initiated as a valuable member of his or her community. Treating individuals with "soul loss" is a major shamanic function, and many of the descriptions of "soul loss" parallel those of PTSD (Krippner, 1997b).

The actual initiation phase is the combat experience of the soldiers' tour. Obviously, there were times of fear and stress in combat. This includes not just avoiding bombs and bullets but also facing the uncertainty of the future. It also includes the apparent inherent unfairness of war, that not all people of service age participate, the extended loneliness, the discouragement of putting one's job and career on hold, the possible betrayal by spouses and lovers, and the loss of innocence. It is the erosion of belief in a just world.

Although the combatants were tested by life's cruelty, other stages in the rite of passage remain unknown. Offering the veteran a grander perspective that extends beyond immediate or remembered experience can give him or her a "telos" or end goal that locates it among a larger field of meaning. The experience of the initiation recalled by the veterans can provide many hours of fertile psychotherapeutic interaction, given that it directs them to the "here and now" and away from the "then and there" of the past.

Without psychotherapy the return stage may never be achieved, leaving veterans marooned in the "then and there" or trapped in a present that is dictated entirely by the past. To do this, the combatants need to discover the value—the grail, the gold, and the treasure—derived from the combat experience. These veterans need to become aware of a "post-traumatic strength" that belongs to them alone. They need to discover within themselves some distinctive character trait or powerful personal attribute that is uniquely their own and integrate it into their present lives. Perhaps this strength will be resilience, or compassion, or irony, or courage. Whatever it might be, this is the reward that has been earned, the completion of their shamanistic journey. This prize may be honored by a small support group or by a large community. Nonetheless, it marks the end of one voyage and the beginning of a new one.

Veterans of the Second World War, despite the gross inhumanity of the combat, had the benefit of a valorized notion of war and its soldiers. Thus, they had a socially reinforced culture of heroism that was more than the petty lip service of present day journalism. During World War II, 464 Medals of Honor were handed out by the U.S. military. In roughly the same amount of time, only two such honors were awarded to Iraq combatants (Donnelly, 2006), and another was awarded early in 2007. One of the blessings and curses of contemporary practices surrounding warfare is that it has come to be popularly viewed as a precise, limited, and professional endeavor. When combat is a technical occupation, heroes are forfeited for paid practitioners. As a result, combatants may suffer similar traumas but within a society that sees it as an occupational hazard.

Upon deeper inspection, most soldiers were able to identify positive values in combat service. Although some felt they fought an unjust war, killed unnecessarily, had been duped by the government, and ultimately were rejected by their society, some inimitable value emerged.

A recruiter in Detroit told Don, who ended up in Iraq, "You are safer on the streets of Baghdad than you are in the inner city of your home town." Don remembered this claim as he dodged sniper's bullets and car bombs, telling himself "You aren't in Detroit anymore!" Nonetheless, he made lifelong friends with his fellow servicemen, he learned survival skills beyond the "street smarts" he had been taught in Detroit, and he brought back an appreciation of life that he had never learned from his family, from his school, or from the street gangs he left when he joined the army.

These veterans stepped up to the plate to defend what they believed. Unlike noncombatants, they put their very lives on the line for the common good of their military unit, even if that was the extent of it. The realization that they, unlike some of the people they knew who were eligible but escaped service for one reason or another, waged their lives for something bigger than themselves and became a beacon of light for many veterans. Realization, however, is just the first step. The combatants also need to take the positive insights gained from their war experiences and transplant them into their lives through conscious self-empowerment that can be supported by cognitive-behavioral, humanistic-existential, and other therapeutic modalities.

Combatants also must realize that, as the rite of passage myths reveal, accepting the call is a one-way ordeal. In other words, they cannot return to their original environment and start over as if nothing occurred. They must take responsibility for their lives, instead of an outside entity, and move from the postulates of the military culture to that of a civilian culture. Armstrong, Best, and Domenici (2006), Leyva (2003), Matsakis (2007), and Paulson (1994) have written first-rate guidebooks describing coping strategies that both veterans and their families can adopt to assist in this adaptation process. These include practical suggestions for spouses, lovers, and significant others, providing instructions on how realistically to assess the situation, create a healing environment, serve as a social support, help establish a regular sleep schedule, serve as a role model when stresses occur in their lives, and maintain a sense of humor when times get rough. If separated, spouses and lovers need to "keep the love alive"; soldiers typically cherish photographs of newborn babies and family members they saw that "one last time" before deployment. When they return, families of troubled veterans must attend to their own needs as well. And it goes without saying that professional help for the veteran is urgently needed if suicidal or homicidal tendencies are present.

Former combatants, as well as their friends and families, need to be aware that the veteran has survived a rite of passage, even thought they might not be aware of that term or what it truly means. At the turn of the nineteenth century, William James (1972), America's first psychologist of note, observed that war can be a preparatory ordeal for the demands of adulthood; it is often "a school of strenuous life and heroism" (pp. 290–291). Even in an era that predated atomic warfare and suicide bombers, James glimpsed the strengths that can surface if combat, with all its horrors, can be reframed in positive terms.

War Games

Children get killed in wars,
which is not good for them.
They should be tickled
and made to laugh,
not killed or made to cry.
I have seen children with rifles
taller than themselves,
very sober looking children
with a sense of responsibility
toward their country.
I'd rather they be irresponsible,
making snow forts and throwing snowballs
like we did.
Is that training for war?
I hope not. I hope it is
just playing in the snow.
In summer we rode our bicycles fast
over rough dirt roads
fleeing and attacking imagined enemies.
We survived, but stunts like that
inspired my braver cousin Raj,
who became a fighter pilot
and did not.

—Tom Greening

7

Civilians at Risk

Although this book focuses primarily on the combat effects of war on servicemen and servicewomen, wars also devastate the civilian population. It is our contention that PTSD among combat veterans needs to be considered in conjunction with PTSD among civilians; not only has the line between the two groups often been blurred, but the two often occur in tandem. Several studies indicate that PTSD and related symptoms are often more prevalent in civilian victims of combat than among combatants themselves. For example, 42 percent of Afghanistan civilians demonstrated symptoms of PTSD in a 2004 investigation (Cardozo et al, 2004). Of some 130 wars waged since World War II, all but two have taken place in low-income countries, killing over 40 million people, most of whom were civilians. Civilians who were not killed were commonly displaced within their own country. The militarization of low-income countries, usually entailing a combination of low intensity warfare with high intensity weaponry, has become the major source of displacement, particularly for women and children. In the past, low-income countries were caught in indirect conflicts between superpowers. Since the collapse of the Soviet Union, however, the major strife has been between smaller (nonstate) political and religious groups. In the twentieth century, more than 63 million civilians have died in wars, many more than the 43 million military casualties (Hedges, 2002).

The second reason for civilian displacement is their desire to leave their countries of origin for better living conditions. This motive stems from the dominant socioeconomic model of development presented by both the International Monetary Fund and the World Bank. All too often, funding decisions leave out large but underrepresented groups of people, decisions that have led to armed conflicts over land, drinking water, health care, and education. Finally, newly formed regimes that purport to offer citizens a choice in their government have been hijacked by new power elites fighting for political and religious control and, in some cases, committing genocide against rival ethnic groups.

Yet, for every refugee of war, there are many more internally displaced persons. The situation in Iraq is just one example. As of 2007, about one-third of upper-class, middle-class, or upper-middle-class Iraq citizens with money or "connections" left the country for safer havens (Hiro, 2007). This exodus robbed Iraq of many of its most talented and skilled citizens, including physicians, of whom 12,000 had fled by 2007. Others remain as refugees in their own country, leaving war-torn areas for more secure locations.

The war effects that precipitate relocation inside or outside of the country take an enormous physical and mental toll. Individuals, families, and entire communities suffer repeatedly from a horrifying spectrum of human rights violations, including death, torture, rape, abduction, injury, displacement, job loss, theft, and an evaporation of even the most basic living conditions. The most common deprivations include "ethnic cleansing," persecution, continual harassment, and intimidation, with the long-term and short-term effects remaining varied and complex.

Even when there are no physical antecedents, mass psychogenic illness can immobilize thousands of civilians. In 2005, in the war-ravaged Russian Republic of Chechnya, dozens of children were afflicted with breathing difficulties, headaches, and physical numbness from what was rumored to have been nerve gas. As a result, schools were closed, political tensions rose, and medical specialists were called in. The official report concluded that the symptoms resulted from "intense psychological pressure caused by lengthy hostilities in the republic" (Bartholomew & Radford, 2007, p. 56). Similarly, terrorism scares have cost businesses and workers millions of dollars in lost productivity and wages (p. 55).

Fleeing forces refugees to cope with a new physical and social environment while experiencing estrangement or loss of family, friends, status, possessions, and cultural roots. Specific risk factors that may lead to long-term disorders include:

- Traumatic events related to conflict after the age of 12 (before this time, the nuclear family usually protects children from the anxiety of war)
- Torture (horrendous experiences by people of any gender or age)
- Violence toward females (particularly severe for young women who may be repeatedly raped in order to humiliate their families and disseminate the aggressors' blood lines into their ethnic group or community)

- Socioeconomic hardship, poverty, unemployment, poor education, and lack of professional skills that fit the new environment
- Problems of marginalization, discrimination, acculturation, language, and communication
- Poor physical health due to lack of food, poor sanitation, and poor health care
- Overcrowding coupled with negative physical conditions, head injuries, and other bodily damage
- Collapse of social networks, resulting in anonymity, estrangement, and lack of social support
- Death of loved ones and fear of additional deaths
- Daily hassles, domestic stress, and conflict-related events
- Failure to cope, especially during the first month following the trauma
- A preexisting history of individual or family psychiatric problems that makes the post-traumatic stress even worse. (DeJong et al., 2003, p. 6)

As we hope is evident, the risks to the general population are great. Yet each culture's shared meanings, values, goals, and customs mean that coping with collective, war related traumas varies in each instance. Hardships for one culture may be the norm for others. The most significant variable is the degree to which the war devastates or interrupts lived lives. With this in mind, certain protective factors exist to promote resilience in each group:

- The presence of a social network, including the nuclear or extended family
- Social support and self-help groups for empowerment and sharing
- Employment or other possible sources of income
- Access to human rights organizations
- Access to recreation and leisure activities
- The ability to perform culturally prescribed rituals and ceremonies
- Political and religious inspiration as a source of comfort, meaning, and perspective for the future
- Refugee camps and centers
- Retaining coping skills, intelligence, and humor. (DeJong et al., 2003, p. 7)

We would include several other resources, such as the ability to at least partially control events in one's life and family, as well as the ability to find meaning in one's suffering (Solomon, 2004). Furthermore, there are organizations such as Veterans and Families Coming Home and Soldiers and Families Middle East Resource that provide community support for veterans, families, and employers.

Control has two dimensions. The first is what one can control by means of autonomy, intention, and action. This includes cultivating food, protecting one's children, and protecting relations within one's community. This type of control is very limited in war situations, leading to displacement. There is another form of control, attributed to one's personal god, gods, or "fate." To simply accept one's "fate" can be very useful for increasing resilience. This personal or cultural myth ("destiny," "kismet," "providence," "fortune") may seem irrational to the secular mind, but it can provide meaning in desperate circumstances.

WAR AND REFUGEE SUFFERING

Most wars are conducted between countries or between rival factions within a country. However, in recent decades, they have taken the new, ominous character of conflicts conducted by states against their own civilians (van der Veer, 1998; Whitaker, 2000). Often, these civilian targets are both poor and from a minority group, having few or no allies, either in their home country or abroad. Since the early 1980s and into the new millennium, wars against civilians have been carried out in such countries and regions as Afghanistan, Algeria, Angola, Burundi, Chinese Tibet, Colombia, El Salvador, Ethiopia, Guatemala, Indian Kashmir, East Timor, Israeli-occupied territories, Liberia, Mozambique, Nicaragua, Northern Ireland, Peru, the Philippines, Russian Chechnya, Rwanda, Sierra Leone, Somalia, South Africa, Sri Lanka, Sudan, parts of the former Yugoslavia, and Zaire (Wright, 2004).

That these are "wars" is not hyperbole. Take the case of Rwanda, where 14 percent of its total population, primarily composed of Tutsis, was killed within the span of three months. In Bosnia, at least 200,000 civilians were killed in "ethnic cleansing" campaigns, with another 20,000 civilians missing and unaccounted for (van der Veer, 1998).

A key strategic goal in this type of warfare is to create terror among the targeted civilian population (Clayton, Barlow, & Ballif-Spanvill, 1998). By manufacturing a state of terror, normal economic, social, cultural, and political relations are disrupted, making it facile for the warring state to achieve its goal: control and subjugation of the civilian population. Further, the wanton destruction of social and cultural institutions, which connect people to their past and shared values, meanings, and goals, has been extraordinarily effective at disenfranchising civilian victims.

The goal of this chapter is to address the suffering of civilian victims of war and review some of the psychotherapeutic approaches useful in the treatment of victims dealing with trauma and unresolved issues. We have worked with civilian victims of war for several decades. Daryl Paulson has used internalized mythic structures with this population, as well as with veterans of the Vietnam War, and had positive therapeutic results. They have often been due to the integration of negative effects of war into the psyches of his patients (Paulson, 1991, 1995, 1997). Stanley Krippner has surveyed the psychological trauma inflicted on civilian populations in five continents, either from firsthand experiences or through interviews with witnesses (Krippner & McIntyre, 2003).

A common thread binding present-day civilian victims of war is that, as a group, they have been unjustly persecuted and, as individuals, they have suffered immensely, with little attention from the world. Generally, their persecution does not happen overnight, but progresses through a series of stages (Bustos, 1990).

Initially, these social and political changes occur in the person's home country, resulting in increasing levels of political repression and persecution (van der Veer, 1998). These stages may include limits to freedom of speech and movement within the country, as well as general intimidation by police, army, or paramilitary groups. These changes are usually met with little opposition as people deny, suppress, or repress the realities of the new situation (Daly & Sand, 1987; Whitaker, 2000). One stage leads to the next, until even the most obtuse citizen realizes that a dictatorship or police state has arrived.

MAJOR TRAUMATIC EXPERIENCES

At some point, social and psychological defenses break down as the political and social conditions worsen (Horowitz, 1998). People experience the abduction or murder of their friends and/or family members who are spirited away in the night or even killed in broad daylight. Survivors vividly describe the trauma of being arrested, detained, or jailed for no substantive reason (Knudsen, 1991; van der veer, 1998). Some of them undergo brutal forms of torture immediately; others experience a more selectively applied torture, designed not only to fracture them physically but also to humiliate and degrade them and undermine their very humanity. The torture takes place in an environment where the victim is helpless and completely at the mercy of the torturers (Dahl, 1989). Thus, torture can be used to promote and carry out a systematic policy of intimidation and destabilization against entire ethnic communities or minority groups. The torture procedures are not only premeditated but are creatively designed to maximize pain and torment (Applegate, 1976).

LIFE IN EXILE

Those who escape to a safe haven in another country are not spared suffering. Life in exile entails major social adjustment issues (Curtis, 2000; Sue & Sue, 1999; van der Veer, 1998). For example, people seeking political asylum generally experience extended periods of wrenching anxiety about whether they will be accepted by a host country or sent back to face imprisonment or death. Nevertheless, they generally feel deeply connected to their home country, and it is only most dire circumstances that prompt their exodus.

Probably the greatest trauma at this phase is the uprooting of their physical, cultural, and social past (Carson, Butcher, & Mineka, 2000; Horowitz, 1998). They are no longer in a comfortable, familiar setting but are trying to adapt to a new environment that is difficult and strange and to a community that is often distant and even hostile. Many people at this stage report feeling a sense of guilt for living while others are being killed or for various morally questionable things they may have done to leave (Daly, 1985; Knudsen, 1991; Pennbaker & Beall, 1986; van der Veer, 1998). Karl, a combat veteran of the Korean War, told us about his feelings of estrangement in a new place. Even though he was not a refugee, there are many resident similarities in his description to that of displaced or besieged civilians.

> Korea was a very strange culture for me, a farm boy from Ohio. The people were friendly but we couldn't communicate at deep levels. The winters were freezing, and the terrain was really rough. Talk about "culture shock"? I experienced it in spades. One day, Marilyn Monroe put on a song and dance show for thousands of troops. I was so far away that I could barely hear her. It didn't matter. Here was someone from home, someone I recognized as being an American who cared for us. When she died, I felt as if I had lost a family member.

Difficulties faced due to complete personal uprooting and living in exile both have been characterized as "culture shock" (Sue & Sue, 1999). This means that people undergo intense and prolonged emotional upheaval, once they realize how "strange" their adopted new culture is and how difficult it is for them to adjust to it. As Sue and Sue (1999) stated, this upheaval is characterized by feelings of insignificance and being lost in these respects:

1. They have lost the love and respect they formerly experienced with friends and family.
2. They have lost their former social and cultural status.
3. They have lost their cultural environment and the many obligations and dependencies that gave their lives meaning.
4. They are adrift among the values of the new cultural environment, values not recognized in their native culture, while the values they bring with them are not prized in the new culture. (pp. 258–265)

There are both intrapersonal and interpersonal aspects of these phenomena. Intrapersonal conflicts usually relate to issues of cultural values and norms at odds with their own. Intrapersonal conflicts lead to anxiety, which often leads to depression or, at least, avoidance. Avoidance prevents integration into the new culture. This engenders the second problem of interpersonal conflict. Interaction with those outside of one's native culture is seriously impeded by differences in both verbal and nonverbal communication. In cases where the victims of war are still within their home country, a clear distinction needs to be made between the ordinary suffering due to war and the suffering that leads to PTSD. All civilians endure pain and grief, and a sizable minority of them develops a dysfunction serious enough to require treatment. Trying to categorize a traumatic experience as "normal" or "ordinary" is, of course, difficult because, generally after the hostilities end, people tend to get on with their lives, often with no evidence of PTSD. As long as they are reunited with their family, cultural group, and familiar surroundings, there is seldom a long-lasting problem. But if a person goes to a different country or a distant part of his or her own country, severe problems may occur. Of course, there is no uniformity among the conditions and reactions to violence, displacement, and torture among civilians. For this reason, both treating and identifying PTSD can be onerous and evasive.

Achterberg (2003) worked with refugees in Kosovo, utilizing imagery, biofeedback, meditation, body movement therapy, and other forms of individual and group work, yet identified "compassion" as the healing vessel that contained all of the techniques and modalities. She concluded, "Life is not about borders, egos, power, or games that will never be won, but our relationship with all living and nonliving things" (p. 312).

Walter's Search

He said he joined the Army
to give meaning to his life,
something his career
as a short-order cook in Alabama
lacked.
The meaning he got was the challenge
of recovering from an IED
and battlefront surgery.
His surgeons learned a lot too,
standing in an inch of blood
as they saved his nose, many of his teeth,
and much of his right leg.
So now Walter is a man,
physical therapy is his job,
and his search for meaning limps along
like the war itself.

—Tom Greening

8

Treatment Approaches to Traumatic Disorders

There are a number of common approaches to treating traumatic disorders. Many of these approaches overlap, with applications appropriate for both combat veterans and civilians. They also apply to individuals who cannot be easily classified as either civilians or combatants, such as the "child soldiers" who fought in the West African civil wars, some by choice, others by force. Once the war was over, it was not uncommon for them to report many PTSD symptoms, especially recurring nightmares of those they had murdered.

PSYCHIATRIC APPROACHES

The psychiatric approach, grounded in neurophysiology and biochemistry, uses prescription drugs as its main treatment aim. In its most basic presentation, it views PTSD through the diagnostic lens of the *DSM-IV-TR* (2000). Additionally, PTSD is often linked with other disorders, particularly depression and anxiety. It stands to reason that if one continually experiences anxiety, it is not long before the quality of one's life disintegrates, and a depressive state ensues (Pine, 2000).

While it is generally agreed that the psychiatric approach is useful, particularly in identifying symptoms, it tends to force a "medical" and biomechanical construction of reality onto a situation that may be better served by broader interpretive methods (Bandura, 1997; Shapiro & Astin, 1998), one that addresses the assumptions, appraisals, thoughts, and beliefs that help people make sense of what they experience (Levin, 2007). The psychiatric approach does not, in our view, offer a holistic analysis of cultural uprooting (Cancelmo, Millan, & Vazques, 1990), although it may be the only modality available in some circumstances (Sue & Sue, 1999). In addition, treatment of certain classes of anxiety, depression, futility, and phobia with pharmacological medications is often dramatic, with few negative side effects (Sheikh & Nguyen, 2000).

Not all mental health practitioners find the psychiatric approach and the *DSM* useful for all civilians and veterans. Burstow (2005) noted that Vietnam War veterans lobbied the American Psychiatric Association for the inclusion of PTSD in the *DSM*, a cause joined by survivors of childhood abuse, incest, and spouse abuse, many of whom hoped that they would benefit from insurance coverage. Burstow, however, has called the category "confused, reductionistic, contradictory, and arbitrary" (p. 429).

Caldwell (2001) also takes issue with the *DSM*, proposing a system of behavioral diagnostic classifications that describe adaptations to a wide variety of distressing and painful adversities. He emphasizes the ubiquity of adaptation in all human behavior, influenced by an individual's biological and constitutional makeup and life experiences. For him, the most serious omission in the *DSM* is the absence of key etiologies, especially the role of developmental aspects of learned fear that threatens, influences, and shapes a person's survival pattern, often grounded in avoidance. The *DSM* cites at least two dozen categories of PTSD; in all of them, the uniqueness of any individual case is muted, usually at the expense of positive lifelong rewards. This is because it is statistically based and grounded in central tendencies described by average confidence intervals, standard deviations, and data analysis (Paulson, 2003b, 2006). The individual survives, but the price paid is a never-ending series of reactions to learned fears as well as somatic complaints, dissociative episodes, nightmares, acute agitation, and an impaired ability to self-structure and self-regulate behavior. This interferes with the establishment of genuine, interpersonal relationships, the ability to find and hold a job, and the capacity to make future plans. Ironically, PTSD is one of the few DSM categories in which an etiology is implied in the term's definition (Krippner, 1997a).

Kirk and Kutchins (1997) go even further than Caldwell, estimating that there are some 175 combinations of symptoms by which PTSD can be diagnosed, and it is possible for two people who have no symptoms in common to receive that diagnosis (p. 124). In a study of 832 patients in a family practice, it was discovered that symptoms of PTSD were often evident in the absence of a traumatic event. Six out of ten patients who described a nontraumatic event as the "worst in their lives" had significantly more posttraumatic stress symptoms for a longer time period than those whose "worst event" fell into a category that psychiatrists would consider traumatic. These life events included marital conflicts, work problems, burglaries, and chronic illnesses. The study's authors suggested that these events may increase overall psychological stress, bringing on symptoms related to an earlier trauma (Mol et al., 2005), a hypothesis reminiscent of our notion of a continuum of clinical and subclinical PTSD types, a spectrum that focuses on symptomatology rather than causal factors for both civilians and combatants.

This tangle of causes and effects suggests that psychiatrists who view human disorders through the lens of biology and neurology do not fully understand the role of shared, cultural intersubjective meaning, personal subjective worldviews, scripts, learning theory, and the lived consequences of different kinds of misfortune. This supports Greening's (1997) assertion that PTSD involves an existential shift caused not only by the stressful event but also a schism between personal experience and reigning social and personal beliefs and worldviews. In our terms, one's personal mythology or worldview is challenged and is found inadequate to deal with the new circumstances, whether the precipitating event is typically classified as "traumatic" or not.

Over the years, Krippner (1997a, 1997b) has observed that psychiatrists are prone to take terms with which they are familiar and superimpose them inappropriately on unfamiliar cultures and situations. Like other hypothetical constructs in psychiatry, PTSD is a part of a human classification structure that seeks to provide order in an infinitely complex world (Gergen, 1985; Kleinman, 1989). The World Health Organization's (1993) *International Classification of Diseases and Related Health Problems* reevaluates what *DSM* calls PTSD, while Lewis-Fernandez and Kleinman (1995) criticized *DSM's* minimal attention to cross-cultural issues. Among cultures, meaning, goals, values, and worldviews are relative, not absolute. Szasz (1991) referred to the entire concept of mental illness as a fabricated "myth," and not in the broader, more positive, sense of the term that we have described earlier. Selye (1974) repeatedly made the point that not all stress evokes distress; some stressful events, especially short-term stresses such as those involved in sports events or public speaking, can inspire or empower people and can even enhance their immune systems.

We continue to employ the term PTSD but with the understanding that there are dangers in medicalizing the complex reactions to trauma. PTSD, as a term, may outlive its usefulness at some point in the future, perhaps giving way to a term such as "traumatic stress injury"; in the meantime, there are civilians and combat veterans who are suffering, and the tentative label of PTSD has succeeded in bringing professional and popular attention to their plight.

DEVELOPMENTAL APPROACHES

Development is often stultified by reactions to trauma, which hamper growth (Goleman, 1995). This is due, in part, to customary defense mechanisms against fear and anxiety, perhaps better described as "protective factors," such as so-called "regression in the service of the ego" (Bandura, 1997; Commons et al., 1984; Mendelsohn, 1987). When the victim is a child or an adolescent, the problem looms larger. If development is hindered, a person is less likely to be able to integrate traumatic experience into her or his psyche (Kegan, 1994). And, in the case of children who are traumatized at an early developmental stage, the obstacles can have more far reaching effects.

Frederick and McNeal's (1998) approach to working with PTSD is eclectic in nature, drawing upon psychotherapy integration (Norcross & Goldfried, 2005), psychoanalysis, Jungian analytical psychology and Neo-Freudian theories, cognitive-behavioral therapy, and many other approaches. Basically, though, their approach is developmental, addressing issues spanning childhood abuse to terminal illness. They assert that "prying memory material" out of the client to keep "dissociative patients symptomatic" can magnify problems by "retraumatizing" the patient or turning him or her into a "trauma junky" (p. 315). Instead, Frederick and McNeal suggest that therapists proceed cautiously in a staged "uncovering," rather than instigating a single act. In the process, "ego-strengthening" provides feelings of safety and stability and educates clients on how to control such symptoms as flashbacks (with medication, if necessary, and often with hypnosis). Hypnotically facilitated psychotherapy can be a powerful resource, often through attempts to put one in touch with past experiences. "Corrective emotional experiences" utilize imagination to evoke positive changes in clients' significant thoughts, beliefs, emotions, expectations, internal structures, and ways of relating—what we have referred to as constructive personal myths. In other words, this "correction" is felt to be a portal for reassigning the valuations of previous experiences, or generating a new framework in which to interpret recurring images. Finally, creativity and socialization patterns will emerge, and often a type of integration may occur that reflects the "sacredness of the process." This "sacredness" is reflected by such mythic statements as "I am becoming the person I always wanted to be" (pp. 322–323). This positive focus on the future avoids the "false memories" that may accompany the dredging up of purported traumas from one's childhood, traumas supposedly "repressed" for many years.

PSYCHODYNAMIC APPROACHES

The psychodynamic approach interprets trauma in terms of a person's interaction with his or her social environment. In this view, trauma is something beyond ordinary experiences that essentially overwhelm the psyche, resulting in numbing or passivity (Blanck & Blanck, 1974; Stolorow et al., 1987). Usually, within a few hours or days of a traumatic experience, one's emotions are stimulated by what has been called an "outcry" period. According to such a model, this is usually followed by a period of denial, with the intrusion of unwanted memories.

As an outcome of his treatment of World War I veterans, Sigmund Freud (1933) developed his own theory on this subject. His understanding was that biological urges of the "id" overwhelm the rational aspect of the so-called "ego." Undoubtedly, what he called the "superego" also exerts pressures of guilt and inadequacy on the psyche, often to the degree that the ego has been immobilized. Allegedly, individuals can successfully repress a traumatic incident, but sooner or later they will relive it in their dreams and fantasies. A major goal, from this perspective, is to work through traumas by building the "ego strength" necessary to allow for a conscious reexperiencing of the traumatic event. This is generally accomplished through a repetitive process of gradual and conscious assimilation of the experience into one's life.

A fundamental problem with this view is that it generally requires more than personal insight and return to events and memories (Corey, 2004). It generally takes time and a highly motivated client in a committed therapeutic relationship to deal fully with the trauma. The psychodynamic view of trauma has evolved a great deal since Freud, centering, to a large degree, in Object Relations Theory (Blanck & Blanck, 1974, 1986; Greenberg & Mitchell, 1983), as well as psychoanalytically oriented and hypnotically facilitated psychotherapy (Brown & Fromm, 1987).

Freud believed that symptoms could only be ameliorated successfully if their underlying causes had been resolved. If not, many psychoanalysts insist that symptoms will be replaced by other symptoms. However, research does not support this conviction, and there are equally compelling psychodynamic reasons why symptom removal is desirable. In support of this post-Freudian revelation, Watkins (1987) has observed that symptom removal may, in fact, strengthen, not weaken, the "ego." His hypnotically facilitated psychotherapeutic techniques have induced clients to mobilize their own resources, stimulating their immunological systems and increasing the production of antibodies through B cell production facilitated via T cell subpopulations, consisting of helper and suppressor cells (Barabasz & Watkins, 2005, p. 214).

FAMILY SYSTEM APPROACHES

A number of practitioners have reported using a variety of family system approaches for dealing with civilian victims of war. The dynamics of those relationships and the roles, rules, and taboos of the family system are evaluated and restructured to meet the needs of the family members and trauma victims (Corey, 2004; Teyber, 2000). Trauma to one or all family members strains the family as a system and compounds existing dysfunctional patterns, communication disturbances, family secrets, overprotection of certain members, or blame.

The routine use of family system approaches in the treatment of war trauma can be exceptionally difficult to manage therapeutically and usually requires lengthy treatment periods. Once treatment begins, the facilitator often discovers that war trauma issues are interwoven within a preexisting dysfunctionality, one highly resistant to change (Corey, 2004; Pennbaker & Beall, 1986; van der Veer, 1998).

Another difficulty arises when family members have been scattered, wounded, or murdered. Nevertheless, measures were used to identify the extent of trauma and, in some cases, improvements due to therapy among adolescents in Angola (McIntyre & Ventura, 2003), survivors of the Rwanda genocide (Bolton, 2003), and refugees of conflicts in the former Yugoslavia (Barath, 2003).

LEARNING THEORY APPROACHES

Reactions to war can be interpreted as the manifestations of learned behavior in which a person is conditioned to avoid stimuli associated with trauma (Bandura, 1997; Wolpe, 1982). On its own, this would not be problematic. More problematic is the generalization of learned behaviors to even the most benign situations. Considerable research and applied practice have been used successfully in desensitizing victims of trauma, through realization that, in spite of one's conditioning, there is no real danger in certain situations. Biofeedback and other self-regulation strategies have been developed to speed up the desensitization process (Moss, 1999). If the body can remain physiologically relaxed, as taught in biofeedback, the desensitization process is greatly enhanced. The goal is to let the body remain relaxed as one confronts the trauma, while soliciting increasing levels of anxiety. For example, one can assign the degree of anxiety a number on a one to ten scale, and then use mental imagery to repeatedly "relive" the stressful situation, with the hope that the assigned number will decrease in severity as treatment continues. Over time, the victim can usually regain a sense of her or his well-being.

Anxiety desensitization is not the same as dealing with one's subjective experience of trauma, and the learning approach usually requires an involved discussion and emotional and cognitive exploration (Bugental, 1987; Schneider & May, 1995). In other words, the phenomenology of the experience, as well as the overt symptoms and reactions, needs attention, because veterans typically avoid talking about their wartime experiences, and, when they do, they do so guardedly and reluctantly (Hayes, 2006,

p. 26). This is an unfortunate situation, because research involving brain scans has demonstrated that articulating feelings may activate the part of the prefrontal cortex associated with language production and suppress the area of the brain associated with emotional distress (Eisenberger, Lieberman, & Williams, 2003). Following a traumatic event, stress hormones become activated and physiologically embed the memory of the event (Winerman, 2006); given this entrenched biological reaction, any type of psychotherapy faces enormous challenges.

COGNITIVE-BEHAVIORAL APPROACHES

Albert Ellis (2001), one of the innovators of the cognitive-behavioral therapies, elevated the human capacity for reason and choice above the power of habit and conditioning (Livingston, 2006, p. 33). Cognitive-behavioral therapies can be very useful, particularly in modifying dysfunctional personal myths and self-talk. If civilians or combat veterans have bought into such personal myths as "I have always been weak" or "I did not see enough combat to be this wrecked," some therapies will be of limited use. Considerable time is required to deconstruct false beliefs that have been accepted as truisms. We have found that an emphasis on acceptance and commitment is useful here. Persuading clients that their beliefs are false or even not absolutely true is often futile, as they always find some way to hold onto them, no matter how limiting. When ex-combatants' self-talk is fused with their identity, specifically cognitive fusion, or their combat flashbacks seem to pull them to the past as if it were happening in the present, they simply cannot examine the situation without overidentifying with it. With mindfulness and acceptance strategies, they can learn to internally view their thoughts as mere thoughts, their feelings as temporary feelings, and their beliefs as personal myths—not absolute truths—and then they can view flashbacks as recall, watching them without completely identifying with them. The process takes some time and is not applicable to everyone, but it can be of immense value. Once the pillars of their conceptual models and perspectives are weakened, cognitive-behavioral therapy is extremely useful; Friedman (1994) feels it is the most effective treatment for PTSD and that recovery is more than likely—provided a skilled mental health practitioner can be found.

Psychotherapy that aims for behavioral or attitudinal changes cannot be ignored. Patients gradually arrive at insights, realizations, and clarity by addressing their intrapsychic issues. However, if the insights gained are not followed up by change, the therapy will have limited scope and efficacy. This is particularly true for such habits as drug and alcohol abuse and can be equally true for avoidance behaviors and pessimistic attitudes.

Other changes can be anticipated as well. If clients no longer fit well with spouses, jobs, parents, religions, or any of their other groundings, they need to move on with their lives instead of remaining in toxic situations. But simply moving on does not give someone license to preserve dysfunctional habits in different situations. To move out of town, get divorced, and change jobs ultimately changes nothing if clients do not face the behaviors and attitudes they repeat and replay.

In part, this is why it is important to place responsibility for the outcome of therapy on the client. A psychotherapist can help an individual find his or her direction, but the client's responsibility is to undertake the necessary work. When returning from Korea with nightmares and loneliness, Washington remarked:

> I was surprised when my therapist told me that she would be a guide for me but that the hard work was up to me. I thought therapy was some sort of magical process where I could just sit back and turn everything over to the therapist. Boy was I wrong!

We have also found that cognitive-behavioral psychotherapy benefits anxious and/or depressed clients who are being treated with drugs, particularly SSRIs. It seems most valuable when a client still has considerable anxiety or depression, even after giving medication a fair trial. Sometimes, the remaining anxiety and/or depression motivate a client to do the inner work necessary for symptom relief. On the other hand, in the beginning, nearly all clients commencing a regimen of psychotropic drugs expect medication to enable them to carry on with their lives in a satisfactory manner. They are in for a rude surprise when side effects, such as hallucinations and unusual bodily reactions, accompany the shift in moods that is the primary focus of medication. When these unexpected reactions occur, a window of opportunity becomes available for the psychotherapist. Kyle told us:

> I wanted to keep my record clean of any visit to a shrink. A few years ago I wouldn't have gone near you guys. But then I realized that medication didn't go far enough, so I booked an appointment with a down-to-earth shrink and I'm finally making real progress.

The strategy of cognitive-behavior treatment is straightforward, whether it is applied to veterans or civilians. A therapist explains to clients that many of their perceived injunctions, the "musts," "shoulds," and "oughts" of their experience are irrational; they are not grounded in the here and now (Ellis, 2001; Ellis & Grieger, 1977). Self-instructions, positive self-talk, "homework" assignments, and reframing are extremely useful to many PTSD victims (Beck & Emery, 1985). The thrust of this approach is that patients are shown how their cognitive and behavioral style, which might have served as a useful defense at the time of the trauma, continues to affect their lives negatively. Through a variety of procedures, they are then taught how to modify or abandon illogical ideas and self-defeating activities. They are then in a position to construct a life philosophy rooted in the present rather than the imagined past (Bandura, 1997). For sophisticated individuals who exhibit emotional sensitivity and intelligence, it is important that the new belief system be grounded in the person's own life experiences, values, meanings, and beliefs. Otherwise, individuals run the risk of accepting worldviews to which they cannot really relate.

Depression among war refugees can also be effectively treated with cognitive-behavior therapy by instilling positive meaning into their devastated lives (Beck et al., 1979). Horowitz (1998) has described the role of defense mechanisms that act as informational sieves for moods, transitional patterns, and general maladaptive behaviors. The goal is to build a sturdy and positive internal structure to replace or augment unstable, irrational, corrosive beliefs that affect mood and behavior. Neither this practice nor any other can claim to revise the events themselves, but they do operate with the powerful presupposition that what is most influential about trauma is not the incident alone, but the gravity it asserts on the orbit of subsequent ideas and beliefs. Refugees may have lost their homes, valued possessions, and family members. Nevertheless, they survived. And their lives need to be reconstructed, beginning with the provision of the basic necessities needed to ensure their survival.

EXISTENTIAL-HUMANISTIC APPROACHES

Learning theory and cognitive-behavioral approaches are, in our experience, critically useful for the desensitization of a surface problem but do not always deal with the deeper aspects of a victim's life (Paulson, 2004). While individuals can ultimately realize they are not physically in harm's way in the new country, no amount of desensitization is effective when they perceive their underlying psychological discord, alienation, and loss as grounded in reality. And the problem is that, all too often, it *is* grounded in reality. A client may leave a therapist's office to return to a home that could be bombed, invaded, or destroyed at any moment. A rival clan or sect may maim or kill the client, as well as his or her children, parents, and spouse. Perhaps the most rational response would be to leave the war zone, but curfews and restrictions might make that action impossible. All too often, civilian war victims realize that they lack the wherewithal to carry out even minimal decisions and exert control over their life direction.

Humanistic-existential psychotherapies hold that it is necessary to build a positive psychotherapeutic bridge between the therapist and the client, developing an "I-Thou" not an "I-It" relationship. Martin Buber (1984), the philosopher who coined those terms, keenly observed that many people interact with others as if they are objects-to-be-used, not people-to-be-savored. The humanistic-existential counselor or psychotherapist realizes that unless there is some common bond between the therapist and the client, psychotherapy remains an intellectual exercise. Deep and long-lasting change is rarely observed, because clients are in a very vulnerable position where trust is essential and rests completely on the solidity of the established relationship. Trust, however, is an emergent property of the client's perspective. If, upon testing the therapist via boundary probes and congruence, the therapist fails in the eyes of the client, deep therapeutic change is unlikely. Instead, clients tend to become complacent and act out previous relationships, like that of the parent-child dynamic. Such a client likely knows what to say to please the therapist but allows only superficial role-playing to occur.

What happens next is usually up to the therapist. This step should not be a haphazard admixture of techniques but a grand scheme that selects methods based on their effectiveness. From the onset of therapy, clients need to feel that they are worthy human beings, not broken castoffs to be fixed. We take the position that the humanistic-existential perspective offers this broad view. Instead of clients coming to a professional to be fixed, both therapist and client need to function in a cocreative process that goes beyond the client's desire to gain relief from symptoms. This perspective is "humanistic" in that it views clients as self-actualizing, resourceful, and capable of making constructive changes in their lives (Cain, 2001, p. 4). It is "existential" in that it helps clients reflect on problems due to lack of meaning in their lives, creating faith in their abilities to discern their own answers (Walsh & McElwain, 2001, p. 253). Hence, humanistic-existential psychotherapies are philosophically grounded, attempting to help their clients grapple with the basic nature and meaning of their experiences, either positive or negative. These therapists realize that their clients exist in a social and historical context and that their choices will shape the situations they encounter in the future (p. 255). Astute therapists will realize that veterans' beliefs may have been dramatically altered by combat and that a holistic approach to rehabilitation is necessary (Decker, 2007).

The grand scheme of therapy includes enabling clients to learn to appreciate and enjoy themselves and others, instead of depreciating and judging. It promotes living in a self-determining, authentic manner, based on who they are or find themselves to be, instead of who they think they should be or who they are told they should be. It is important that they develop their neglected or overlooked personality traits, as well as increase their freedom and power by accepting responsibility for their lives. Finally, they must be aware of psychological activity both inside and outside of themselves.

Some therapists may feel more comfortable applying aspects of positive psychology (Seligman & Csikszentmihalyi, 2000; Snyder & Lopez, 2002), helping their clients discover their "signature strengths." The purported difference between humanistic-existential and positive psychology is that positive psychology claims to ground its practices in empirical studies conducted within the framework of mainstream science. However, humanistic-existential therapy is also based in empirical, quantitative evidence (Elliot & Greenberg, 2001; Koole et al., 2006; Rogers et al., 1967; Truax &

Mitchell, 1971), clinical practices of various authors (Willis, 1994), qualitative evidence such as interviews, case studies, and phenomenological data (Clarke, 1996; Giorgi et al., 1983), as well as existential philosophy (Boss, 1979). From our point of view, humanistic-existential psychology is more comprehensive than positive psychology because it is grounded in several philosophical traditions, while also encompassing a wider range of research methods and paying more attention to the "dark night of the soul" experiences, "spiritual emergencies," and wisdom from cross-cultural literature and arts (e.g., Buddhism, Native American). Nevertheless, positive psychology must be recognized for its formulation of novel interventions (such as "learned optimism" and the "recrafting" of love, work, and play experiences) and its impressive body of research data on such topics as life satisfaction, virtues, and happiness (Seligman, 2002, 2005).

We feel comfortable using both positive psychology and humanistic-existential therapies simultaneously, as the differences between the two perspectives are outweighed by their similarities. Both take the position that psychological well-being needs to be studied in its own right, not simply as the absence of disorders and distress (Peterson & Seligman, 2004, p. 65).

Both positive psychology and humanistic-existential psychotherapy are exceptionally practical for dealing with PTSD among veterans. Both advocate approaches based on learning theory and common sense. Examples include having veterans reconnect with friends and families, find ways of dealing with stress (such as meditation, yoga, exercise, dance, expressive art, and sports) that minimize medication regimens, and circumvent the use of alcohol and illegal drugs. Also, they advocate practicing imagery to "rehearse" appropriate behaviors (such as meeting new people, applying for a job) and putting skills developed in the service to civilian use (such as team building, reacting swiftly to challenges, and taking pride in one's accomplishments). Veterans need to congratulate themselves for their positive accomplishments and not brood over setbacks and failures. And a sense of humor can aid all of these ways of recovering from the ravages of war (Armstrong et al., 2006). For example, Garry Trudeau's cartoon strips about soldiers who have served in Iraq and Afghanistan often deal with PTSD, amputees, and traumatic brain injury—yet have won praise from readers from across the political spectrum (Gettelman, 2007).

Self-love and self-care can also be practical and sensible. Veterans can pick up their old hobbies, watch humorous television shows and movies (while occasionally taking a "holiday" from media news that could be upsetting), attempt new skills (such as cooking, athletics, artwork, or gardening), visit museums, go to musical events, read novels, eat healthy foods, volunteer for community service, and keep a journal or chart their progress on a computer file. This journal (or computer file) could cite the activities, places, people, and situations that trigger flashbacks, coping mechanisms when symptoms recur (such as deep breathing, using mental imagery to reduce the severity of the symptom), as well as list rewards for accomplishments (eating out, going to concerts, buying a new tool, upgrading one's computer) (Armstrong et al., 2006; Matsakis, 2007).

Invariably, when combatants begin to explore existential meaning, the topics of religion and spirituality arise. Our position is that therapists should explore their own religious convictions and spiritual experiences, forming a personal mythology that includes them, and that will serve as a platform for discussing these topics. Many therapists are not members of an institutionalized religious group but see themselves as spiritual, acknowledging that they operate within a framework that includes something greater than they are. Clients need to be encouraged to explore for themselves the connections they have to this spiritual realm (Krippner, 2005). However, religious doctrine is not an excuse to avoid taking responsibility for one's life. Instead, the goal is to find a profound relationship with one's spiritual convictions and forge a connection with what one considers the sacred, holy, or cosmic. This integration of spiritual matters into psychotherapy is exemplified by Decker's (2007) eclectic treatment model, which is a masterful blend of cognitive exposure, psychoanalytic considerations, trauma focus, Gestalt work, existential concerns, and a basic spiritual perspective. From our point of view, this model reaches deeper dimensions of the human psyche than the so-called "faith-based" treatments that are religiously doctrinaire and that might breach the wall between church and state that is central to American democracy (In the Capital, 2007).

Koole, Greenberg, and Pyszczynski (2006) have identified five basic existential concerns: death, isolation, identity, freedom, and meaning. The psychological confrontation with these concerns occurs most dramatically in the aftermath of extremely negative events "whether personal ones...or more globally significant ones like the terrorist attacks of 9/11" (p. 212). To assist mental health practitioners' work with what the *DSM* refers to as "religious or spiritual problems," the Sidran Institute has developed a training curriculum and programs especially geared toward members of the clergy, who are often the first professionals sought out by traumatized individuals (Hook, 2005).

Profound meaning resides in Buddhism, Hinduism, Taoism, Islam, Judaism, Christianity, and other institutionalized religions or belief systems for many clients. The field of transpersonal psychology (Vaughan, 1995; Washburn, 1994, 1995; Wilber, 1995) studies these meanings and how they provide profound dimensions to human existence. The term "transpersonal" refers to experiences in which one seems to transcend one's everyday identity, often establishing a connection with spiritual agencies. We believe that the transpersonal aspect of psychotherapy is especially useful for many veterans with PTSD and ignoring it may limit an entire world of potential growth. As Tick (2005) has observed in his masterful book, *War and the Soul,* the symptoms of PTSD can diminish or disappear when veterans are reconciled with their "deepest moral and spiritual connections about the sacredness of life" (p. 282). Restoration of the soul may heal not only the self but one's community as well.

In our experience with PTSD cases, the most damaging effect of war trauma is the loss of the empowering personal myths about a traumatized person's control of interactions with her or his environment (Paulson, 2004). When individuals feel that they have little control over the course of their lives, the negative effects of trauma are accentuated (Shapiro & Astin, 1998). From an existential perspective, finding positive meaning in war experiences is a major challenge (Paulson, 2004). For instance, asking a woman who has been raped by a soldier and become pregnant to find an upside to her condition is an absurd insult. Her situation makes her vulnerable to rejection by the community, not only because she is considered "poisoned" and "tainted," but also because, in some way, it is alleged that she "brought on the event" (Pappas, 2003).

Treating individuals who have experienced these situations is delicate and fraught with difficulties. Moreover, many victims harbor the personal myth that God is punishing them for their impiety (Richards & Bergin, 1997). The therapist is often caught in a no-win dichotomy. If victims modify their thinking, they lose much of the cultural mythology that has provided them with life meaning. Yet, until they reframe this perspective, they remain victims not only of war but of their own thinking. These kinds of damning bifurcations extend well beyond the limited case of rape. They emerge when a shopkeeper's store is bombed, when an office worker's car is stolen, or when a teacher sees her school destroyed by insurgents, sometimes "youth soldiers" who once were her own students.

Often an existential perspective is helpful but needs to be combined with other approaches (Paulson, 2004). War victims have, more than likely, experienced "too much reality" and, through this experience, are acutely sensitized to the brutality and sheer meaninglessness of not only their lives but of all lives. For many, a doctrinaire, "faith-based," religious perspective has limited effectiveness for one of two reasons. First, as previously suggested, individuals may feel as though they are being punished by God for some transgression. Often, the specific transgression cannot be identified, or, because it seems to be so minor to the therapist, it is discounted or ignored. For example, not saying one's prayers or not donating enough money to the local mosque, church, or temple can be viewed as the transgression that caused the strife. To a therapist, this might be seen as an inessential fiction to be discounted, while to the client it is a source of his or her suffering.

The other common reaction is total hatred of the "enemies" for their actions and existence. While anger is often easier to work with than internalized guilt, it has a tendency to fester and grow, swallowing more and more of the victim's worldview, motivating some to become terrorists themselves. The psychotherapist's or counselor's existential or spiritual approach can hardly provide long-term therapeutic benefit in most of these instances (Richards & Bergin, 1997). Humanistic psychology's "hierarchy of needs" has emphasized that "lower order" needs, such as safety and security, must be met before "higher order" needs come into play (Maslow, 1971). There are instances where humanistic-existential counseling needs to assist clients in their lived world, helping them find a modicum of protection, and meet such basic needs as food, clothing, and shelter. Therefore, the mental health professional needs to form partnerships with aid workers in devastated areas to help provide basic necessities.

Once basic needs have been met, existential and spiritual approaches, if life-affirming and positive, can be combined with other therapies, notably those based on learning theory and cognitive psychology. Anger and revulsion are understandable, and these feelings can be expressed verbally, through dance and art and in psychodrama. Eventually, mental health professionals may be able to help their clients reconstruct personal mythologies, incorporating broad-based affirmations that include forgiveness and reconciliation, reconstructing lives that have survived the vicissitudes of war and trauma.

After

"This is the part I didn't want to see."
—Sgt. Kendall Sorensen

After the fun, after the shooting spree,
this is the part we did not want to see—
Two groups of victims on a smoking plain,
one armed with tanks, the other armed with pain.
Reluctantly, the conquering hero sees
his own defeat in eyes of refugees,
while shattered children trapped in lives of fear
are asked to trust their fate to some emir
whose bathrooms are adorned with unearned gold
to symbolize new order wrought from old.
Revenge against revenge—it does not cease.
The desert storm has brought no rain of peace.

—Tom Greening

9

Keys to Treating Trauma

Experience gained by Daryl Paulson through counseling Vietnam combat veterans, as well as Vietnamese, Middle Eastern, and Latin American war victims now residing in the United States, reveals a series of crucial keys to psychotherapy in general: the client must be heard truly and be taken seriously by the therapist (Teyber, 2000). Victims need to tell their stories, expressing their pain, their rage, their despair, their guilt, and their hatred (van der Veer, 1998). As they tell their stories, often repetitiously, they need to be reassured that they are heard, that they are valued, that they are respected, and that they are appreciated.

Paulson (1994, 1998, 2004) has developed a therapeutic approach in the treatment of veterans, victims, and refugees of war that consists of a cognitive approach that reframes the situation as a mythic rite of passage. However, it is contraindicated in the early stages of therapy, when anxiety, depression, and feelings of loss are intensely experienced. Early in the therapy, clients may not be ready to take a retrospective look at their trauma and reconstruct a live narrative. Later in the course of therapy, when the client has dealt more with the traumatic experience and is somewhat desensitized to it, it is more beneficial to introduce the rite of passage perspective (Paulson, 2001).

Rites of passage and the mythic structures that contain them are not fables or falsehoods when used in this context. A rite of passage, from an internal perspective, is a self-constructed framework that serves to organize one's traumatic life experiences in a coherent structure that clarifies and defines the meaning of one's unique experiences (Tick, 2005). These cognitive maps can provide meaning to the past, definition to the present, and direction for the future. War itself can be conceptualized as a rite of passage; at the same time, recovery from the ravages of war is a more arduous rite, especially for civilians. It is easier to bomb a school than to build a school; it is easier to destroy than to create. Counselors and therapists must work to help clients "build" and "create" their own cognitive maps. It is no easy task.

USING INTERNAL MYTHIC STRUCTURES

Campbell (1968, p. 3) identified three recurrent cross-cultural phases present in the "hero's journey"* and similar mythical rites of passage: separation, initiation, and return. These are the three segments of the hero's descent into the horrors of the unknown from which he or she attempts to bring back new insights and important truths for the community.

The separation phase, or "call to adventure," signifies that destiny has summoned a person for a rite of passage. In terms of "the call," this is the initial challenge to that individual's former conceptualization of the life event. If he or she did not consciously choose the event and feels as if he or she was "chosen by fate," then the event is viewed as the motivating force behind the person's situation. It is the point where a transition between the former life (pre-trauma period) and a passage to a new life (post-trauma period) begins. It is a liminal period in which the person is thrown off-balance and is "betwixt and between." Many indigenous tribes who value balance and equilibrium saw this phase as a dangerous crossing, but one that—if traversed—could strengthen the soul.

The initiation phase is the experience of being removed from one's customary surroundings, being arrested, assaulted, and tortured, facing death, and having fought back or escaped. It is a very difficult period when one has little or no control over the events and their outcomes and a period of intense and physical testing in which the person must confront circumstances and survive (Paulson, 2004). The person is essentially in an unfeasible situation yet must endure. In this phase there appears to be no future, only a painful present. Yet, it is a present that is pregnant with possibilities if one is resilient and resourceful.

The return phase includes the therapeutic process in which individuals deal with the traumatic experience (Paulson, 1991, 2004). It involves working with the traumatic experience, as well as assigning meaning to the experience that can be used as a source of new wisdom. Optimally, these insights are shared with a support group, a neighborhood, or a community.

The return phase is also an opportunity for integrating one's pre-trauma and post-trauma lives. It is possible that those individuals, while suffering horribly from their experiences, can reach a greater level of well-being than

---

*"Hero" may be interpreted as oneself.

could have been achieved without the experience (Paulson, 2004). In essence, they have derived value that is greater than they might have had they not experienced the traumatic event. Notable examples are Victor Frankl (1956) and Elie Wiesel (1996), both of whom gained considerable wisdom from their internment in Nazi concentration camps, wisdom that they shared with the world community.

As time goes on, these people still recognize the horror of their trauma, but they often view it as one of the most useful experiences or lessons in their lives. It may be the case that, had the trauma never happened, they would have continued to exist without any deep investigation of life's meaning. At its best, it can be a momentous "wake-up call," one that can benefit the individual and those around them (Paulson, 2004). And, chances are, in dealing with war issues, trauma victims will also be forced to deal constructively with other intrapsychic issues that they would not have addressed without the trauma. In this way, survivors of war may have the clear purpose of helping others in similar situations, although not everyone completes the cycle in this manner.

William, a World War II veteran, left Italy "with a feeling of unfulfilment . . . . It was like arriving at the railroad station of a great metropolis and never getting off the train" (Kaufman, 2006). He vowed that he would "one day get off the train," and 45 years later, he returned to the site of battle, performing what we would consider a "rite of passage." William walked along the bank of the Arno River and viewed the Leaning Tower of Pisa, reenacting, in his imagination, a battle that never took place, because his battalion had been stationed on the wrong side of the battlefield.

William was not the only veteran of World War II who felt incomplete. Children of combatants often recalled their parents' refusal to talk about the war. Gawne's father fought in the Brittany campaign, was severely wounded, and returned home to recurring nightmares. His son later observed that everything seemed reduced to "just a uniform hanging in the back of the closet." The son of another veteran told his father that he had "shut down the part of you that remembers too well how it feels to huddle in a hole and be shelled. You are going to forget that. You are going to make yourself forget" (Freeman, 2005, p. 23). Several of these children have written books and created Web sites as a means of honoring and preserving family histories.

Jed, who fought in Vietnam, returned to the United States not only with a sense of emptiness but also to the contempt of the American public. Rather than suffering in silence, as many of his comrades were doing, Jed returned to Vietnam, devoting several years to working with the "children of the dust," the offspring of U.S. servicemen and their Vietnamese girlfriends, whom the Vietnamese treated vilely. He reunited some of them with their American fathers and found schools and jobs for others, either in Vietnam or abroad. He told us, "Once I started to work with these boys and girls, the war finally came to an end for me."

Yet, for every civilian or veteran who completes the hero's journey, there are those for whom the journey ends in limbo. By casting their dilemma in mythological terms, we hope that we have brought attention to the importance of completing life rituals, finding some closure to life's narratives, and closing what some psychologists call a "Gestalt" or wholeness. On the one hand, one is always on an excursion of one sort or another. For most people, this excursion takes the form of a spiral, as one completes one loop of the spiral, another emerges. Far too many people, many of them trauma victims, get stuck in one of the lower loops and never transcend the groove in which they have been jammed for years if not decades.

WHAT WE HAVE LEARNED FROM VIETNAM COMBAT VETERANS

We have used a variety of treatment options that we find of immense value in assisting combat veterans. However, for finding positive meaning in endeavors that appear to be a rational mistake, reframing the experience as a rite of passage can be helpful. Paulson (1994) reframed his Vietnam experience in this way to find meaning. He also underwent much one-on-one psychotherapy, so we do not recommend using only the reframing method. But let us tell you the stories of several Vietnam veterans, weaving Paulson's war experiences throughout. Paulson fought as a marine in Vietnam and, like so many other veterans of that war, suffered severe psychic injury from the nightmare of death in which he participated. Paulson's story is hauntingly similar to the stories of other veterans of the war, including the call to duty, the initiations of boot camp and early field experiences, the brutal encounter with the enemy, and the return home.

With the modern technological advancements in warfare, it is still the common infantryman, or "grunt," who fights the bulk of the war. It is the infantryman—still primarily male—who must experience the physical, emotional, and mental anguish of war: being sick, being wounded, facing the tension and anxiety of impending death, and dealing with the deaths of others on a daily basis. For the modern infantryman, like his predecessors, life will never again be the same. No longer can he dismiss death as an event far in the future. Even if he survived the war, he would know always that death is but an instant away. No matter where he is, no matter what job or position he may hold, no matter whom he marries, no matter how financially secure he is, he will always know, deep in his heart, that life on this earth holds no permanence for him.

For the most part, his worldview is contrary to the worldview of his peers who did not experience combat, those who were not exposed to its brutal forces. For the noncombatant, death is deniable; for the combat veteran, it is an overshadowing truth. While the noncombatant's worldview is generally very predictable—graduating from high school, entering college, marrying, raising a family, working, and ultimately enjoying life in retirement—the combatant's worldview usually is one of living in an unpredictable world that is undergoing constant, threatening change. He has seen so much death, so much suffering, and has been forced to live so closely with insecurity that he can no longer feel secure. Often, the veteran feels his life has no positive meaning, no purpose, and no direction, once he has experienced war.

This meaningless state, Paulson (1994) argues, can be corrected with the positive use of mythology and initiation rites. In a number of mythological sagas, the initiate/warrior/hero (1) was "called" to enter the adventure, (2) began the "journey," (3) completed a series of "adventures," and (4) upon completing these adventures, gained greater knowledge and wisdom that could then be applied to his daily life. However, the predominant problem for the Vietnam combat veterans, and the Iraq combatants as well, is that the knowledge each veteran gained from the war was not recognized or respected by either his culture or himself. Ironically, he completed the combat initiation experience but did not know it held the key to an initiation into a larger life, one that holds potential meaning for his life.

We espouse the theory that, by participating in war, the combat veteran participates in an initiation rite. For him, accepting this theory may be central to his making positive psychological gains. If he does not do this, a perpetual, existential crisis will exist, that is, life will have no meaning for him (Paulson, 1994). Paulson (1994) continues:

> Intense feelings of despair, stemming from lack of positive meaning from their combat experience is a recurring situation faced by many combat veterans with whom we have worked. In other words, they are convinced that there was and is nothing useful to be derived from war. They feel, as do most Americans, that the United States did not win any political, economic or strategic victory. It only killed many of its young men.

The majority of combat veterans, particularly Vietnam veterans, were unprepared for the psychic trauma they experienced; this included being torn from the secure fabric of their community and fighting a war for an unknown purpose. The lack of psychological support from their country while serving in Vietnam was painful and traumatic, but being attacked, put down, and protested against by their peers for their involvement in Vietnam was excruciating.

The story of one veteran, Joe, clearly defines this situation. Joe had grown up on a farm in Kentucky and was a peaceful, laid-back farm boy. After high school graduation, he worked on his father's farm and was preparing to marry his high school sweetheart. But Joe was also a poor boy, unable to get a draft deferment. Thus, shortly after graduation, he was served a draft notice. Joe had absolutely no desire to go to Vietnam, but he felt a moral responsibility to defend his nation from attack, so he joined the U.S. Army. He was drafted into an army infantry division and sent to Vietnam just in time for Christmas. There, he learned about the horrors of war. He learned what it was like to see comrade after comrade killed. One moment, they would be laughing and joking with him with a twinkle in their eyes about what they would do when they left Vietnam. The next moment, they would be dead, lying in the grass or mud with a poncho covering them until they were picked up by a chopper and taken to "Graves Registration." His friends were now cold and gray-looking, their eyes staring vacantly upward.

Joe ultimately survived Vietnam and was exuberant about going home and marrying his high school sweetheart, who had waited for him. Upon his return, however, things were not the same. The sweet smell of the summer's clover no longer made him glad to be alive. Being with his sweetheart no longer brought him joy and happiness. He was now burdened with unfinished business. Every night, the faces of his dead buddies visited him in his dreams. He saw their gray, cold faces, eyes open, staring out into space. He was in pain. His sweetheart turned away from him, marrying a guy she had been seeing while he was in Vietnam. His parents kicked him off the farm for his drinking. He tried college in Louisville but was seen by many as a war criminal. Within four months of starting college, he dropped out, beginning a clouded, 10-year ordeal of running from himself, drifting from town to town and bar to bar.

This story, while unique to Joe, is similar to the stories of other veterans. While one's past cannot be altered, one can begin to make sense out of one's war experiences. One can turn one's life around.

As previously stated, one approach is to reframe or refocus feelings of despair and hopelessness and find positive meaning in the war experience. In this context, veterans can discover who they are, where they are going, and where they fit in. That is, they can put meaning into their lives.

Meaning operates not only *in* one's conscious awareness but *outside* it as well. The meaning carried outside of one's awareness has a powerful effect on how one feels, thinks, and acts. The way in which one acts or lives may be thought of as one's personal mythology. In this sense, myths are not just stories, but constellations of beliefs, feelings, and behaviors organized around a central core or theme; these constellations can help or hinder us in comprehending our lives in meaningful ways and in feeling connected with the universe.

Many mythological motifs portray the "hero" as a warrior, having to proceed through the initiation experience alone. To a great degree, combat veterans, particularly Vietnam veterans, also had to deal with *their* experiences alone. They left their communities alone. They endured combat training alone. They contended with precombat anxiety alone. Alone, they dealt with their thoughts of being killed in battle. They proved their worth to their combat units alone. No one cheered them upon their return; they were again alone. Being alone, then, is something with which combat veterans can identify. Because our society will probably never welcome them home or provide meaning for their involvement in the war, they must strive to develop their own personal meaning from the war, a meaning unique to each warrior. Personal meaning is possible, especially when viewed as a male initiatory rite. Jungian psychologists have long known that when one is told a mythological story, he often can stand away from it *psychologically,* extracting and incorporating some personal meaning into his life from the myth.

Recall that three recurring themes are identified in this work: the call to adventure, the initiation, and the return. The call to adventure—the separation phase—consists of leaving the known behind and entering the adventure, or new dimension, in life. The initiation phase is the actual series of life events that one must experience before passing into the new dimension of life. The return is experienced only after a successful initiatory passage into the new developmental stage of life. The experiences and knowledge gained from this journey are passed on to others in order to aid them in their lives.

For example, let us look at the ancient male puberty rite. Prior to the call, both boys and girls generally helped the mothers with domestic chores around the campsite. When boys entered the puberty phase of their lives, they were "called" or separated by the tribal men to be initiated into manhood. In this case, separation was usually dramatic and, sometimes, violent. In some societies, tribal men would come and physically seize the boys from their mothers. The boys entered an initiatory period where they were stripped of their formal identities and forced to endure initiatory brutalities, such as having certain teeth knocked out, being tattooed, or being circumcised. Through this process, they were accepted as one of the men, which was a major social advancement. Now they were the hunters, the ones who provided food for the tribe. They "returned" to the tribe as men, where they could tell others of the experiences and the insights gained from the initiatory ordeal. In other societies, the transition was not as violent: boys would live together in special structures, and would receive tutoring in the skills that would ensure their passage into "manhood." Similar rituals were often constructed for girls, on either a group or an individual basis.

In Paulson's (1994) words:

> During my senior year in high school, 1966, I was deeply infatuated with a girl who really did not care about me. I was discouraged over my lack of success with her, bored with school, and could see no reason to go to college. I was unskilled in any kind of trade, such as carpentry or auto mechanics. I felt a sort of "power" telling people I was thinking of joining the Marine Corps after graduation.
>
> If I did not go to college, I would be drafted. My peers perceived this as the ultimate failure. To be drafted was in the category of being a bum, and bums

were used as "cannon fodder" in Vietnam. Successful men would let the unsuccessful fight the war. At the time, however, that perception did not bother me.

In February of 1966, I saw the John Wayne movie, *The Green Berets,* and I was intrigued by the adventure. I saw a way to escape my boredom. Since Russia and China were said to be aggressively helping North Vietnam, I believed that World War III would be starting any time and that I might as well face the end fighting instead of hiding. There was also the glee of defiance. I could finally show my parents, my teachers and my fantasy girlfriend that I was tough and did not need them. So I joined the Marine Corps on the 120-day delayed program. That is, I joined the Marine Corps with four months of high school to complete before graduation. Ten days after high school graduation, I found myself getting ready to go to the Marine Corps Recruit Depot (MCRD), San Diego, California, for boot camp.

Most of us who joined or were drafted into the military had a vague sense of apprehension, but the experience was still weeks or—at least—days away. There was still time to party and play a tough role with our friends.

I doubt that any of us realized just what was in store for us, and as we got closer and closer to the MCRD, I noticed our joking and laughing became less and less frequent and intense. That we were now in the United States military was becoming reality. It was no longer an abstract concept. Right now, we were owned by the government, by the Marine Corps; it could do with us what it chose for our entire enlistment. For us, this realization was very sobering. Our lives, as we knew them, were over. What would be next? What would military life be like?

As I looked out of the 727 Delta airliner on our landing approach to San Diego, I made a commitment to myself that although I was unsure of what lay ahead, I would not screw up. Then we landed. As soon as we got off the plane, we were loaded into buses and driven to the MCRD, where we reported for duty.

So far, things were not so bad, and since it was about 2:30 a.m., we were directed to a temporary staging area where we could sleep until morning. That morning I woke up to the peaceful whine of a small propeller-driven aircraft cruising through the air overhead. I was in a state between sleep and being awake, and since I grew up near an airport, I felt as though I was at home listening to an airplane. Abruptly, I was brought back to reality when a drill instructor marched into the squad bay yelling, "Get the hell out of the racks, you pukes! You goddamn maggots!" He started yanking recruits out of their bunks yelling, "This ain't no picnic, girls! Get the fuck up!"

We were dumbfounded. What was he talking about? What were we supposed to do? Two more drill instructors came into the squad bay, also yelling and screaming about what miserable-looking pukes we were. A hippyish recruit next to me had a scraggly beard, with which a drill instructor became obsessed. He walked over to the recruit, pulled his beard and told him if he did not have it gone in fifteen minutes, he would set it on fire with his cigarette lighter. Then he dragged him out of the room to the barber shop. He yelled for the rest of us to follow him down the stairs to the courtyard to have our hair cut. One at a time, we sat in the barber chair and had all our hair shaved off. It took about nine seconds to get a Marine Corps haircut. Then we were told to line up and get a shower in the receiving barracks next door. There, 87 of us were instructed to remove everything we were not born with and place it in the plastic sacks provided. We were then issued a small bar of soap each and marched naked to a communal shower. All 87 of us were cramped into a shower stall facility that would comfortably have held about 12 men. But the drill instructors kept yelling and screaming, "Shower up! Assholes to belly buttons, girls, get your asses in there and get cleaned up!"

After showering, we were issued underwear, socks, tennis shoes, a sweat shirt, utility trousers and a utility cap. We had no identity now. We could not recognize each other. We had no individuality, no sense of identity, and no contact with the outside world. We were totally separated from our communities, parents, friends, wives and girlfriends. Looking at each other without ever talking, our eyes asked: *What had we gotten into?*

Over the next several weeks, our spirits were broken. We were constantly humiliated and harassed. Finally, we lost our ability to care. We were dead to our past lives; they were but long ago dreams. We had no hopes or aspirations beyond just getting through the moment. Clearly, we were experiencing what is known in mythology as the "Dark Night of the Soul."

After about three weeks of living in dread and despair, however, we began to identify with the Marine Corps. It seemed as if we had had no other life, as if we had always been in boot camp. We noticed that the drill instructors also began to change their attitude toward us. We were now called "men" and "Marines" instead of "girls," "pukes," or "scum," and we began to live up to it. We learned to march; we learned to fight; we learned to work together. We were preparing for our own initiation experience, that of combat as a unit, as a military machine.

INITIATION

Paulson (1994) continues:

Once we completed our infantry training, we were destined for South Vietnam. Although we had not actually experienced combat, we thought we had a pretty good idea of what we were getting into. We had heard war stories from returning veterans. We had viewed report after report on the nightly news. We had seen trauma after trauma in movies with actual combat footage, but we were in the precombat stage of the initiation experience. We were committed to the adventure, and there was no turning back. We, the mythological heroes, stood alone in this adventure. This was a time when we thought about dying, about leaving our parents and loved ones, and about going to a foreign country to lay down our lives for America.

It was a time when I started talking to God. I had had to go to church and Sunday school all my life, and I had pretty well ignored the whole thing. Now, however, faced with the very real possibility of dying in Vietnam, I started to talk to God. I had a conception of God being a wise old man sitting on a giant, gold throne. I told him I would protect the United States from attack and do a good job—so good that he would be proud of me.

Over and over, I wondered how it would be to really experience combat. Was there a lot of shooting or just a little? What was it like to be mortared? Rocketed? Was it non-stop, 24-hour fighting? Could I kill another human being? If I could not, would I be hanged as a traitor? If I were killed, would my body be lost? Would it be mutilated? Would anyone remember me?

I even dreamed about combat. Dreaming I was walking on patrol, I found that it was not so bad, just as Sergeant Rock of the comic book found it.

One friend of mine decided to go on a perpetual party and drink his fear away. As we waited to go, he would "party hearty" as he called it, for it was his last chance. We did not have much time to dwell on how combat might be, for we were flown to Vietnam very quickly. A four-day layover in Okinawa, and then we were sent on to Da Nang Air Base where we were immediately assigned our in-country units. We certainly had doubts about our performance in combat, but our morale was fueled by our training in boot camp. We definitely felt that we had control over our combat destiny—whether we lived or died. Our thoughts were based on our boot camp logic: if we did everything we were told and did not screw up, we would live; if not, we would be shipped home in a body bag, dead. However, we were scared to death. Then the day came—the day we had to go on combat patrol.

Many of us were killed during this period, because of our inexperience in combat, but for those of us who survived our first experiences of combat, a psychological transition occurred: total despair. In my first two weeks of combat, our radio man was shot through the head just in front of me, while on patrol. He had moved into the path of a bullet probably destined for me. He was talking to another unit, and then it was over. He was gone. Just like that. He was simply "tagged" and "bagged," that is, he was identified by his unit and put in a body bag to be sent home. Just like that. I saw seventeen of my comrades who were coming in on a helicopter for a ground assault killed by a direct hit of a 121 mm rocket—all killed. Just like that! At the end of those two weeks, I watched six seasoned veterans destroyed by an incoming mortar round as they ate their C-rations. Just like that, they were gone. They were tagged and bagged. From my standpoint, combat was far too ruthless, random and absolute for me to be able to predict or prevent my death.

In classical mythology, this portion of the initiation often was referred to as the Road of Trials. It is during this period that the hero is severely tested. I, too, was tested during this 13-month ordeal, by continually witnessing young friend after young friend brutally killed, and by killing Viet Cong and North Vietnamese Army (NVA) members as if they mattered no more than rats, gleefully enjoying their suffering and pain. I was becoming progressively numb to my humanness by living this life. Soon there was no boundary between the war and myself. Now we were enmeshed, the war and I—united in this senseless butchering. My proud motto became, "Kill all the gooks, let God sort the fuckers out!" I had become a true killing machine.

I recall an incident at the An Hoa Combat Base during the 1969 Tet Offensive. One night—and it was at night when so much of the actual fighting occurred—we were hit by an NVA force. They attacked and overran a portion of the compound. About 35 NVA had broken into the camp and were looking for the communications bunker to blow it up. We bounced hand flares into the night sky to see them. We laid down a massive barrage of M-16 rifle fire, M-60 machine gun fire and M-79 launched grenades.

At one point, we were supported by a .50 caliber machine gun located on the main observation tower. Very quickly, we killed every one of the NVA and shredded them into what looked like hamburger. That is how massive our fire power was against the group. The next morning, we went over to the NVA bodies and took turns taking pictures of our kill. It was a joyous time. We had "kicked ass," and we felt good about it. We had a body count delivered to our doorsteps. We scraped up the hamburger-like bodies and laid the chunks and bits and pieces along the main road to the camp. It was a warning to the Vietnamese people who were working on the compound filling sand bags not to betray us. This was a time when we wished we could kill every one of the Vietnamese. That would solve our problem. It is incredible that we could have regressed to such a primitive way of functioning in such a short time. Life had no value except the saving of our own.

Still, during times alone, I wondered just what I had gotten myself into. I knew I was in a situation way over my head. What I was doing and how I was doing it somehow did not seem right. I was so terrified that I would never again see a friendly face, a face of one who would care about me and not try to kill me. I knew I was deeply, emotionally wounded, but I was determined to survive at all costs or, at least, kill as many NVA as I could before I was killed.

Since I was new to combat and ignorant of the actual ways of combat, I knew that I would not survive for long.

I prepared to accept my death as well as I could. As I have said, I clearly saw that it did not matter how proficient I was; a random rocket or mortar hit could end my life in an instant. This was not an abstract threat of tomorrow or next week; it was 13 months of "now," 13 months of wondering if I would be alive to eat the next meal, to see the next sunrise or the next sunset. I began hoping that since I would surely die, I would get it over soon, rather than prolonging my suffering through the end of my tour. This, I found later, was a prominent attitude among the infantrymen.

In mythological motifs, the hero experiences an encounter with what is called the father figure. The father figure is psychologically important in these stories because he is the force who fiercely guides the hero through the trying times of the initiation. The father image, his guidance, and his strength were also present for us. After having proven ourselves worthy (still alive after a number of battles), we were "taken in" by a more experienced combat veteran, "the father." This person acted as our guide and took an active role in teaching us to survive combat.

A leathery old Marine took an interest in me and taught me how to survive. He taught me the laws of combat; I learned the sound differences of incoming and outgoing mortars and rockets, and I mastered the art of "walking point" without being killed or getting the entire squad killed. In Vietnam, walking the point was dangerous. It meant one walked 25 to 50 meters in front of the rest of the patrol. It meant the point man was the first to get shot, step on a booby trap, or set off a mine. To me, it was an exhilarating experience that not just anyone could do. I had to be prepared and tested for walking the point by "the father." If I failed the test, I would be swiftly killed. If I passed, I was one with the father; I was competent and potent.

I remember vividly the first time I walked the point. I felt a strong connection to the NVA. I had to pit my survival skills against theirs. There was no one to hide behind or to take lessons from now. It was an exhilarating, yet terrifying, experience, knowing that death could come to me or the entire squad at any given moment if I failed.

In addition—like the heroes in mythology—after suffering and enduring and surrendering to apparent utter failure, we were assisted by supernatural forces. For me, this assistance came in the form of "intuition." I actually began to feel warnings about dangerous situations before they occurred. I was truly amazed at how these extra "survival senses" seemed to develop as I needed them.

For example, during the 1969 Tet Offensive, I was again at the An Hoa Combat Base with my unit, awaiting helicopter transportation to a very hot, bloody battle taking place in an area called Elephant Valley. Elephant Valley was a treacherous place, and we dreaded going there. I was very preoccupied with what kind of shit (combat) was going on there, but the weather was bad and we could not go that night. I had a very strong feeling of impending danger while lying in my tent. I could not sleep, my heart raced, my anxiety escalated, and a voice inside me said, *Leave the tent, now!* I gathered my flack jacket, helmet, ammunition and poncho, and I walked to the perimeter trenches, where I tried to sleep. About two hours later, our compound was overrun by NVA. During this attack, our camp was pounded with hundreds of high explosive rockets and mortar rounds. The ground shook from the impact of these rounds; a series of violent fire explosions engulfed the entire northern side of the compound. We thought we would never survive the night, as we repelled wave after wave of NVA attackers. Finally, by morning, they retreated.

I was so tired and sore that I limped back to my tent to sleep. When I got there, I was shocked to discover a huge hole in the tent, directly in line with the spot where my head usually rested on my cot. A boulder, approximately three feet across, lay on top of what was left of my cot. That boulder would have killed me had I stayed in the tent. From that time on, I depended on supernatural aid to keep me alive. Time and time again, intuition assisted me in surviving the initiation of war.

Superstition was common in the infantry. A lucky rock, chain or saying made the difference in whether one *thought* he would live or die. One of my friends carried an empty beer can that Raquel Welch supposedly drank from during "The Bob Hope Christmas Special" at Da Nang. As long as he had that can and could hold it to his chest, he was safe. Another friend felt he had to write in his journal every day. If he missed a day, he was in danger. Another person from Tennessee wore a raccoon tail on his helmet. He felt that as long as he had that amulet, he would be spared. Yet another felt that if he did not eat the pound cake in the C-ration can, he would be spared. He had seen too many people killed after eating the pound cake; it was a bad omen. Sometimes the supernatural aid almost made us shudder. At one time, we believed that we could control our destiny by "just trying harder." However, as we saw the gruesomeness, swiftness and finality of death, we thought we would never "make it"—never survive the combat. At some point in the initiation process, however, this changed. We began to see that you were not killed until it was your time. Our motto became, "When your number is up, you're wasted—but not a second before." This brought us some comfort. There was reason and purpose to the apparent random killing. We were part of a larger system and would now die only when it was our time. How could such a perceptual change have occurred? One would think mere chance was the arbitrator of life or death. The more shit [combat] you saw, the worse were your chances of surviving. This was how we first perceived it; but as we survived situations that were "unsurvivable," our perceptions changed. Let me explain this with some examples.

Larry, an army artilleryman, was in his tent with eight other men. Suddenly, his camp took five 121 mm rocket hits. His tent took a direct hit, killing everyone in it but Larry. He was not hit by any shrapnel. He was burned and had both eardrums ruptured, but that was it. The 121 mm rocket, a very lethal weapon, is considered to have an absolute kill range of 50 meters. Larry had been about eight meters from the rocket crater. His number was *not* up.

Another instance is from my combat experience. During the 1969 TET offensive, my unit, part of the 5th Marine Regiment, was camped at An Hoa, which was about 35 miles northwest of Da Nang. It was a horrible place, and NVA ran rampant. John B., John O. and I had survived the major area operations as members of "Task Force Yankee." Now this was over, and we were going back to the 1st Marine Division rear for a little rest and relaxation at China Beach.

Before going to China Beach, we were assigned to a work detail for several days at the 1st Marine Division headquarters. This was a welcome assignment, because it kept us out of the bush at An Hoa. On the second and last day of our detail before going to China Beach, I noticed that John O. and John B. were unusually moody. They were bitchy. How could this be? We were going to have some fun at China Beach. For lunch we ate some warm ham and cheese sandwiches and drank "cold" Coca Cola. This was the life—why could we not be office pogs (administrative personnel)? We laughed about them having it made. But I had a gut feeling that something was bothering John B. and John O. I asked them about it, and they responded that there was nothing wrong. I worked alongside them, folding tents, all afternoon, but there was some barrier between us. That night we were in the 1st Marine Division's Supply office—supposedly a very safe place. I told John O. and John B. that the club opened at 7:00 p.m. and this would be our chance for some cold beer and fun. In An Hoa, the beer we drank was hot and foamy. Because of its consistency, it just would not stay down. Here, at the club—a real club, a shack in which *cold* beer was served—things could be different. Drinking would be fun instead of an ordeal; it wouldn't be a struggle to keep hot, foamy, biting beer settled in your stomach.

John 0. and John B. were not interested! We had a fight, and I stormed out of the office and headed to the club. On my way, I heard an explosion. My heart plummeted to my feet, for I knew it was incoming. When I heard the second and third explosions, I ran for the lines. I knew we were in trouble, even if the office pogs here did not. Then the sirens went off. About an hour later I heard that the Division Supply Office was hit and two marines were killed. I wondered where John 0. and John B. were; I wondered who bought the ranch up there and kind of laughed to myself that it served "them office pogs" right. Then I heard that John 0. and John B. were the ones who were killed, and I was needed to identify them. I could not. I just could not bear to see my two best friends destroyed. I had been closer to them than to any humans on the planet. We had suffered together on patrols, been through TET together, been drunk together, and relied on each other to pull and force the other through combat, when one of us could go no more. We had each been jilted by a girlfriend; we shared this agony together. We had shared hopes of going to college together, and now it was over. They had been taken from me. From my pack I removed the fifth of R&R we had planned to share at China Beach; I drank and held back my tears and drank and held back more tears—tears that would not be shed for another six years—and drank and drank. Visualizing burying them safely and lovingly in the deep blue sea, out of harm's way—respectfully watching them peacefully descend to sleep through eternity—brought me comfort in my sorrow.

The next morning I found out that both John 0. and John B. would have been safe had they not panicked and run away from the bunker into an open room, where they met the mortar round. To this day, I cannot explain why two seasoned combat veterans ran from a bunker into a room, separated from everyone in the office, to be killed. They were the only ones killed. Truly, their numbers were up and mine was not. These experiences were very powerful and brought us to a more peaceful, fatalistic stage. When your number is up, it's up. There is no death before that time.

The hero meeting the goddess is another mythological motif encountered in many tales. The meeting of the goddess occurs only after the hero has endured many trials and has proven himself worthy. The goddess' function is to provide the hero with both bliss and comfort. For me, once I came to terms with my combat situation and accepted it, I was free to just *be.* Gone were most of the fears of being killed, for now I accepted that if it was to be, it would be. I no longer felt responsible for survival. If I was killed, that was simply the way things were intended to be. My number was up.

Once the hero enters this stage, the actual initiation is nearing completion. He had survived everything the war could present to him and had not crumbled. It was during this period that the combatant felt most comfortable being an infantryman. He was no longer an initiate; he was a full-fledged combat veteran.

THE FALSE RETURN

Paulson (1994) continues:

For those of us who survived the "Nam," our day to leave the country finally came. We were going back to the WORLD—a name we gave to the United States—home to round-eyed, friendly, and affectionate women, home to a world where the streets were asphalt-paved and there were flush toilets, hot and cold running water, food other than C-rations, and plenty of cold beer.

Unlike the mythological hero who—after going through the initiatory ordeal to find the gold, the golden fleece, or the grail—brings back his trophy to share with all, the Vietnam veteran brought back no treasure. That is, he attained no positive knowledge (treasure) that he could share with the others in his community. When our 707 landed at El Toro Marine Air Station, which had been deactivated, I was secretly preparing for a hero's welcome. I think all of us reasoned that we would get a doubly strong welcome because we had fought in spite of the absence of any explicit government plan to win the war. For example, congress and/or the president would decide to bomb North Vietnam one week, but stop bombing the next. This on-again, off-again strategy was terrible for our morale. We would often wonder, *Why the hell are we here if our leaders cannot make up their minds whether to fight the war or bail out?* Given these unusually hard conditions, we now thought we would be rewarded.

We landed and walked out of the plane to our homecoming reception. I saw *three* people waiting for us. That was it! They were Marine wives who had volunteered to serve cookies and Kool-Aid to us. Where was everyone else? Where were the women to welcome us home? They should be here, I thought.

Once in the air terminal, we were escorted to waiting military buses and driven to Camp Pendleton Marine Base for discharge or reassignment. During the drive, some college-age people screamed obscenities at us and flipped us the bird. I can still remember their yelling something about our being "warmongers."

At Camp Pendleton we were swiftly processed and bused to Los Angeles International Airport to schedule flights home. At the Los Angeles airport, I went to a bar to have a couple of drinks while waiting for my flight. This was an especially big event for me. It was my first legal drink in the United States and in a bar, for now I was of age, 21. I felt like being friendly, so I tried to start a conversation with two women sitting next to me, but they ignored me. Then I tried to talk to a couple of guys, but they, too, ignored me. It began to dawn on me that no one cared that I had served in the Vietnam war. I felt like a misfit.

The lack of care and concern for what I had been through was even apparent with my friends when I arrived home and went out drinking with them. Things were different. I noticed not only that they did not care about the war, but that I was now different from these guys. They were caught up in being "cool" and contriving to attract women. I just did not care. I had just seen hundreds of U.S. servicemen killed; I had also seen hundreds and hundreds of North Vietnamese soldiers killed and had tried to kill as many of them as I could. I had faced thirteen months of not knowing if I would die that day. Now, to worry about my hair or a woman seemed petty and meaningless. To protect myself from the meaninglessness of this life, I found a friend that night. It was a friend who would keep me calm and mellow for the next two years. That friend was beer.

The first several weeks back in the states were also hard on me when I had to describe the Vietnam experience to my friends. After a friend asked me, I thought to myself, *how could I describe that* hell *in words?* I felt anger, frustration, fear and hate, all welling up inside of me. I felt like beating the table in utter frustration, but instead I calmly took another drink of beer, said, "It was real bad," and left it at that. But I knew—not only consciously, but to the center of my being—that something was terribly and painfully wounded within me. My friend did not really care. He was more interested in collecting information to support his anti-war beliefs. For me, however, it was different. He had opened up a huge wound inside me. I recalled the friends from my unit whom I saw killed—John O., John B., Jose, Peter, Jocko, Fraize, Rocko, Pork Chops, and Glen. What had they died for? They died for nothing—nothing but bullshit. I took another drink of beer...and another...and another.

I think all of us veterans shared a sense of condemnation. We felt a kind of deep guilt that sent terror to the very core of our being. If we had been wrong about the war, were we not similar to Nazi criminals? Was there really a reason to keep on living? How could we live with ourselves, having seen and experienced all the brutalities of war and survived it, only to realize that our involvement served no positive purpose? I sensed the overt damage within myself. I remember fantasizing about how warm and caring I would be when I got back from Vietnam. I would find that special woman and devote my life to our relationship. The entire time I was in Vietnam, I thought to myself how nice it would be to be held by a warm, loving woman, to watch her laugh and smile as I teased her. I would fantasize over and over what it would be like.

When I did return, things were different. I found that I did not really like to be with women; they made me nervous. To be held by a woman made me feel very vulnerable. Instead of feeling good, I would feel terribly sad and afraid in her arms. It was almost like being a little boy again, in need of a mother to hug away my pain. But I was 21 years old; I was too old to need a mother figure. Since these vulnerable feelings were, I thought, a sign of my weak character, I began avoiding any closeness with women.

I did find that I could get close to a woman when I drank. Drinking made relationships with women much easier; I did not feel vulnerable and could use them for sexual gratification. After all, what was a woman for, except to fuck? Many other veterans I talked with shared this experience. In fact, our new motto became, "Find them, feel them, fuck them, forget them." We had to distance ourselves from any meaningful encounter with women because we felt that we could not share with them what we had experienced. How could you tell your girlfriend what it was like for you to shoot another human being? How could you tell her how vulnerable and scared you had felt, never knowing if you would live another hour the whole time you were in Vietnam? How could you tell her what it was like to kick dead NVA soldiers because you were so angry at them for killing your friends? I was afraid to tell any woman what it was like.

How could I tell her about the horror I felt watching a dump truck taking the corpses of seventeen of my friends to be embalmed? How could I tell her what I felt when I watched their blood drip and flow from the tailgate onto the ground? How could I tell her how deeply I hurt, of the agony I was in, and how gnawing my suffering was? How could I tell her that the pain and guilt followed me like a beast tracking its prey? How could I tell her that the pain hounded me at night, during the day, and even while making love? What would she think of me if I told her? I feared that if any woman knew this about me, she would freak out, go into convulsions, vomit, and totally reject me for being such a disgusting human being. What was I to do? I did what seemed best: I drank and drank and drank.

So did most of the other veterans I knew, and since we drank so much and so often—while pretending it was partying—it was hard for others to recognize it as a way of masking our own pain. But God, it was there.

Then one day, it happened. I had an anxiety attack. I was sitting in an accounting class when I suddenly felt as though I were dying. My heart began to pound; I was becoming dizzy and my eyes would not focus. I began gasping for breath and sweating profusely. I began to "freak out." I walked out of class, pretending everything was okay, and went immediately to the student health service. There, however, the doctor who examined me could find nothing wrong with me. To me, this meant that something very serious was wrong with me. I began to relive feelings of being near death, as I had been in Vietnam. This totally confused me.

After suffering about five more panic attacks and running to the doctor, he sent me to a psychiatrist. I did not relish the idea of having mental problems, but I needed to be spared from this new form of suffering. When I saw the psychiatrist, he disinterestedly asked me what my symptoms were. I told him, and he prescribed two kinds of tranquilizers, as well as an antidepressant, and told me to take it easy. That was the last thing I could think of doing, I was so distraught with my life. I tried, though. I tried to enjoy target shooting with my .22 rifle, but I began to physically shake so badly while aiming, I could not shoot. Shooting had been my favorite pastime, and now it was gone. I just could not endure it; it made me too tense.

I tried to go on relaxing picnics with my friends, but I became too uneasy, even with the tranquilizers, to enjoy the picnic. I kept feeling that someone—the enemy—was hidden in the trees, stalking me, just as I had felt in Vietnam. At times, I became so tense and anxious on the picnics that I would have to drink a couple of belts of whiskey just to get through the ordeal.

No fear impacted me as much as the fear I felt during thunder storms. Even though I knew thunder was caused by lightning, the sound of thunder would send me right back to Vietnam. It felt as if I were undergoing a rocket attack. I would have to drop to the ground to protect myself from incoming.

In mythological stories, after the hero has successfully completed his initiatory experience, he returns to the world to share his newly acquired knowledge with the common people, in order to be of service to them. It is in this situation that he is the hero. Yet, for the returning Vietnam combat veteran, there was nothing of value which he could share. There was only pain, frustration, and anguish. And instead of being treated as the hero, he was shunned by his friends for being a veteran; he was shunned by the World War II and Korean veterans for losing the war, by the hippies for being a warmonger, and by himself for allowing himself to be duped by his country. Vietnam was not a war to save the enslaved Vietnamese people; it was not fought to protect America. It was a cruel joke and a cruel turn of fate for the veterans who fought it. It seemed just one more thing that he had screwed up in his life.

Faced with the agony that there was no positive meaning (or Grail) to be found in participation in Vietnam, I was thrown into an existential crisis. My entire world began to collapse. I could only suffer and drink and suffer and drink and suffer and drink. My world continued to fall apart, as I realized and felt to my core that my involvement in the war was for no positive purpose. Over and over in my mind, I lamented how I had trusted the government and how it had betrayed me. Over and over, I asked myself, how could the politicians have done this to us?

Plagued with guilt, I tried to find a place where I could go for forgiveness, to get away from this hell. I felt too guilty to go to God and church, for I had killed, I had injured, and I had tortured my fellow human beings with intense delight. No, I could not go to God or church, for I had too much blood on my hands. I reasoned that no one wanted me now, not even God, for I had killed His children.

I felt completely alone and totally isolated. I lived in an alien world with which I could not communicate. I did not fit in with the other college students, since I was a Vietnam veteran, but I did not fit in with the military, either. I spent a little of my time studying, but most of my time I spent drinking to assuage the pain of life's all-too-obvious meaninglessness. The recurring visions and dreams of the killing I had seen and the killing I had done began to intensify. I just could not stop visualizing—and reliving—the emotional scenes of my comrades' deaths. Even the alcohol was not taking the edge off. I could not sleep, and I could not bear the pain of being awake. I could only suffer and hurt and despair over the meaninglessness and aloneness I endured, but even these were not as painful as the guilt.

One night, I found my way out. I looked at my loaded .38 caliber revolver with perverse pleasure, thinking that I could end it all. My suffering would be over in a flash, and I would have the last laugh. One 158 grain hollow-point in my brain, and it would all be over. But as I looked at my gun, I thought about the Biblical Job's suffering and how it had been for a purpose. Then I thought about my comrades who had been killed and the despair they would feel with no one to tell their story. I started to cry and then decided to stay drunk until I found a psychotherapist who could help me. For the next year and a half, I remained mostly drunk. Incredibly, though, I finished college and went to work for my father. Even more incredible, I got married. However, the marriage made me feel so guilty, because I did not love the woman, that it made me seek out a psychotherapist in earnest. This time I found the one I was looking for, one who not only knew psychotherapy, but who cared about me as a person.

Returning to mythology, we note that, unlike the mythological hero, the Vietnam hero's return was not his physical return from the war. When he returned physically, he had one more obstacle with which to contend in the initiation process. This is a critical point. The vast majority of people, veterans included, think that the physical return from Vietnam was equivalent to the "return" of the hero in mythology. Hence, the majority of veterans to this day are in a sort of limbo. They are in a hellish state, caught between a war that is over and a society that does not care about their story, even though they need society's help in being reintegrated into the social fabric. The real return for most of us, then—if we had one—began only after we dealt with what we had done in Vietnam. That took place in the therapist's office.

THE REAL OR ACTUAL RETURN

Paulson (1994) continues:

After being back in the United States for some time, many Vietnam veterans realized they could no longer escape their emotional agony through denial. They were no longer in Vietnam, nor had they "returned" from the war. They were stuck in a wasteland, in a pseudo-return. As their pain affected more and more areas of their lives negatively, they had to admit to themselves that they were in deep trouble that was only getting worse.

So many Vietnam veterans were caught in a dilemma. How could they be brave, strong men if they could be victims of emotional suffering? To be a victim of pain and suffering and to admit it was the equivalent of being a pussy or a wimp.

For me, this period was, in many ways, more painful and traumatic than actual combat had been. During this time, I had to face the dark side of my personality, the side that had participated in the killing and maiming of other human beings and had witnessed the brutal killing of friend after friend.

Because I had had a very negative experience with a psychiatrist a few years before, I was in no frame of mind to trust another one. I remembered how cold and uncaring that psychiatrist had seemed and how dehumanized and worthless I had felt from the encounter. I had felt like a giant rat that the psychiatrist studied with indifference. My emotional pain mattered not at all to him, for it was only a biochemical imbalance. To protect myself from another psychological disaster, I tested and retested the new therapist to see if he merited my trust. Eventually I began to trust him and to deal with some of the war issues which plagued me.

I had to experience the war all over again; this time, emotionally, I had to face the various combat situations I had been holding in. I had to acknowledge that I had killed and had done it with great satisfaction. One major area of guilt for me was that I had tried to kill 21 NVAs as a personal birthday present to myself for my twenty-first birthday; having killed only 20 1/2, I was extremely upset. Someone else had finished off the twenty-first NVA for me, and I was credited with only one-half a body count for that one.

In therapy, I had to experience the tremendous guilt of what I had done and the even greater guilt about how willing I had been to do it. I realized that had I been a German soldier in World War II, and had I been asked to gas Jewish prisoners, I unquestioningly would have done so. I would have justified it, thinking, *our leaders know what is best.* In therapy, I recognized that I had never given any serious thought to what I was doing in Vietnam. I learned the need for responsibility. Even though I had given no thought to what I did in Vietnam while I was there, I was still responsible. With this realization, I was very remorseful. This position was very sobering, but while I was in the pit of my despair, something wonderful happened. I read about the writer of the religious hymn, *Amazing Grace*. The writer had been a Negro slave trader who participated in many Negro slave killings before he experienced a religious conversion. The words of that hymn struck a deep chord in me, resonating within me to create deep feelings I had not experienced before.

Amazing Grace, how sweet the sound
that saved a wretch like me!
I once was lost, but now am found,
was blind but now I see.

I really identified with those words, not from a religious posture, but from a forgiving stance. I, too, felt like a wicked *wretch,* and I, too, could be forgiven. Realizing that, I began to ease up on myself and stop condemning myself so ruthlessly. I began to accept that I had not done a lot of noble things in Vietnam, but I had done the best I could do at the time and that I would not be a willing stooge again.

In one of my psychotherapy sessions, I described how John 0. and John B. were brutally killed. Because I was so emotionally close to them, their deaths had a major impact on me. While describing to the therapist the death scene, it became as vivid as it had been when it was occurring. I could see the illumination flares burning all around me; I could smell the burned gun powder in the air; and I could feel the ripping pain in my heart when I was told my two best friends had just been killed. I began to cry in the psychologist's office and felt embarrassed, so I held my tears back as best I could. After the session, when I had to drive to a city about 100 miles away for a meeting, I let the tears come. As I drove down the highway, the agony and pain of losing my two friends resurfaced. This time, I did not hold back. I cried and cried, for the entire 100-mile trip. When I got to the city, I was so drained from crying that I immediately checked into a motel and went to bed.

The next morning when I got up, there was an amazing change in my perception. I could smell breakfast cooking, and it made me feel peaceful and good, reminding me of when I was a young boy at home and my mother cooked me breakfast. Also, the people staying at the motel now seemed "friendly," though I did not talk to any of them. Even the birds gathered on the lawn seemed to be friendly. I felt connected to my body and connected to the universe. This was the beginning of my psychotherapeutic "cure" from Vietnam.

As I began to examine my life, I found that I did not trust myself, even though the severe degree of my anxiety was lessening. My core fear was that I felt I needed to protect myself from getting lured into another Vietnam experience. I also felt that I had to protect myself from drinking and from wandering into situations where I might be tempted to lose control. To protect myself, I constructed a very potent component to my personality that I termed the "survivor." I view the "survivor" as a domineering, judgmental part of my personality that kept me in total self-control, always striving to do the right thing. To someone who has never experienced making a mess of his life, control is probably no big deal. For me, however, the only thing I desperately needed was the security that came from total control and domination of my impulses. In order to control all impulses, I kept myself at the mercy of the dominating survivor part of me, which was safer than having any choice, since there was the possibility that I might screw it up. Control was assured by my generating scary physical symptoms, such as heart palpitations, intestinal upsets and acute anxiety when I would venture out of the control of the "survivor." These symptoms effectively kept me from venturing into areas where I might react spontaneously and be at the mercy of my impulses—out of control. I learned to avoid most things fun, because fun meant out of control.

Letting go of this ultra-protective behavior was very difficult for me. It meant I would have to take responsibility for my life, something I just did not have the confidence to do. How could I trust myself to be responsible for my life when I had screwed it up so badly? I had killed human beings and enjoyed the feelings of power I derived from it. I thought women were of value only as sex objects. I had lied and cheated to get my way. How could I trust myself to take conscious control of my life? This was hard, but I slowly, hesitantly tried. It was a very painful process at first, but as I took more and more risks—as well as the responsibility for their successful outcome—I began to develop increasing levels of self confidence. For example, I began to go out with my friends to the bars to dance. I had tremendous impulses to drink, as well as to avoid being responsible for my actions, but I found that I could say no to these impulses and deal with my life. God, it was hard, but I really did it.

One of the greatest insights of my life was realizing that I and I alone had responsibility for my life. While I *knew* I could manage and direct my life, I had trouble *doing* it. Yet, I did do it; I was learning.

I have discussed choice, responsibility and self-control with many other veterans and found we share a common pattern. Prior to examining our lives, we professed to be in charge of our lives, but we clearly were not. We were running our lives on automatic pilot, the automatic pilot of our conditioned responses. This automatic behavior was based on our previous life experiences, in which we drew upon our interactions with our parents, our heroes, and various other significant authority figures in our lives. We thought their influences were our own, but they were the ideals of others with whom we identified. We were living our lives based on the insights of others. For most of us, even when we clearly saw this through psychotherapy, we hesitated to let go and choose for ourselves—authentically. Being aware of and taking full responsibility for one's choices and actions is very, very scary when one is not used to doing it. We were not comfortable taking responsibility for our choices, because if we were wrong, we felt out of control and guilty. We would then lose confidence in our ability to live our lives with self-control.

Several mythological motifs pertaining to the hero's quest actually describe many of the behavior patterns seen in Vietnam veterans. Because these myths are so useful in predicting one's behavior, we can look at them and ask, "Who or what does control our lives?" As previously stated, most veterans live their lives on automatic pilot or in acting out learned behaviors. We feel comfortable with these actions, and when we become consciously aware that much of our lives are lived from these learned behaviors which are now unconscious, we have the option to change what we do not like. When we try to change our ways of living, however, we get extremely tense and anxious because we feel uncomfortable making choices, carrying out those choices, and having to exert our willpower to see them carried out. We are just too used to protecting ourselves from dangers which really do not exist.

I had solved the problem of living my life by turning it over to an idealized, fabricated part of my personality. I built it based on the models provided me by authority figures in my life. This action reduced my tension and anxiety about choice and responsibility, because I did not have to consciously deal with any decisions. My internalized authority figure did it for me. But the price I paid for this selling out of myself was a life filled with unhappiness and anxiety. When I recognized what I had done, I began to drop this mask and revert to my authentic self and live my life as I was. It was at this point that I began my "return" journey.

I began to accept myself as I actually was, not as I should be. I recognized that while I was not the toughest person in the world, neither was I the weakest. I was not the smartest person, but I was not the dumbest, either. I began to accept my emotional sensitivity, ultimately even viewing it as a positive attribute. I gave up the idea that I had to be cold and insensitive in order to be a "man." I also accepted that I had intuition, creativity and imagination, which I had considered to be character flaws at one time. I discovered that I could not categorize myself as a particular kind or type of person. I was what I was. While it was difficult to do, I allowed myself, more and more, to be me—the authentic me.

Often in mythological stories, upon finishing the initiation experience, the initiate had two choices concerning his next step. He could refuse the "return," thereby not sharing his discoveries with others, or he could return, sharing his wisdom and knowledge—his treasure—with others.

A minority of combat veterans have made the return passage and integrated themselves back into society. They have something of positive value to offer others in our society. This is the critical point. From an outer perspective, the combat veteran brought nothing of benefit back to society, but after a successful passage of psychotherapy—or sorting out the experience alone—the veteran did bring back an assortment of treasures to share with society. What were some of these treasures?

First, there was self-acceptance. That is, the veteran learned to fully accept himself as he is. He may not approve of what he did or how he did it during the war, but he has accepted his involvement in the war as well as accepted who and what he is.

For me, this was a very difficult task. I felt that accepting my actions was the same as approving of them. But as I realized that I did what I thought was necessary at the time and did the best job I could, I found that I could accept my involvement. I acted in the context of the situation in which I found myself. Unfortunately, I was wrong, but once I discovered that I was wrong, I changed my perspective. I could not go back in time and change what I had done in Vietnam, but I could leave the past in the past and go on with my life in the here and now.

Jonathan, a former Marine infantryman, had a similar story. For fifteen years after he returned from combat, he grieved and grieved for his friends who had been killed. During those fifteen years, his life was in limbo. Finally, he entered into psychotherapy and ultimately had a revelation leading to the realization that that portion of his life was over. No amount of grieving could ever change the past or bring it back. With this realization, he accepted his present life situation, left the past behind, and went on with his life. Another category of personal treasure gained by a number of veterans is the ability to be self-directing. Unfortunately, many of the Vietnam veterans are so preoccupied with their pain and suffering that they are not in direct control of their lives. They are instead controlled by feelings and impulses. They are literally like leaves in the wind, blown this way and that at the mercy of the environment.

The combat veteran who has successfully completed the initiation and is in the return phase discovers that he needs to control and direct his life consciously, if he is ever to be happy. When he gave up self-direction, he was running from the mythic, cruel horn of the world. This maneuver was self-defeating; it reinforced his lack of self-direction and strengthened his avoidance of the world. As he took control and directed his life in a manner that was in his best interests, he gained self-confidence and self-esteem, which promoted his ability to direct himself.

In my case, self-direction came from a strategy my therapist provided. I call this the "Ed Shubat meditation"—named after the clinical psychotherapist who presented it to me. It goes like this:

Reassure myself that I am a growing, self-actualizing human being. Specifically, I am a human being who is a biological organism, who takes care of himself physically, emotionally, mentally and spiritually. I deal with situations (physical, emotional, mental and spiritual) from where I am, as I am, instead of from a preconceived position.

I learn to deal with myself from a position of what is best for me, taking into account the background of what needs to be dealt with. I evaluate my experiences, being flexible, and act accordingly.

I make attempts at dealing with and processing various experiences. I take risks and carry out the decisions I make.

I judge and evaluate those decisions, choosing which best fits me as a person. I develop self-confidence over time from dealing authentically with these experiences.

I give positive regard to my humanness, as well as to the humanness of others, and recognize that I will make mistakes in my growth process.

For eight years, I meditated on this daily and was rewarded by becoming even more self-directed, even more authentic, and even more autonomous.

Another personal treasure many combat veterans who returned successfully brought back was a firm sense of responsibility. No longer could the veteran allow someone else to think for him. He had to make his own choices about what he liked, what he wanted to do, how he felt about something, and where he stood. Although it is very enticing to take no responsibility for one's life, one's choices, and one's life situation, to a large degree for the veteran, the consequence of letting someone else be responsible for him is the very reason he struggled so after Vietnam.

During the Vietnam war, many of us believed the U.S. government's propaganda—at least, at first—that we were fighting to save the Vietnamese people from communism. Ultimately, though, we found that our government had lied to us. When I first got to Vietnam, I was pro-war. I believed we were there to fight the communists who were threatening the world. But we were not fighting to save a race of people; we were fighting to protect our own government's blunder. When I discovered that we would take a hill at the expense of six or seven Marines, just to do the same thing over again the next month, I realized that something was wrong. I realized that we were not fighting the war to win it.

Also, another area where we Vietnam veterans were duped was in killing the enemy. Ultimately, most of us killed the NVA, or "gooks," as if they mattered no more than rats. We had successfully been able to dehumanize the entire Vietnamese people. Yet, when we expressed our guilt, many people back home tried to justify our actions by having us rationalize that we had to do it—kill them or they would kill us.

Maybe so, but how many of us veterans ever considered what we were doing? We were just following orders. Many times I have thought to myself, this is how the Germans could have gassed millions of Jews, Slavs, and others during World War II. They, too, were following orders. This is a point to really consider. I suggest that the reader consider this question: "How far would I go, following orders?"

Those veterans who have successfully returned have had to deal with their involvement in Vietnam and take responsibility for their actions both then and now. To be aware of how one affects other human beings and not knowingly take advantage of them is a sign of being responsible for one's life. This includes lying to women just to get "a piece of ass," cheating on one's wife, or acting in ways which are self-defeating. This is one of the gems the combat veteran—the combat veteran who has successfully returned—can share.

Please note that taking responsibility for our actions is not the same thing as self blame. Naturally, the veteran tended to blame himself for screwing up his life based on his actions in war. His motto often became, "war did this to me." As he began to acknowledge that he must take responsibility for his problems stemming from war, he found that, because he got himself into this situation, he had the power to get himself out of it. This realization gave him a tremendous sense of self-empowerment.

Another treasure gained by a number of Vietnam veterans was the realization that they were a valuable part of a web or network of interpersonal relationships. A common occurrence with most "returned" veterans was the tremendously valuable feeling of genuine care and concern of others about their well-being. Many veterans recall that when they were in the most unbearable pain and when they had been rejected by almost everyone they knew, there were usually to be found one or two people who stood behind them through thick and thin. Interestingly, it was not until the veterans were on the road to psychological recovery that they were able to acknowledge openly that if it had not been for those persons who really cared, they never would have made it.

In my own case, after I returned from Vietnam, I was rejected by everyone I knew. I was sure my friends could sense the pain I was in, especially since I had to stay drunk. I still remember that one of my close friends confided in me—at the lowest period in my life—while we sat in a bar drinking, that I was really "fucked up" and not fun to be with anymore. I knew this, but I did not know what to do about it or where to go for help to solve my dilemma. Had he stabbed me with a knife, the pain would have been less.

It was not long, though, before my wife became overwhelmed with my problems, as did my friends. No one felt comfortable with me, since they could not relate to me, and ultimately very few people wanted to be with me. However, one person did stand behind me. He was the third psychotherapist I saw. Even today, I shudder to think what would have become of me had Ed Shubat not taken more than just a "professional interest" in me. I am sure I either would have killed myself or had to be institutionalized. That psychotherapist—whom I did not even like at first—was my total, psychological support system. He was behind me when I quit drinking, when I went back to college and needed help from the VA to finance the endeavor, and when I went to graduate school; he was my best man in my second marriage. Finally, even when he was within days of dying from cancer, he still was there for me. Just before he died, I asked him to find me when I die, if there is an afterlife. He assured me that he would. To be truly appreciated for "me," in spite of my life's background, was a real treasure.

Self-reliance was reported by a number of veterans to be a tremendously valuable gained asset. Self-reliance came to these men because they had to face combat "alone"; they had to face death "alone"; they had to return to America and put their lives back in order "alone." Because they were used to being alone, they did not require the constant support and reassurance that so many of their noncombatant peers needed when making life transitions or adjusting to situations beyond their control. For example, these veterans did not get in a major turmoil about what the recession would do to them. Most reasoned that if they survived Vietnam, they could survive any economic downturn; those who worked in the corporate world believed they could survive the corporate wheeling and dealing. Some reported that they did not become emotionally immobilized when their wives left them. If they could survive Vietnam, they could survive a divorce. There just was not anything life could deal to this person that could be worse than what he experienced in Vietnam. To illustrate this, my story continues.

THE PROOF OF THE PUDDING IS IN THE EATING OF IT

Paulson continues his story, now as a microbiologist in civilian life:

Late in the summer of 1991, my professional world was collapsing. I had worked for the same medical product corporation for ten years. Starting as a privately owned company with five employees, it was now owned by a large blue chip corporation and had a staff of more than seventy. I began my career as a bench microbiologist, worked my way through the laboratory, and finally started and headed the Food, Drug, and Cosmetic Evaluations Department. But my spirit was broken. I had succumbed to the ambivalent attitude prevalent in the corporation. No matter how hard I worked, no matter how many new innovations I brought to fruition, neither my people nor I benefited. The fruits of our labor went to the CEO's inner circle. I quit trying to make things change and just waited for whatever would happen to happen.

The Tuesday following Labor Day, I was asked to come into the CEO's office. When he asked me to sit down, I knew it was the end. As he read me a prepared document, my heart dropped through the floor.

Daryl, I regretfully inform you that your services will no longer be needed as of September 13, 1991. This termination is not a reflection of your work, but of economic necessity.

Even though I had known this was coming, I was floored, angry, and disappointed. I put myself down for working in the business world, and then I began to question my value as a person. What was wrong with me? I wanted to work, I wanted to contribute, but I wanted to be treated fairly—not as a pawn. Was this asking too much? Did I not count? Did my people not count? I was dismissed from the office as quickly as I had been summoned. Embarrassed about being fired, I hurriedly left the facility and drove around the city to regain my composure.

New fears began to surface—what would I do? There were no other laboratory complexes in Bozeman, Montana. How would I make the payments on the house, the car, and the charge cards? What would I tell my wife and children?

Then, as I continued to drive, a very peaceful feeling came over me. I was relieved that my horrible experience with corporate America was over. I was free. I would never have to work for a corporation again. I decided to change careers. During the past ten years, I had positioned myself for a second career by completing a doctoral program in psychology. Because I did not want to go back to corporate life, I decided to become a clinical psychologist, a transition that I felt would be relatively easy.

During my training in psychology, I had the good fortune of being exposed to many useful personality models, particularly psychosynthesis. Psychosynthesis, thought of as the art of integrated living, was first described by Roberto Assagioli, an Italian psychiatrist. His work focuses on the integration of the mind, body, emotions, and spiritual components of human beings. In this training, I learned not just to identify with my personal or ego self but also to connect with my total self, which Assagioli labeled the "transpersonal self." For me, the connection with my total self took the image of what I call "Big D," or Big Daryl. Big D accepted me, supported me, and understood me, even when I did not. Big D, while being inclusive of me and accepting of all life, was also very much me—a much larger me than my conscious self.

After I decided to go into psychology, I became more settled and comfortable. Toward the end of the week, I decided to discuss my situation with Big D. I rode on mountain trails muddy from the melting snow, got off my motorcycle, sat under a tree, and just let myself be. After some time, I asked Big D for guidance. Because I wrote these internal dialogues in a notebook, I will share them with you.

Daryl:
What advice can you give me about beginning the psychology practice?

Big D:
First, relax. Everything is okay. This [losing your job] is not the end of the world. You are finding your way in the world. You did not fit at [the past job]. You need to do your own thing, that is, to develop your own laboratory service company. Psychology is a way, but not yours...your way is that of building a laboratory, you know it. Go slow; think of what is right for you, not how to avoid your anxiety of starting a lab...Do not try to make your company based on a book or an authority figure but centered in you. You have the training, you have paid the dues, now just do it. You will succeed.

I was stunned by Big D's advice. What did I know about the business world? I hated it. I thought Big D had made a mistake, but I soon realized the significance of the message. I could start my own business, and I would. I had a mission, and it was a mission that mattered. That day, BioScience Laboratories, Inc., was conceived. To cite an old aphorism, the proof of the pudding is in the eating of it.

I had but $3,297 to my name, no financial backers, no real entrepreneurial business experience, and no co-workers to support me—I had only myself. But when I thought about it, that was a lot. I had my education, an undergraduate degree in business, and graduate degrees in microbiology, statistics, and psychology. I had the ability to keep going in spite of fear, which I had learned while serving in Vietnam with the U.S. Marine Corps. I had ten years of corporate experience, including sales. I had drive and energy, the will to succeed, and creativity as well as common sense.

Fifteen years later, BioScience Laboratories, Inc., has three laboratories and nearly 50 employees. I'd like to share some of the keys to my successful transition, many of which are the "treasures" earned through my initiation rite.

GUIDANCE FROM MY TOTAL SELF

I feel it is very important to have an honest, deep relationship with oneself. This, of course, entails getting to know who you are, what you like, what you want, what you need, and how you feel about yourself and others in your life. It is replacing the "shoulds" in one's life with the real needs and wants.

My search for myself began after my combat experience in Vietnam. Having killed human beings, lost most of my ethical values, and then returned home psychospiritually bankrupt, my alcohol abuse and despair forced me to deal with the issues in my life, a process that culminated in the ability to tap into the resources of Big D for guidance. I found tremendous strength, wisdom, compassion, intuition, and insight upon which I can draw from this part of my being.

FRIENDS

After I lost my job, not one of the other 72 employees maintained any contact with me. My support came from friends outside the corporation. One, the owner of a local medical laboratory, helped me find a basement space at a local medical clinic to rent very cheaply. He helped me convince the building manager to put cabinets, shelves, and lighting into this laboratory space and amortize the costs over two years. Because it was impossible for me to purchase supplies on an open account (large supply houses want trade references, and I had none), my friend allowed me to order supplies via his laboratory account.

Several friends at the local state university arranged for me to use laboratory equipment inexpensively. These friends and their support were critical in the successful launch of BioScience Laboratories.

MENTORS

I place great value on a business mentor, a father figure, if you will. Although I did not have one while building BioScience, I had had one during the early period of my corporate experience. While earning my advanced degrees, I had learned how to survive in the academic setting, but in the "real world" of business, I was ineffective. For example, when I first started with the corporation, I tried to complicate microbiology and statistics to show my "brilliance" instead of being of service to clients. I was unable to communicate with clients at a useful level. This, of course, made my value to the corporation very shaky from the outset. Fortunately, Rod, a wise, successful entrepreneur and, at that time, the executive vice-president of the corporation, took me under his wing. Fortunately, I listened.

Rod taught me, by example, how to truly serve customers by meeting their needs. He taught me how to talk with people, a skill he further reinforced by persuading me to join Toastmasters International. He also showed me the importance of psychology, especially to understand myself.

Finally, Rod showed me how to support and nurture myself, something every leader needs to do, for when you lead, the strokes cease to come to you from others. You must give them to yourself. In short, Rod showed me how to be a servant-leader. I am deeply indebted for his training, even though I have not perfected it.

PAST EXPERIENCES

For me, the Vietnam experience, which held mostly negative memories, was very important in the success of my business. I enlisted in the Marine Corps upon graduation from high school in 1969 and served with the 1st Marine Corps Division north of Da Nang. During this period, there was little popular American citizen support for the war. Hence, like so many others who served there, I felt totally alone and isolated. I had to face my precombat anxiety alone. I had to deal with my fear and anguish of being killed—alone. Finally, I had to deal with my life upon coming back to the United States—alone. No one was there to cheer me or support me when I returned home.

Much of the creation process of my new venture had to be done alone. I had to ferret out customers, design the working structure of BioScience, face an empty bank account—alone. Worse, I had to live with my terrors of going under and failing in this pursuit—alone.

Fortunately, I knew how to suffer and keep going in spite of my "gut-wrenching" fears and others' dire predictions. In Vietnam, many times I just wanted to lie down in the mud and die, but the part of me that I call the survivor would take charge and scream internal commands to me to keep going. I kept going in Vietnam, and I would keep on going in my business. I would endure and succeed.

PERSISTENCE

I knew at the beginning that the initiatory passage from corporate employee to entrepreneur building an organization from scratch would be fraught with trials and tests. I had the endurance to make the passage, and I had Big D for continuous guidance. I found it a lot easier to keep going when I *knew* there was purpose and meaning to the struggle.

I slowly secured jobs, and I made enough money to keep the doors open. During this time, I routinely stayed up until 3 or 4 A.M. and went back to work at 8 A.M. But business was starting to develop.

Three months into the business, I hired my first employee, a major step. At first, employees were nervous about working for a company that was, for the most part, just an idea. However, as they realized that I was committed to the endeavor and that progress was being made, they too became committed to this endeavor. This experience has been repeated for each of our employees as we have grown.

MISCELLANEOUS SOURCES OF SUPPORT

Several books provided me with additional courage and direction. One was Og Mandino's (1974) *The Greatest Salesman in the World*. Hafid, the main character, was a poor camel boy who dreamed of becoming a success-ful salesman of carpets and robes. His trials to sell just one robe encouraged me to keep going. He struggled, he was scared, but he kept on going; and so did I.

Another book that spoke to my heart and soul was Napoleon Hill's (1937) *Think and Grow Rich*. His anecdotes of endurance, persistence, patience, and learning from experiences helped me.

For financial advice, I did not rely on the knowledge I received in business school. BioScience Laboratories was in no way financially secure enough to employ financial ratio analysts. What really paid off for me was studying the book *The Richest Man in Babylon* by George S. Clason (1955). I followed a very simple strategy that worked—to save 10 percent of everything my busi-ness earned. From this simple procedure, I was able, in the space of one year, to purchase a computer system, two sterilizers, and a complete assortment of laboratory equipment. These purchases had a snowball effect. Because I had more equipment, I was able to do more kinds of work, which allowed me to generate increasing levels of business.

At the outset, I made the decision to develop a people-centered business and not allow the terrible injustices and deceptions that had been forced on me to be forced on my employees. I chose to provide a place of nourish-ment for employees, where they could grow professionally. I designed a workplace where employees can use their own unique creative abilities to perform the required work.

This endeavor has been a tremendous learning experience. It has been a challenge as well as an original creation—a creation where people do mat-ter, where the quality of work matters, and where we can contribute to soci-ety as well as to each other.

It has now been more than 15 years since I began BioScience Laborato-ries, Inc. I have made many mistakes on the path. Over the years, I have felt cheated at times for excess anxiety and a constant feeling of doom—all caused by Vietnam, I lament. Yet, without the military experience and with-out participating in Vietnam and learning to suffer and suffer but still con-tinue, I could never have done it. Yes, the war was a huge cost to me, but I also acquired huge benefits.

CHOOSING A PERSONAL PATH

Paulson's story continues.

One of the most difficult tasks for a returned combat veteran is to live an authentic life. This requires courage. Courage is the ability to attend to some task in spite of gut-wrenching fear. But that ability depends, to a large degree, on where one is in one's life. Thirty years ago, I thought courage was going to fight in the Vietnam War instead of going to Canada to dodge the draft. As a

Marine Corps enlistee, I was facing the reality of going to war and the possibility that I would not come back alive.

When I first got to Vietnam, for me, courage meant being able to kill—to shoot—another human being, a "gook"; as we called them (the North Vietnamese Army and the Viet Cong). But I was not in Vietnam long before I viewed courage as the ability to keep on fighting in spite of the frank absurdity of the war. For example, I clearly remember my anguish over taking one hill, losing six or seven men, and after a month or so, abandoning it, only to retake the same hill a month later.

After returning home from the war, unable to "fit in" with my noncombatant friends, I coped with the alienation the only way I knew how, by drinking and drinking and drinking. I had become guilt-ridden and defensive concerning my involvement in the war, particularly because I could not see any clear purpose in it. There was no courage here—only utter despair. Yet, it was not long before courage meant entering counseling. I could no longer deal with my life. The inner resources I needed to confront, in therapy, those things I had done so willingly in Vietnam were many times greater than those I actually needed to fight in Vietnam.

And, to this day, I think one of the greatest tests of courage for me (as well as the greatest joy) was to allow myself to discover who I really was at my core. I find that this is true, too, for those I counsel, if they stay in the process long enough.

One of the first acts of courage in counseling is to acknowledge that one is essentially "alone" with one's subjective experience. No one else sees things exactly like you, no one feels exactly like you, and no one can know you exactly the way you do. But, out of this aloneness, a client finds his or her real Self, a discovery that eventually provides a tremendous amount of satisfaction. Discovering one's real Self takes time; it is not usually an instant discovery.

To proceed in therapy, in spite of one's doubts and fears about what one will discover within, requires not only a high level of courage but a persistent level of courage. This is often a time when an individual realizes he or she cannot go back to the "old" ways of living but does not feel comfortable with the "new" ways. This is the time to reach deep within for the will to go on, despite the feeling of existing "in limbo."

Often, as individuals in counseling discover and begin to accept who they are authentically and to truly become that person, they find that they do not "fit in" with their peers any more. The things they used to do, the places they went, as well as the people with whom they liked sharing these things are no longer enjoyable. This is a lonely time, requiring courage "to begin anew" and to live in accord with a new-found inner truth.

I am reminded, at these times, of Dietrich Bonhoeffer, a German Lutheran theologian who was safely outside of Germany and Hitler's Nazi reign of terror in the late 1930s. He returned to Germany to live in accord with his inner truth. He resisted the oppression and the systematic extermination of the Jews, Slavs, homosexuals, gypsies, Communists, petty criminals, the mentally handicapped, and other "inferior" people. He could not ignore this inhumane action. He had to be true to himself, which meant he had to stand up for what he believed.

Consequently, he was executed in 1945, which was, for him, "the Cost of Discipleship." He understood courage to be living authentically in *this* life, by serving humanity openly, justly, and with dignity, not awaiting his reward in the next life.

At times when danger threatens to paralyze us, suddenly, from the mysterious depths of our being surges an unsuspected strength "enabling us to place a firm foot on the edge of the precipice," and confront an aggressor calmly and resolutely, standing by our convictions at all costs. Courage to be oneself comes at a price. It is not free from negative repercussions. Those who walk away from a toxic job, leave a bad marriage, or stand up for what they believe often pay with pain, loss of profession or profit, and, sometimes, even the loss of their lives. Courage to be oneself, then, is not only the discovery of who one *is* authentically, but also demands that one *live* authentically. That is, one makes one's *own* choices, listens to one's *own* voice for guidance, and acts based upon one's *own* tastes and preferences while taking into account the impact of one's actions upon others regarding what one perceives as just and fair. Courage to be oneself requires a committed, conscious relationship with oneself—deepening to the very source of one's Being. It requires seeking one's deepest inner truth, no matter where that journey may lead. And it will, no doubt, wind through a variety of experiences:

- the depths of traumatic pain;
- the heights of spiritual insight;
- unresolved childhood issues;
- denial around addictions and compulsions;
- the dynamics of the family system;
- the struggle with life values and choices;
- decisive social and political action; and
- the healing of relationships with self, others, and the world.

Finding the courage to be oneself enables one to forgive others for failing to understand and even respect human beings. It also allows one to forgive all humanity for its senseless cruelties imposed upon those who "do not fit in." The courage to be oneself fosters the self-empowerment necessary to grant that forgiveness.

Finally, courage to be oneself also, at times, requires self-sacrifice. Consider the case of Gary and Mary Jane Chauncey and their 11-year-old daughter Andrea, a victim of cerebral palsy. The Chauncey family were passengers on an Amtrak train that crashed into a river while crossing a bridge hit and weakened by a river barge. As the railroad passenger car was sinking, the parents managed to push Andrea out through a broken window to rescuers, but at the expense of their lives. Consider the case of Dave Sanders, a 47-year-old teacher and coach at Columbine High School in Littleton, Colorado. He assisted at least 24 high school students to safety, even though he had been fatally wounded by two bullets to his chest, unleashed by two deranged students in their quest to kill. He could have run away and saved himself for he was in the teachers' lounge, far from the shootings. But he did not.

In the future, I think, we must find the courage to come together as humans, seeking mutual understanding and acceptance. Such courage requires that each of us step out of the safety of our familiar dogmas, policies, and group biases, and decide authentically what is true, what is right, and what is just. Most of us have searched for the courage "to do the right thing," in temples, in churches, in science, in medicine, on earth, in heaven, and even in hell. But, in the end, sometimes in despair, we come back to ourselves—where the whole search began—and find that all each of us has been seeking without abides within our very selves. It is our own authentic Self—our Source of Being—and it was there all the time. It just takes courage to recognize it.

THE HARD ISSUES OF LIFE

Many war veterans on an authentic path continue to find life hard, that is, hard to live with self-awareness according to their own inner dictates. Some of the most difficult problems combatants encounter, as do all other humans, are the unfairness of life, the finality of death, the despair of divorce, the pain of betrayal, the grief of losing an intimate other, the anguish in trying to establish a quality life after combat, and the terror of facing a terminal disease. Many who have tried to live authentically drift back into a worldview of meaninglessness—back to where they began. These times are hard for anyone, but for the combatant finding him or herself in a "spiritual desert," not knowing where to go for nourishment, it is gut-wrenching. And, even those who find meaning through fellowship and religion run a risk of splitting their lives into two compartments, spiritual and mundane, thereby constructing their lives in ways that are more difficult to live authentically (Assagioli, 1965; Cortright, 1997). Answers to these problems are not usually easy or simple, particularly because one must try out new behaviors and be successful with them before real self-change and psychological growth can manifest themselves (Bandura, 1997).

Yet as hard as change is, facing life directly, as it is phenomenologically experienced for the client, takes not only much courage but persistent courage. Much of our work has been with combat veterans who find it particularly hard to find positive meaning in their lives. They find the normal personal and cultural-psychological defense mechanisms inadequate to contain their lack of meaning. This is generally not the worldview of the general public, who are secure in the roles, rules, and taboos of the culture. That is, until they have a close brush with death, confront a serious illness, or lose life's meaning. Then their cultural and personal defenses no longer tend to work for them either.

Counseling and psychotherapy can be immensely helpful in assisting individuals during these times, given they have not lost meaning. If meaning, from the client's perspective, is missing, generally little progress will result in counseling. Victor Frankl (1956), a Jewish psychiatrist, discovered the importance of meaning to individuals while he was interred at two Nazi concentration camps during the Second World War. Frankl noticed repeatedly that when individuals lost their life's meaning, they would usually die.

EXISTENTIAL SPIRITUALITY

Traditional religious practices are the source of meaning to literally billions of human beings around the world. Their religion provides meaning, direction, and purpose in life. However, one does not usually confront "Being" via an authentic personal confrontation unless one's life is in crisis.

In these cases, the counselor or therapist has an opportunity to counsel psychologically, as well as spiritually guide a person into a deep encounter with "Being," or more generally, "what is." Here, encounter with "Being" is a quest for self-understanding that, according to Heidegger (1962), allows one to become what one already is, a being who understands "Being" directly. (Heidegger's understanding of his own "Being" kept him from renouncing his Nazi party membership; hence, one's "search" does not produce unequivocally benevolent results.)

Several common themes are encountered in one's search for "Being." First, the encounter is authentic and personal. The rituals and shared beliefs that describe "what is" no longer work to explain "what is." Instead, one needs to encounter "what is" directly. And, in order to do this, one must allow whatever material is present in the unconscious to emerge to consciousness. This is an exceptionally painful process for a client.

Additionally, most persons in industrialized cultures have been overacculturated. They literally have been programmed how to act the "right way," go to the "right places," and be with the "right people." Although there is much value in enculturation—in fact, it is necessary—it is often overly restrictive for a person. To counteract this, combatants are urged to listen to their own voices, not their superegos—society, parents, or other authority figures—in order to make their own decisions, to act in their own ways, to be responsible for their own actions, and to feel ever more in touch with their "Being."

Tillich stated that authentic spirituality is one's existential passion for encountering the Infinite—one's ultimate concern. Existential encounters with "Being" are not centered outside oneself but within one's "Being." And these have little to do with academic or religious knowledge, but rather, occur through a direct phenomenological interaction with "Being." Authentic encounters with one's self require a committed, conscious relationship with oneself, with the very source of one's "Being" (Paulson, 1993, 1999a).

In seeking a direct encounter with "what is," it is a good idea to begin the search where one is in one's life, instead of where one should be (Assagioli, 1965). And where one is in one's life depends upon one's inner values, beliefs, experiences, goals, and aspirations, as well as values shared within one's culture, concerning worldviews, meaning, and direction (Daniels & Horowitz, 1976). In searching for one's own truth, we advise one to pay due respect to the "great ones," Christ, Mother Mary, the Buddha, Krishna, and the Prophet Mohammed, but acknowledge that one must find out for oneself "what is" (Chaudhuri, 1965). In this process, one reportedly experiences, often for the first time, what it feels like to be oneself authentically— down even to what one's arms, legs, and teeth feel like from within (Washburn, 1995). Additionally, what one authentically feels and values about one's life becomes important in discovering positive meaning. And it is important to note that one should seek to discover how one feels about this or that, not how one should feel (Paulson, 1993).

As the encounter with "Being" progresses, one is metaphorically able to "rest"—to let go into one's very being—and to just "be" (Washburn, 1995). When issues surface to consciousness, a person is free to attend them or not, depending upon what one chooses to do. And, over time, it appears that, as suppressed and repressed emotional issues are dealt with psychologically, genuine insights from one's deeper source of "Being" surface to consciousness, making the entire introspective process deeply valuable and worthwhile (Boorstein, 1997; Paulson, 1999b; Washburn, 1994, 1995).

Let us now explore what the actual contact with "Being" may be like for those who experience it. Direct confrontation with one's ultimate concerns and ultimate meaning in life generates huge amounts of existential anxiety, for one does not know for certain "what is," if one will find any positive meaning at all, or if one will be sent into a spiraling, downward trajectory to meaninglessness and utter despair (Fingarette, 1963; Grof, 1975, 1985, 1988, 1998; Washburn, 1995). Metaphorically, many seekers report feeling as though they were alone in a snow blizzard or a thick dark fog, unable to see anything clearly, and unable to gain any sense of bearing (Metzner, 1988). This anxiety is not mere tension; it is total gut-wrenching and all-consuming terror and confusion (Washburn, 1995). There appears to be nowhere to go for escape, for both cultural and personal defenses are broken. There is no ready-made belief system to subscribe to now, only confrontation of the Ground, which appears to threaten absolute nonbeing (Washburn, 1995).

This period of existential anxiety has also been called the "Dark Night of the Soul" and the "Night Sea Journey," for one is not only alone, but all is unknown (Campbell, 1971). Predominant feelings reported are that one is on some dark planet somewhere in a dark corner of the universe, where one is utterly alone, where there is no one to know how one feels or that one even existed (Angyal, 1965). One's meaning, direction, and purpose evaporate. Nothing makes sense. All appears to be lost. Yet one must continue the journey (Campbell, 1968).

Raw courage is needed to continue, because this is a period of no exit; one knows one cannot go back to former ways of being, but feels one cannot go forward either (Campbell, 1968; Grof, 1985). And it is at this point where traditional existential encounters stop. That is, one must face death and destruction alone, and one is alone in a meaningless world, except for the meaning one gives it. Yet in this aloneness, one is free to choose the way one "is."

We do not think that most existentialists went far enough in exploring this encounter with "Being." A surprising number of individuals we have studied find that, within this apparent chaos and aloneness, a deeper, more solidly grounded self emerges. This Self knows things "for sure." Individuals experiencing this "self" perceive their day-to-day egoic self as being a part of this larger self (Paulson, 1993; Whitmore, 1991). This Self, while not generally interpreted as the "Ground of Being" in any absolute sense, is perceived to be a direct link to, as well as a part of it. In fact, many individuals no longer feel a need to contact the Absolute Ground of Being, once they discover this aspect of themselves. They feel connected "enough" with "what is" through this self-sense to provide not only relief from groundlessness, but also an existential *knowing* of "what is." That knowing is sufficient not only to bring meaning into their lives, but literally to infuse their lives with it.

When one has contacted the deeper self, one finds that there are no set spiritual goals to be pursued, directions to follow, or techniques to use (Paulson, 1993; Whitmore, 1991). There is, however, a growing ability to experience this self directly as one's own Being (Brown, 1993). This self is not a symbol of oneself, but a constantly emerging "Being-ness" of oneself (Paulson, 1993). This deeper self is not perceived by the person as emotionally needy, controlling, directing, judgmental, or self-righteous. In fact, an overwhelming majority of subjects we have studied report that this self-sense seems not to care if one even listens to its voice. But those who do hear its soft, friendly, accepting voice find it loud and clear in revealing truth.

This self obeys no tradition, set of rules, roles, or taboos, nor does it make them for the personality. It is creative, authentic, and wise, knowing what troubles the individual, even before he or she asks (Assagioli, 1965). To many, this sense of Self appears as an "other," while at the same time, as oneself (Vaughan, 2000). At no time has it been explained as an "it"; but rather, as what Martin Buber termed "thou" (Buber, 1958; Firman, 1996). Contact with this Self is truly a spiritual event in that, through this connection, one intuits egoically that *everything* is as it should be (Paulson, 1995).

Yet there are individuals who do not discover a deeper self. Our research has revealed that they feel themselves touching their *Source of Being,* which they generally state is a "life-giving mystery, a rejuvenation, or energy infuser" beyond any self-sense, yet not separate from it (Paulson, 1993). By merely becoming aware of that mystery directly, they feel grounded and solid within their lives. It is like being fed or supplied nourishment from the "river or spring of life."

Revenge

The moon is low and casts its shadows long,
and in this gloom what God can say I'm wrong?
My truth is that I am my father's son
and seek revenge and honor with his gun.
The man I'll kill would kill me if he could—
His father shot my father in this wood.
The unmarked grave is covered up with snow,
and vengeance is the only law I know.
The moon is low, and soon the sun will rise
but not until the killer's first-born dies.
Thus as a son I'll show what I am worth,
and so we spend our meager time on earth.

—Tom Greening

10

Alternative Approaches to Treating PTSD

Throughout this book, we have emphasized the spiritual aspects of PTSD, which is as much of a "soul disorder" as a "stress disorder." Krippner has personally studied many indigenous practitioners, shamans, and folk healers who deal with a condition they refer to as "soul loss"; we have not equated this problem with PTSD but there seems to be an overlap. Traditional Chinese medicine treated a loss or imbalance of "chi" energy through acupuncture, diet, massage, and herbs, including the burning of "moxa" on acupuncture points or the body's "energy centers." A number of psychotherapists, counselors, and body workers have utilized these energy centers in a variety of practices collectively known as energy psychology or "EP" (Feinstein & Krippner, 2006, pp. 299–307).

EP can be described as an approach to treatment, therapy, and self-management that stimulates these hypothetical energy centers for the purpose of changing specific attitudes and behaviors. Many EP practitioners claim to have treated PTSD successfully. These practices typically combine mental imagery and/or verbal affirmations with the stimulation of acupuncture points to effect attitudinal and behavioral changes. Feinstein, Craig, and Eden (2005) tell the story of Rich, a hospitalized Vietnam War veteran disabled by insomnia, haunting war memories, and fear of heights, the latter due to some parachute jumps made during combat operations. During treatment, he was asked to imagine a situation involving heights; his fear level increased immediately. While holding the image of these stressful events,

Rich was asked to stimulate a number of points on his skin by tapping them with his fingertips. Within 15 minutes, Rich reported no fear reaction; the therapist tested this report by having Rich walk onto the fire escape on the third floor with no resulting anxiety.

The therapist then asked Rich to retrieve several of his most intensive combat memories, using the same tapping procedure. These were "neutralized" within an hour; Rich still recalled the experiences but they had lost their emotional charge. The therapist taught Rich several tapping procedures as homework assignments. Within a short period of time, his insomnia had cleared, war memories stopped intruding into his awareness, he discontinued his medication, and he had checked himself out of the hospital. A two-month follow-up indicated that Rich was still free of the height phobia, the insomnia, and the intrusion of war memories. Several war veterans in the same hospital were treated with similar methods, reportedly achieving similar results. It is clear that the claims of EP need to be investigated by outside observers; if this modality proves to be an "empirically validated approach" (Roberts & Yeager, 2004), its short-term treatment time could rehabilitate many combat victims in a cost-effective manner.

From a neuroscience perspective, PTSD is the result of hyperarousal, which destabilizes the amygdala and autonomic nervous system, resulting in exaggerated anxiety, inhibitions, and agitation. Flashbacks are particularly problematic because there is no sense of distance between the traumatic event in time or place. The corticohippocampal networks have not been able to contextualize the somatic, sensory, and emotional memories with the networks of the autobiographical memory (Cozolino, 2002). Additionally, during flashbacks, the amygdala's fear networks are activated. The amygdala's dense connectivity with the visual system of the brain likely accounts for the visual hallucinations experienced during flashbacks. Finally, a decrease in regional cerebral blood flow in the left inferior frontal and middle temporal cortex, "Broca's area," during speechless terror is often reported. PTSD victims may have this neurobiological component at its core.

EP is often combined with other forms of therapy such as traumatic incident reduction (TIR), a short-term treatment procedure for PTSD and related disorders (Volkman, 2004). TIR operates on the principle that a permanent resolution of a case requires the recovery of repressed memories rather than mere catharsis or coping. It purports to take a "person-centered" perspective, finding out what made the triggering (or "root") incident traumatic from the client's viewpoint (Gerbode, 2004, p. 2). The client is encouraged to express and experience the traumatic incident fully, enabling the incident to be "discharged" at which point it becomes a past, rather than an ongoing, incident. The client tells and retells the TIR practitioner everything he or she remembers about the root incident, each time "peeling off layers of thoughts, considerations, emotions, decision, and opinions" (p. 13). The incident or incidents undergo "reframing" and "cognitive restructuring" often accompanied by "imaginal flooding," sometimes facilitated by hypnosis, Gestalt work, and "desensitization."

TIR therapists claim to obtain lasting results in as little as two or three hours; in one research study yielding favorable results, the average length of time per session was 71 minutes (Carbonell, 2004). In this study, TIR was compared with two varieties of EP treatments (i.e., thought field therapy, eye movement desensitization and reprocessing), both of which require very little verbalization and which claim to "interrupt" the post-traumatic reaction" on a physiological level. TIR, in contrast, claims not to "interrupt" the reaction but to "extinguish" it (p. 118). Despite the differences among therapists and treatment modalities, "all of the clients felt subjectively better after treatment" (p. 117). No long-term follow-up data were provided, making this study far from definitive. However, one of the treatment modalities, thought field therapy, was credited by the chief medical officer of Kosovo for rehabilitating 105 victims of ethnic violence (Feinstein, Craig, & Eden, 2005, pp. 14–15).

Eye movement desensitization and reprocessing (EDMR) requests that a client focus on several aspects of a distressing experience. At the same time, the client's attention is grounded on some form of bilateral stimulation such as eye movements, tapping, or sound stimulation (Shapiro, 1993). This combination of dual focus and bilateral stimulation is felt to generate a reduction in the emotional charge associated with the distressing experience, desensitizing the client. As this desensitization occurs, the client is guided through a process of cognitive restructuring in which the personal meanings associated with the disturbing experience are transformed (e.g., "I am in danger" becomes "I am safe now"; Dorsey, 2005).

Proponents of EMDR point to compelling research data supporting the long-term effectiveness of the technique and claim that it has demonstrated differences between pretreatment and posttreatment measures of brain physiology (Lansing et al., 2005). Proponents claim that so-called "talk therapies" attempt to train the left frontal cortex (the verbal/conscious part of the brain) to override an already aroused right limbic system (i.e., the emotional/arousal part of the brain), the area directly accessed by EMDR (Dorsey, 2005). Earle-Warfel (2005) has proposed a model of PTSD based on chaos theory; for her, EMDR and EP may be effective because (according to chaos theory) only slight perturbations of a few crucial neurons may be needed to alter the stability of whole neuronal systems.

Thought field therapy (TFT) is another form of EP that claims to be based on the network of "meridians" that connect the acupuncture points described in traditional Chinese medicine. TFT claims that in the case of traumatic stress a perturbation creates a break or disruption in the circuitry of the chi circulating in the body's meridian network. In other words, negative emotional conditions such as fear or anxiety produce disruptions in the body's "energy system," which, in turn, give rise to higher levels of stress. A study of ten survivors of motor vehicle accidents with severe PTSD symptoms yielded reports of improvement after only two TFT sessions for half the group. Furthermore, brain-wave assessments before and after TFT treatments indicated that the clients who reported the most improvement manifested decreased right frontal cortex arousal, as well as other positive changes (Swingle et al., 2004).

EP AND PERSONAL MYTHS

EP, if it is effective, does not rely on the stock concepts of psychotherapy, such as insight, behavioral rehearsal, or attitudinal shifts. The fact that EP is fairly brief indicates that the client's relationship with the therapist is not the predominant factor in reported benefits. Instead, its benefits often are attributed to nonspecific factors such as expectancy, suggestion, and enthusiasm. The significant shifts in psychological test results usually are chalked up to the fact that a retest generally yields more favorable results due to the tendency of scores on the second test to fall back toward the average scores (the "regression to the mean" effect). The psychophysiological changes are more difficult to explain in conventional terms, and future research might extend what has already been initiated. The case could be made that these changes are the result of the stimulation of the skin's energy points, and the subsequent signals that are sent to the brain.

Because personal myths, both helpful and harmful, are associated with bodily function and the brain's chemistry, Feinstein and Krippner (2006) have presented a five-stage program for combining EP and self-managed mythic change for PTSD and other disorders.

1. In the first stage, the survivor of a trauma begins to realize the limitations of the prevailing myths that are the most resistant to change because they have become rooted in traumatic experiences. For example, the personal myth, "I will never be able to establish a close relationship with anyone" is clearly dysfunctional and irrational. It is recommended that the person who holds this myth provide a score of from 1 to 10 while he or she engages in self-talk on the topic, replacing the old myth with a challenging myth such as "If I change my attitudes and behavior, it is possible for me to have a close relationship with someone." Technically, this approach is known as the Subjective Units of Distress Scale and has been used in numerous stress-reduction studies. In this case, however, the combat veteran or civilian survivor breathes deeply several times, inhaling energy and exhaling stress. After ten cycles, another number is brought to mind; several cycles might be required to reduce the number from 10 to 6, from 9 to 2, or some other number.

2. In this stage, the old myth and the challenging myth are compared. Personal experiences supporting the belief that close relationships are impossible are contrasted with evidence to the contrary. Specific examples of closeness can be

brought to mind, as well as specific plans to resurrect these past experiences for future action. Again, deep breathing is an effective relaxation technique, although various EP manuals provide directions for "tapping" specific acupuncture points to facilitate the process. However, practitioners of "mindfulness meditation" can work toward the same goal by being "mindful" of intrusive dysfunctional myths and releasing them as part of their meditative process.

3. The third stage involves an imaginary dialectical struggle between the old myth and the challenging myth. This encounter can be "acted out" with a voice given each statement, or the dialogue can be written or imagined. This time, however, deep breathing would be counterproductive because one wants to be alert and energetic, not calm and relaxed, while the drama is played out. One should pay close attention to the body's reactions as each myth has its say; it is likely that the challenging myth will provide more feelings of energy than the old, torpid, negative statement.

4. The fourth stage closely examines the old myth to see if there is any portion of it that is worth saving. Perhaps there are people with whom closeness is not a wise option. Perhaps one should move slowly when embarking on a new relationship. Challenging myths, or countermyths, often are overly ambitious and unrealistic. As the two myths are examined, one can breathe deeply and can assign numbers to evaluate the distress associated with each myth. Typically, a new myth will emerge that combines the best parts of the old myth and the challenging myth, and this new myth will yield a low number on the distress scale when its implications are understood.

5. The final stage is a careful formulation of the new myth. For example, it might state, "I am capable of having close relationships, but I need to move at my own pace so that I experience success rather than failure in this endeavor." Once again, imagination is called upon as the veteran or civilian plans a step-by-step procedure to bring the new myth into his or her life. An energetic dance can serve as a ritual to anchor the new myth, and an affirmation can prompt specific behaviors that will ensure positive change. In the language of positive psychology, one has moved from learned helplessness to learned optimism. In the language of humanistic-existential psychology, one has undergone an existential shift that has the promise of providing greater meaning in one's life. And from the cognitive-behavioral perspective, the veteran or civilian has begun to think differently so that one can act differently.

We have used the term "myth" throughout this book from a psychological point of view. We prefer it to such terms as "script" or "belief" because they omit the emotional tone that is implicit in "myth." A myth is not only given lip service, it is felt in the gut. EP procedures are extremely controversial, and our inclusion of them does not imply our endorsement. However, they are brief, they are cost- and time-effective, they are easily learned, and, if they demonstrate their effectiveness, they could provide relief for many veterans and civilians for whom conventional psychotherapy, for one reason or another, is not an option.

TERROR IN THE NIGHT

Throughout this book, we have described a continuum or spectrum of disorders resulting from war. Clinical PTSD is the most severe, but there are subclinical cases that have escaped a formal PTSD diagnosis. In addition, there are many people who manifest symptoms of PTSD but with no clearly identifiable trauma as the precipitating cause. A common denominator across this spectrum is the frequent occurrence of frightening dreams or nightmares. Sigmund Freud could not fit nightmares into his notion that dreams represented unfulfilled wishes; eventually he decided that they represented a "repetition-compulsion," a tendency to repeat what had been experienced. The Gestalt psychologists thought of nightmares as unsuccessful attempts to complete a "Gestalt" or wholeness in their lives. Other theorists have looked upon nightmares as desires for punishment, childhood fears that resurface during sleep, or simply as a side effect of indigestion. Some otherwise well-informed psychotherapists confuse nightmares with night terrors, abrupt awakenings in the middle of the night, often accompanied by violent body movements and screams for help. However, these disorders of arousal are fairly common among children and represent glitches in the brain's sleep and dream mechanisms (Galvin & Hartmann, 1990, pp. 233–235).

Night terrors often include episodes of sleepwalking. But frightening dreams usually occur in what is called "rapid eye movement sleep," that stage of sleep marked by eye movements as well as immobility of the large muscles. As a result, sleepwalking, erratic bodily movements, and long episodes of talking almost never occur during nightmares. The nightmare is usually detailed and vivid, lifelike and filled with sensations—sights, sounds, and pain, the latter being rare in typical nighttime dreams. A veteran of the Korean War told us about his recurring nightmare:

> I was back in Korea. Bombs were going off and were exploding all around me. My buddies were screaming. One of them died right in front of my eyes. I was hit in my arm. I could feel the blood running down to my fingers. And the pain was dreadful.

Nightmares of combat veterans and civilians with experience in war zones are similar. They contain few of the symbols and metaphors that characterize other dreams. But some people with PTSD have night terrors as well and only recall the pain and terror that accompanied the experience. In addition, there are occasional bursts of imagery just before a person falls asleep and just as they are awakening. For most people, these are pleasant and even fantastic in nature. For the PTSD victim, these twilight episodes can be as terrifying as the nightmares that occur later in the night. One common feeling that permeates all of these nighttime experiences is a feeling of helplessness; one is in danger and lacks any sense of power or control.

A team of mental health professionals interviewed citizens of Kuwait, four years after the Gulf War. One out of four Kuwaitis were still suffering from PTSD; children were still experiencing a variety of behavior problems, and both adults and children reported frequent nightmares. One woman related a recurring nightmare to the team:

> We are at home and the Iraqis come to our house. They break the windows and storm in, searching everywhere and demand to know where [my brother] is. My two little children are crying. One soldier is pointing a gun at each of our heads one by one, saying he will shoot us if we do not tell where he is hiding [but] we do not know. The soldier pulls the trigger and shoots my son, then my daughter. I wake up screaming.

In waking life, the Iraqis did come to the woman's house and held guns to everyone's head while they asked about her brother. They never shot anyone and eventually left. This nightmare represents fears of a situation that night have occurred but did not actually happen; hence, nightmares are typically realistic but they do not always mirror actual events (Barrett & Behbehani, 2003, p. 138). However, they may "hijack" ordinary dreams; a pleasant dream can be disrupted and overshadowed by the nightmare. At other times, the nightmare may interweave multiple events into the same narrative, including traumatic experiences that occurred several years apart (Peters, 1990).

INTERVENTION FOR NIGHTMARE SUFFERERS

Many repetitive post-traumatic dreams arouse suspicions that they are predictive of an event that might occur again, increasing the survivor's anxiety. A mental health worker needs to respect the survivor's belief system while assuring her or him that such nightmares are common after a life-threatening experience and that they rarely, if ever, predict future events.

Once the survivor understands the nature of her or his nightmares, a number of interventions are possible. Some can be used in combination with other issues, such as "survivor guilt," the feeling of self-reproach that one did not deserve to have lived while so many neighbors or companions died. The interplay of survivor guilt with a nightmare not only disrupts sleep but may exacerbate other PTSD-related problems that can impair daytime functioning (Coalson, 2006). A skilled clinician can help reframe the nightmare so that it can be used to explore and resolve guilt and other conflicts. Grant, a Vietnam War veteran, reported this dream:

> I'm lying in an open casket. I'm wearing my dress military uniform with medals on my chest. I'm aware that I am alive but not moving. A young Vietnamese boy walks slowly past the casket looking at me. I wake up disoriented and fearful.

Grant acknowledged how this nightmare triggered intrusive memories of a war experience for which he felt extreme guilt. He revealed that a small Vietnamese boy had approached his position during fierce city fighting. Grant had been separated from his unit and thought he was surrounded by the enemy. Alone, and afraid that the boy would report his hidden position to the nearby North Vietnamese soldiers, Grant shot the boy. Soon after this ordeal, Grant began to have this nightmare.

Grant's therapist helped him to reframe the nightmare, looking at it as an invitation to seek new understanding and insights for unresolved conflicts, as an affirmation of inner strength and stability needed to face a difficult personal issue in civilian life, and as an honest attempt to express an unresolved issue. These strategies helped Grant develop new perspectives about the nightmare. Instead of seeing his presence in the casket as punishment, he identified the wounded warrior part of himself as "stuck in a casket of guilt" from which he could now extract himself. The Vietnamese boy was now seen as an opening to "release his hold on the boy's spirit." Grant later went to his church and, during confession with a priest, sought forgiveness for his actions. Dreamwork and its follow-up resolved the guilt and the occurrence of the nightmare (Taylor, 1992, p. 135).

Halliday (1987) has developed a variety of practical techniques for nightmare relief including cathartic techniques, alterations of the story line, desensitization procedures, and "fear and conquer" approaches. In the latter instance, the dreamer is encouraged to confront his or her tormentors and vanquish them. Sometimes, "lucid dreaming" can be learned and the dreamer can become aware while the dream is going on (Galvin & Hartmann, 1990). Lucid dreaming is not easily attained, but someone can simply "redream" the dream upon awakening, and fight the oppressor in his or her imagination.

Stanley Krippner has used several of these approaches with nightmare sufferers, many of them trauma survivors.

1. Upon awakening from a nightmare, and while the emotional feeling is still present, redream the most terrifying part of the dream and make face-to-face contact with the oppressor. Ask, "What are you doing in my dream?" If the answer is, "I am here to punish you," reply, "I have had all the punishment I can take, and I don't want you in my dream anymore." Imagine that you have access to a weapon that will kill or maim the oppressor and strike the foe with all of your force. But if the answer is, "I am in your dream to teach you something," ask what the lesson is to be, being wary that this may be a clever ploy rather than a compassionate offer of help. If the dream character is sincere, listen carefully to the advice and carry out an activity in waking life that manifests it.

2. Spend some time drawing or painting a scene from the nightmare. You do not have to have artistic talent to carry out this activity, but making an exterior

representation of an internal experience often brings some control and understanding to the nightmare. The field of expressive arts therapy has developed many treatment procedures for PTSD; working with nightmares in this manner illustrates the effectiveness of expressing images from one's dreams or imagination.

3. Write a narrative about the nightmare, and then act it out playing all the parts. Not only will this desensitize you to the nightmare, but you might discover that some of the dream characters resemble yourself and some of your character traits. Hence, the nightmare may reflect not only the traumatic experience but some childhood experiences that predisposed you to PTSD.

4. Use self-suggestion before falling asleep. Tell yourself, "Tonight I will have a restful sleep. If I have a nightmare, I will use a story-line alteration or a face and conquer procedure to reduce the negative effect of the nightmare." It may take more than one night for self-suggestion to be effective, so do not give up if the results are not immediate.

5. Place a "dreamcatcher" above your bed. These artistic productions are part of Native American lore and are created to protect children (and sometimes adults) against frightening dreams. They are available in craft stores, or you can make your own. They often take the form of spider webs and are thought to "catch" intrusive spirits who trigger the nightmares. Even if you do not share this particular belief system, there is an expectancy effect involved in obtaining a dreamcatcher and ritually placing it in a strategic location. I have a number of dreamcatchers from various parts of North America that I use myself or give to nightmare sufferers. If nothing else, they add a decorative note to one's bedroom and, like each of the other procedures I recommend, turn the nightmare sufferer from a victim to a person capable of self-management.

6. Finally, give your nightmare a title. Keep a journal or a computer file of nightmares. This is another attempt to externalize the nightmare, and to exert a modicum of control over it. As time goes on, the title might need to be changed. What was "Punishment for My Sins" might become "Forgiving Myself and Others."

GROUP WORK FOR NIGHTMARE SUFFERERS

Some PTSD survivors work well in a group setting. Coalson (2006) has done considerable work with groups of clients suffering from PTSD finding that this arrangement has many advantages over one-on-one psychotherapy. A group can serve as a "safe haven" where clients feel comfortable revealing frightening nightmares, share hidden dilemmas, and experience emotional reactions in a supportive environment. It is necessary to establish parameters for how a dream will be discussed and interpreted. Coalson has found that the most prudent method is to allow clients to be the interpreters of their own dreams. Other group members may offer feedback but in a prescribed manner. Group members, when talking about someone else's nightmare, are encouraged to preface remarks with words to the effect that "if this were my dream, this is what it would mean" (Taylor, 1992). In this way, challenging and confrontational statement can be made in such a way that they may be accepted or rejected by a client. Such an approach often helps clients feel safer, less defensive, and more willing to share their nightmares with others.

Feedback and observations from others can increase understanding of dream images, amplify the nightmare's message, and assist with identification related clinical issues. For combat veterans and civilian survivors, recounting the nightmare may open up a host of related issues that the individual had been reluctant to share with anyone. Coalson (2006) has developed a procedure that involves three successive levels of intervention, allowing for integration of different approaches. First, there is the initial discussion, one designed to describe the nightmare and better understand it as well as related issues. Second, specific interventions are introduced, such as the face and conquer approach. These provide a further reduction of nightmare distress. Finally, follow-up therapy engages and resolves identified cynical issues that have emerged during the presentation of the nightmare. In one instance described by Coalson, the story-line alteration technique was utilized:

> Karl, a Vietnam combat veteran, survived two helicopter crashes while serving as a door gunner. More than 20 years later those experiences continued to haunt Karl in a fearful recurring nightmare about helplessly falling.
>
> Karl attempted to fly rather than to fall, and it he did fall he tried to land in some interesting, beautiful location. This intervention was combined with sandplay, guided visualization, and hypnotically facilitated psychotherapy. During a two-year follow-up, the dream had not returned.

Another group member, Bernard, who had served in Vietnam, told the group how he had made an effective story-line alteration to treat a recurring nightmare:

> I'm walking through a hallway. In the hallway are three red doors. I open them in succession. Behind each door are different images reminding me of a war zone trauma. I open the third door and suddenly awaken, feeling horrified.

Bernard changed one detail. He changed the color of the first door from red to blue, his favorite color, one which reminded him of peace and tranquility. His nightmare continued to recur, but with reduced intensity, and without the distressing images behind the doors. The first door retained its blue color, and eventually the nightmare discontinued altogether.

Recurrent nightmares are a common symptom of PTSD among both combat veterans and civilian survivors. Many dream researchers suspect that neurological networks weave dream images through emotional connections (Hartmann, 1999). In much the same way, a nightmare might connect the dreamer to other issues in his or her life, issues that can be explored in either an individual or a group session.

PSYCHOTHERAPEUTIC POSSIBILITIES OF VIRTUAL REALITY

Dreams have often been compared to the technology known as virtual reality, a procedure that outfits individuals with goggles and headphones, placing them into a setting far different from the office or laboratory where they are actually located. The U.S. Office of Naval Research and the University of Southern California have joined forces to develop a treatment procedure for PTSD, one that shows great promise for combat veterans as well as for civilian survivors.

The veteran being treated wears goggles over his or her eyes and dons headphones. Using scenes from Iraq or Afghanistan, the veteran seems to be placed in the sights and sounds of battle. But a therapist can activate or remove the sounds of gunshots or the sight of smoke, depending on the client's reaction. The guiding concept is to reintroduce the clients to the experiences that triggered their trauma gradually, until the memory no longer incapacitates them. This is similar to exposure therapy, desensitization, flooding, and a variety of other behavioral techniques that have the client repeatedly relive the frightening experience under controlled conditions to help her or him work through the trauma. But virtual reality therapy is high-tech and resembles a video game. Indeed, many veterans played video games before joining the armed services, and this type of therapy is uniquely suited to them. The "gaming" aspect of the treatment helps to lessen the stigma associated with seeing a psychotherapist.

The suitability of virtual reality therapy may be assessed by the measures that clinicians often use to assess PTSD. The first is a trauma exposure measure. It lists a number of different traumatic events that the client may have experienced, such as combat, accidents, or sexual abuse. Some clinicians go a step further and ask when these events occurred, and others try to assess the degree of exposure. Questions might include the time of the experience and whether the client felt his or her life was in danger. The other type of measure typically asks the client to identify symptoms that might be connected to the traumatic experience. Our continuum includes subclinical cases of PTSD as well as PTSD symptoms that do not seem to be associated with a specific trauma. These measures are useful to differentiate these types of problems and to plan a therapeutic program accordingly.

If virtual reality therapy is reminiscent of a science fiction scenario, the twenty-first century may yield even more remarkable treatments for PTSD. Pharmacologists are developing drugs that might eliminate traumatic events from one's memories. Optimally, these drugs would be administered immediately after the combat trauma, preventing the event from being incorporated into the combatant's long-term memory (Goldman, 2007; Restak, 2003, p. 145). This treatment might also be effective if administered while the veteran is recalling or imagining the incident. Memories are vulnerable; they can be strengthened or weakened by careful targeting during psychotherapy. As a result, these drugs, if perfected, could reconsolidate memories in a more favorable manner. Brain scans could indicate whether the traumatized veteran's amygdala is switched on or off. The next step would be to treat nightmares and flashbacks chemically, erasing or altering certain memory molecules.

Some observers might claim that this type of treatment is too impersonal. However, it would take place within a psychotherapeutic context with highly trained practitioners. In a world where seven out of ten students in northern Baghdad suffer from trauma (Palmer, 2007) and half the children in both Israel and Palestine have frequent nightmares, daring procedures and bold healers are urgently needed.

Falluja Corpse

I will lie here,
buried below Falluja
for a long time.
Being dead,
I am in no hurry.
You can collect those other corpses,
rebuild the city above me
and proclaim victory.

I watched with amusement
as they used a grappling hook
to drag Ali away
because they were afraid
he was booby-trapped.
They don't know the real meaning
of that word.
They don't know how much explosive
I have packed inside me.

I am a patient man
with a long memory
and nothing else to do.
Even from this awkward position
I will conceive many children
who will honor their father.

—Tom Greening

11

Remembrance

Like other holidays of remembrance, Veterans Day is yet another spiritually bankrupt day off for most people. To veterans though, it can be the catalyst for a dramatic return to traumatic events. Douglas, one of our interviewees, recalls his service in the European theatre vividly, especially on Veterans Day. He went through several intense campaigns and battles, losing comrades and seeing others permanently disabled. However, he told us that he has never manifested any symptoms of what is now referred to as PTSD. Furthermore, he does not know many of his combat buddies who did, even though they served in some of the same menacing theatres. The two he recalled having recurrent nightmares had liberated prisoners from concentration camps, which lends strong support to clinical data indicating that PTSD can result from witnessing abuse perpetrated on others, or observing the effects of abuse.

As we have noted, there is a saturation of books detailing first-person accounts of war, and all of them with unique tenor and objectives. For some the writing is the therapy, and others have no difficulty returning to their memories of war. However, some World War II veterans were not as fortunate; Danny told a journalist that it took him 55 years before he could talk about his combat experiences even in passing. Despite his military decorations and his combat record, he never married or had children. He sighed and said, "I missed a lot of life because I could never adjust."

There is the well-known case of Ira Hayes, one of the six men who raised the U.S. flag on Mount Suribachi on Iwo Jima in 1945, an iconic event captured by Joe Rosenthal's famous photo, and portrayed in the 2006 film,

Flags of Our Fathers. Hayes was hailed as a hero, but began drinking when he returned to Arizona, paying his bills with a series of menial jobs. He was arrested for drunkenness some 50 times and died at the age of 32; his body was found face down in a pool of water. A neighbor recalls:

> Back then, people didn't look at alcoholism the way they do now, and the post-traumatic stress treatments didn't exist. You have to wonder what his life would have been like if he had the help that's available today. (Smith, 2006)

Hayes's comrade-in-arms, John Bradley, also survived the war but was assailed by nightmares and once expressed his wish that "there had never been a flag on top of that pole" (Schickel, 2006, p. 102).

For those who came of age in the 1960s, Veterans Day represents the tremendous price an entire generation paid in lives lost and the social unrest stemming from the Vietnam War. More recently, Veterans Day, for many, centers on the Middle East and the United States' involvement in Iraq and Afghanistan. Even so, civilians prefer to pay their respects at an emotional distance. They prefer "the fog of war" because this "fogginess" keeps them from the lucid acknowledgement of the dead and mutilated soldiers and civilians it leaves in its wake.

For the combat veterans of any war, Veterans Day is a different experience. It is a day to remember young friends whose lives were drastically abbreviated. For those with PTSD, their nightmares can be contaminated with the faces of dead comrades. Is it any wonder that many of them withdraw into themselves, hide their medals, and refuse to talk about the war? Corliss (2006) has commented that their war experiences have made them, in their way, "the living dead."

Support groups, such as the Vietnam Veterans Against the War, and films, such as *Born on the Fourth of July* (1989), assisted many in bringing these "living dead" back to life; the real-life protagonist of the film, Ron Kovic, was there and knew what he was talking about. So did members of Vietnamese Veterans Against the War who contacted the eminent psychiatrist Robert Jay Lifton (1979) who helped them open up storefront treatment centers for "rap sessions," a model for the VA community treatment centers created in 1979. Noah, a Gulf War veteran, remembers his treatment at one of these VA facilities fondly:

> I have been a VA mental health patient since 1997 with great results. The VA has helped me immensely....For example, last night I was having my usual nightmares but at the end I was healing the same people that I wounded. I was going enemy by enemy, not letting them die. I took care of them. I started [to give them] intravenous fluids, pressure dressings, shipped them to the nearest combat hospitals. I woke up confused but not sad. I had a smile on my face.

Noah also enrolled in a Family Constellation Therapy group, one that emphasized role-playing and group processes. His progress may have been the result of both types of support.

For Paulson, Veterans Day recalls the combat operations in which he participated with other Marines at An Hoa Combat Base in South Vietnam. A great deal of blood was spilled in these areas, but, also, emotional bonds were forged between combat brothers, bonds that were so strong that they could not be imitated.

Just who are the veterans this day celebrates? They certainly are not "natural-born killers" or "crazy losers." Rather they are human beings who had plans, wishes, values, and aspirations. For the most part, they were, and are, young and filled with ideals, fired by aspirations, and fueled by the dream of contributing something meaningful. For many of them, that meaning centered on protecting their families, friends, and nation from attack, as well as protecting weaker, besieged cultures from their stronger oppressors. Yet, in their exuberance they are incredibly vulnerable. The people who serve our military are at the whim of the politicians and government officials who send them into harm's way, not always with adequate preparation or good intentions, but only the thin aegis of patriotism.

There are older veterans, too. Many in the reserves are old enough to have abandoned the illusions of youth. They are not out to right the world, but to supplement their income. Little did they know that they would compose a majority of the armed ranks in Operation Iraqi Freedom. They ventured into harm's way, although they may not have agreed with the war. They went because it was their duty.

Certainly, there are those who conspire to attack America, and there is a real need for a strong military. However, in combat, many men and women give their lives, and the survivors pay their own price. After facing the onslaught of bullets, mortars, and rockets, killing others at close enough range, and delighting in the payback for dead friends, the world of these combat veterans will be forever different. They can repress and ignore what they have seen, but many who were searching for an adventure after high school or college will anguish in a hell devoid of meaning or purpose, hamstrung by their own memories.

Unlike people of their generation who never went to combat, no veteran can deny the reality of death. It becomes the lynchpin of reality. They realize that feeling secure in life is a fantasy. So, why plan for anything long term? Life can be taken away in an instant, just as the lives of their friends were taken. Flashbacks of their dead friends come and go. One moment a friend was smiling and joking around; the next moment, he was lying prone on the ground in a sticky pool of blood, eyes open, staring straight ahead out of a grey, sunken face, waiting to be transported to Grave Registration. This was someone's great joy—a son, a daughter, a husband, or a wife. They were as real as anyone, as significant to someone as you are to your loved ones. But they are no more. Vera received this letter from her fiancée, Paul, when he was serving in Vietnam:

> There sure has been a lot going on here. Both Bravo and Charlie Company were almost completely wiped out two weeks ago, and we were next, but didn't go to operation. Just a few days after one of our new guys set off a booby trap—a 250 pound bomb—it killed five, and wounded four. It was the worst thing I've ever seen. When it went off I looked up and saw arms and legs flying in the air, and one landed right next to me.

In war death becomes a megalithic presence, no longer somewhere in the future, but now. It is greeting a sunrise and wondering if you will be alive to see the sunset. And, if you do survive to see it set, then you ask if you will be alive to see tomorrow's sunrise. This is the life of those who were in combat, and it is the life of those in combat now. Rather than resembling hardened killers, they seem, for the most part, more like homesick kids.

Many men and women have served. It is our shared and solemn duty to make sure that, for those who serve and wager their lives, we ensure the legitimacy of our wars, and take responsibility for their repercussions. The reasons for going to war must be openly presented, embraced, and viewed as just, as noble, and in America's self-interest. And, finally, we cannot rely on the poor, the marginal, and the confused to fight our wars. All of us—politicians, farmers, businesspeople, bankers, doctors, and carpet cleaners—must share equally in the burden of actual combat or support those who do. We would support a program of national service similar to those found in several other countries of the world. This service need not be in the military; there are several governmental (e.g., the Peace Corps) and nongovernmental agencies (e.g., volunteer services for veterans and other marginalized people) that need help. The United States is in a critical phase of its history, and its survival is the responsibility of every citizen. It is either all or none.

Throughout this book, we have recorded the contributions and comments of female veterans, beginning with Krippner's cousin Marcia Lou Gates, who served as an army nurse in the Second World War. Women now fill 15 percent of U.S. military ranks, and there are regularly mandated workshops on preventing sexual harassment and assault. Each batallion contains a person trained to respond to complaints. In the Vietnam Conflict there were 7,500 female soldiers and in the Gulf War, 41,000, generally in combat support roles that were often in harm's way. By 2007, some 160,000 female soldiers were serving in Iraq; many of them have been killed, maimed, or diagnosed with PTSD.

In a controversial article for the March 18, 2007, *New York Times Magazine,* Sarah Corbett claimed that rape and attempted rape exceeded combat trauma as the cause of PTSD. Corbett quoted Abbie, a member of the Wisconsin Army National Guard, as saying, "You're one of three things in the military—a bitch, a whore, or a dyke. As a female, you get classified pretty quickly." As a result, women have the extra burden of having to defy stereotypes, especially those marking them as too fragile for military duty. Another stressor, for many women, is concern over children left at home.

These stresses produce complaints such as "my brain is not working," "nothing is ever clear," and "why can't I remember things?"

Corbett's report was criticized because it was based on a handful of female soldiers. Nonetheless, it identified two of the VA PTSD programs as treating women exclusively, generally with prolonged exposure therapy. Sexual molestation in childhood was identified by Corbett as a predisposing factor for PTSD, and female reservists were especially at risk because they had not imagined they would face combat in Iraq. It is clear that considerable research is needed if female soldiers, reservists, and National Guards are to be adequately served if they develop PTSD. Presently, the lack of useful information regarding female veterans reflects an overall gender gap in the PTSD literature (Kimerling, Ouimette, & Wolfe, 2002).

Let's Try Everything

Back then
I was a young and sheltered American,
but I remember the newsreels:
Refugees on broken roads
trod east, or was it west?
How many of them
got to a safe place?
The nuclear menace
is not like a Stuka—
It doesn't bomb and strafe
and then disappear
into an April cloud.
No baby carriages
are overturned,
no car radiators
are riddled with holes,
no one is dying
in a muddy ditch.
Since Hiroshima
roads are wider,
cars are faster,
but our modern freeways
become more crowded,
like our minds.
We refugees
escape neither east nor west
and April clouds do not hide
what we know.

I'm told that
despair alone
does not empower.
Before the radioactive dust
stuffs us up,
let's try singing
a loud, inspirational song
with quavering voices.
Let's try acting,
if it hasn't been too long,
as if we had choices.
Let's try
everything.

—Tom Greening

12

Gold Along the Path

Most of this book's previous chapters concerned veterans who have already returned, and the positive meanings or lessons many of them derived from their experiences. This chapter consists of suggestions to those who are stuck in the labyrinth, and provides a possible map for the maze. Traumatic brain injury is the most common physical trauma suffered by U.S. troops in Iraq. Veterans in one study who believed it was appropriate to hold in their emotions, be self-reliant, and dominate women had less favorable views toward seeking psychological help. But men who focused on their careers, success, power, and competition showed greater improvement one year after hospitalization. The "inner narrative" (what we would call "personal mythology") appeared to be the key to recovery (Good et al., 1996).

Our first suggestion deals with guilt, for veterans who think their characters are flawed because they were afraid during combat, or because they did not see as much combat as they thought was necessary to justify wrecking their lives, or because they felt that they enjoyed the killing too much. This is the tyranny of holding personal myths about the way "things should be." These myths are dysfunctional and destroy the life direction of too many veterans. What should or should not have happened needs to be replaced with "what did happen" and "what is happening now." If the veteran with PTSD cannot walk down a street alone, no belief in what should have happened will change her or his situation. Ultimately, the moral valence of their actions is not tied to these judgments, nor is the success of their lives. But a veteran, no matter how painful the endeavor, must own her or his role in healing. To be honest with oneself—that one is stuck in a living inferno—is necessary. And the suffering afflicts the weak and the strong alike.

In Paulson's case, when he returned from Vietnam he tried to keep the pain and rage inside by drinking. In his words:

> I felt that since I was a Marine, I *should not* have any pain. I forgot that I was a human being beneath the "Marine cloak" and could not destroy my fundamental nature. Being human, with feelings, I was allowed to hurt without having to justify my pain. This was hard because my combat veteran friends, as well as my family, advised me "not to think about it," "just be strong," or "don't let it bother you." Yet I thought about my pain every minute of my waking day. I tried to be strong, but I felt so vulnerably weak, and it *did* bother me. Their advice was offered in love and out of their despair over my condition, but it did not work. I became increasingly alienated from myself. I split myself into essentially two beings—what I *should* be versus what I felt I *was*. It was not until I hit the bottom and felt like taking my life that I admitted to myself the agony in which I was living.

Nate used similar terms to describe his PTSD symptoms, saying, "I feel sometimes like I have lost the ability to be myself" (Jaffe, 2005).

This brings us to the second point. Once the veteran admits that he or she is in an agonizing situation, it is time to seek psychotherapeutic help. There are many counselors and therapists, but only a few who will have the necessary "therapeutic fit" for each veteran. Rarely will the first therapist a veteran sees have the proper tools or demeanor suiting that person. Therapeutic fit refers to the reciprocal relationship in which there exists mutual caring, positive regard for one another, common respect, and basic trust. The therapist might be a qualified and credentialed psychiatrist, psychologist, social worker, marriage and family counselor, vocational counselor, pastoral counselor, or "life coach"; but the "fit" is more important than the title on her or his office door (Armstrong, Best, & Domenici, 2006).

Kevin, an Army mortar man, described the process:

> When I started having anxiety attacks, I was referred to a psychiatrist by the emergency room physician. I told the psychiatrist that I was in deep conflict over the Vietnam thing. He was not so concerned with that, but concentrated on my symptoms. He gave me a prescription for tranquillizers, anti-depressants, and sleeping pills.
>
> Everything was pretty good for a week or two, but I could tell the valium was not working so well any more. So the psychiatrist upped the dosage. Each time he increased the dosage, I would be alright for another couple of weeks, but then I would start to feel anxious again. I found that I could dull some of the edge of the anxiety by taking a couple of drinks of whiskey. This cycle went on for one whole year. I was heavily dependent on tranquilizers and alcohol, and I re-focused from Vietnam to just keeping my tension down.
>
> Finally, I went to another psychiatrist in a large city, to see if he could help me more. The same cycle was reinstituted. Then I joined a transactional analysis group. The men and women in the group, I could feel, cared about me. I was

not just a "thing." The leader of the group asked me many questions about a how I felt. I could not believe it! Things were so different. I quit the group because it moved too fast for me, but I did check out a clinical psychologist, and for some reason, I stayed with him for a few sessions. I did not like the guy at first, but after a couple of sessions, I began to trust him. He did not push me faster than I wanted to go, yet he would not let me continue with my bullshit without confronting me. We worked through the Vietnam thing together and even parts of my early childhood, which had kicked off much of my trouble. My advice to others is to stay in the consumer mode. Do not trust a therapist about whom you just have a bad feeling. About three months is the limit I would see someone without seeing positive results. Then go to someone else until you find one that can help you.

Veterans will generally know when they have met a therapist with whom they can have that therapeutic fit. The process is very similar to getting to know people. With some people, one can spend only a little time, revealing very little, prevaricating to avoid being corrected or belittled. With others, one can reveal all and still feel accepted. The latter is the state for which the Vietnam veteran is wise to search. Until he or she finds it, few therapeutic advantages are available.

The third piece of advice to veterans undertaking therapy is not to expect a miraculous recovery. As a veteran describes and relives the situation that caused his or her pain, a great deal of conflict will arise. This grief is not more in a series of needless agonizing nuisances, it is an inevitable trial required to surmount the impasses in one's life.

Paulson recalls:

When I first started to reveal to my therapist what I had done in Vietnam and how guilty I felt, I thought for sure that he, too, would abandon me. I could visually see him clutching his throat and gasping in horror as he fell from his chair over the disgusting, disgraceful things I had done in Vietnam. When I did tell him and felt he would kick me out of his office, he merely said, "Thank God that is out in the open now." He did not reject me.

Over the next several months, however, I felt the agonizing torture and pain of having to relive some of my experiences. It was pure hell—pure hell during the sessions and pure hell after the sessions. It was pure hell second after second, minute after minute, hour after hour, day after day, until I had worked through it. Then most of the pain vanished, just like that.

Knowing that pain is to come does not make it easier. It must be experienced in all of its breadth and depth.

The fourth suggestion is that one can better live out the ordeal with a support system. Combat veterans need to recognize that during the course of therapy they will experience a great deal of tension and anxiety. There will be times when they will feel off-base, not know where to turn, and be confused about themselves. This is part of the route, and the reason a support system is critical. A social group offers veterans firm ground to support their efforts to find themselves. They can then explore what is necessary for their particular therapeutic situation without fear of rejection. This awareness has an incredibly stabilizing effect on the veteran. Juan, the Army infantry officer, describes his experience this way:

> When I came back from Vietnam, everything was different. I did not know who I was, what I was, or where I should be going in my life. I was off balance. But since I was perceived as a tough combat veteran, I felt that if I told anyone how off balance I felt, I would somehow be a very weak person. So, at first, I played the role of a tough infantry officer. But I become more and more cynical, more unhappy, and more confused. I wanted to drop the whole stage performance and tell everyone, including myself, how scared and miserable I was. But where could I go? There were no support systems that I knew of at the time. So I found another answer, that of drinking. I began to live my life with a little on-going "buzz." It blunted the sharp sting of life's cruel horror. But soon I found myself drinking more and more. Within two years, I was a drunk. I was hospitalized in an alcohol treatment program and during that time, something marvelous occurred. Several representatives from Alcoholics Anonymous (AA) visited me. I decided to join AA and, to my surprise I found a very supportive group of people who had "been there." They had hit the bottom in their lives and now were working their way back. They gave me the strength to deal with Vietnam just by being accepting. I could question my motives, my life, anything, and they did not judge me. After I had this support base, I used it to launch my life. I quit drinking. I learned a lot about the benefits of a support group from that experience.

The fifth point is for veterans to be patient and nurturing with themselves and their therapeutic task. Recovering from an emotional disorder is a bumpy road. One day it will seem as though the conflict evaporated, and the next day might be crippling. Peaks and troughs, though frustrating and painful, are intrinsic to the therapeutic process. It is important to remember that it is not an ordeal of useless suffering. Paulson continues:

> I can remember my own experience of the road to recovery. I would go out on picnics and outings but find myself very uneasy. I would imagine that the North Vietnamese were behind the pine trees, stalking me. I would imagine that lightning storms were incoming rocket and mortar attacks and that exploding firecrackers were rifle shots aimed at me. I felt this way even when I was in my biofeedback desensitization program and knew that the enemy was not stalking me, lighting was not a rocket attack, and firecrackers' bangs were not gunfire. I still strongly felt as if I was under attack. This was very confusing for me. One part of me knew that nothing was wrong, but the other screamed "Under attack!" I would have periods when I could enjoy life without the fear of being killed, but they were always followed by a panic or anxiety period when I was not sure whether I was really in danger. Finally, as I let the panic attacks just happen and began to nurture and support myself, they began to die down and almost completely diminished.

The sixth and final point is to acknowledge and accept that giving up the pain of combat is not easy. Combat veterans live their distress for so long that it becomes an integral part of them. As they get better, however, they will need to give it up. It is a difficult process, for as terrible as the pain is, it is familiar, and losing it may feel like a kind of amputation. Thus, the transition itself is often anxiety-producing. As veterans learn to give up the pain and accept the fact that they really can have a productive and happy life, the resistance to healing subsides.

Often people who have not been emotionally wounded wonder why it is so difficult to give up the pain and suffering of a traumatic disorder. Because veterans have experienced so much pain in their lives, they grow accustomed to it and often think that life itself is inevitably painful. They do not relate to people or lifestyles of self-fulfillment and self-actualization because their personal mythology sees the world as one of total danger. Most of their day is concerned with maneuvers to protect themselves from peril and annihilation. In their world sincerity is a trap or a ruse, one that prevents the development of real relationships. And while this constructed reality is distorted, it is their reality.

As veterans gradually learn to give up their defenses they usually feel vulnerable and tend to reerect their defensive posture to the world. Gradually, though, as time goes on, they let go of their protective strategies until at last they choose to pursue their health, respecting their honest desires, wishes, and aspirations, instead of fortifying themselves. Personal mythologies replete with suspicion, distrust, and guardedness gradually give way to personal mythologies that emphasize positive thinking, optimism, authenticity, and trust.

These changes, however, are usually the result of a very slow process and need to be respected as such. As veterans learn to take small risks over time, they build their self-confidence and feel more comfortable asserting themselves. The study of 15,000 Civil War veterans resonates with what we have described in this book; observing battlefield death, being wounded, and undergoing captivity all placed combat veterans at risk for "nervous disease." The younger soldiers were especially vulnerable (some were listed as nine years of age). We now know that the regions of the brain that support motor and sensory functions mature earlier than do higher-order association areas, such as the prefrontal cortex. Immature nervous systems were especially vulnerable to PTSD, and they still are. The more things change, the more they stay the same (Putnam, 2006).

So what do we see as the major themes in this book? We have provided vignettes from interviews with combat veterans from half a dozen U.S. wars, police actions, and operations, combat veterans who fall somewhere on the PTSD spectrum, most of them at the extreme end with diagnosed cases of post-traumatic stress disorder. We have included sections on civilians with PTSD because the nature of war has changed; the number of dead and injured noncombatants now far exceeds those who fight the world's wars. We have provided the standard definitions of PTSD and have noted that it is not a perfect construct. We have described our continuum of related disorders, stressing the variability and the importance of individual and cultural differences in diagnosis and treatment. We have placed considerable emphasis upon existential and spiritual aspects of PTSD, even suggesting that "post-traumatic soul disorder" might be an apt descriptor. We have urged that the focus for female soldiers move from one of weakness and vulnerability to one of strength and accomplishment. Finally, we have attempted to describe post-traumatic strengths; gold can be found among the dross if one knows how to mine it.

In 1990, the celebrated author Barbara Ehrenreich gave a presentation on war and warriors to a group of sociologists, and, although supportive and interested, they reminded her that war had run its course. The Cold War had ended, and they informed Ehrenreich that war was a subject of only historical interest. Later that same year, the United States was at war in Kuwait and Iraq, and a little more than a decade later, in Afghanistan and again in Iraq. In the intervening decade, several ethnic, political, and religious wars were initiated, with no end in sight. Ehrenreich's (1997) subsequent book, *Blood Rites,* is one of the most insightful analyses on the passions involved in warfare and why habitual conflict will be difficult for the human species to terminate. Acts of war typically are designed to evoke "shock and awe"; massive destruction constitutes a demonstration of collective virility.

The premature conviction that war is obsolete has a venerable history of its own. The introduction of the gun, and later artillery, seemed to promise levels of destruction so immense that no state would want to risk them. After the bloodletting of the Napoleonic Wars, Auguste Comte and John Stuart Mill predicted that war would phase out as nations turned to industrial production. World War I was "the war to end all wars." World War II introduced atomic weapons and similar optimistic slogans. Since then, there have been nearly 200 wars of various shapes and sizes, taking the lives of more than 200 million combatants and civilians (Ehrenreich, 1997, pp. 225–266).

At the same time, however, organized human resistance to war has been on the rise. The practices and passions of war have been the province of the warrior elite, and popular opposition to war largely has taken the form of opposition to this elite group. Ehrenreich commented, "It is a giant step from hating the warriors to hating the war, and an even greater step to deciding that the 'enemy' is the abstract institution of war" (p. 240).

An outstanding 1972 documentary film, *Winter Soldier,* which included first-person accounts of Vietnam veterans' guilt and trauma, could not find a distributor for 33 years (Atkinson, 2005). However, in 2005, the Public Broadcasting Service aired a film titled, *A Soldier's Heart.* One segment of it included an interview with a Marine sergeant who opened fire on an Iraqi civilian as she was reaching into her handbag for a white flag, while approaching the sergeant's checkpoint. When he realized his mistake, he broke into tears, crying over her dead body. Thereafter, he was unable to carry out his duties. Such are the consequences of modern warfare. And such is the nature of the enemy against which the fighters for peace will mobilize if war trauma, at last, is to take its place with the plagues of the past, rather than remain a malignant malady of the present.

In its modest way, we hope that this book has provided enough data in the form of research, case studies, and first person accounts to demonstrate the traumatic effects of war upon those who survive it. PTSD and related conditions exact an atrocious human toll. PTSD can be diagnosed, although imperfectly because it represents a continuum of clinical, subclinical, and related cases. PTSD can be treated, although many of those who most need help refuse to request it, and others who want help simply cannot find it. Most importantly, PTSD (and the wars that trigger much of it) can be prevented. The fate of the world depends upon how sincerely and how energetically humankind devotes itself to this task.

A Poem for All Nations

On a slowly collapsing balcony he sits
Begging for the noise of whirlwinds
To cover his tears.
Five thousand years of war
Nothing new
His family this time
What's left of it.
A call from the embassy finally comes
Still missing
They do not care
He does not expect them to.
Slumping back to some tea
He sees in a cloud a face like his mother's
When she was young
And then a lady too still
Beneath the cedars below
Her hair somehow untouched and soft
And the left side of her face.
In the silence of the courtyard
A child still unaffected smiles.
He waves to her through burning eyes
And descends to rock the ghostless shell.

—D. Michael Schmidt

References

Achterberg, J. (2003). Afterword. In S. Krippner & T.M. McIntyre (Eds.), *The psychological impact of war trauma on civilians: An international perspective* (pp. 1–14). Westport, CT: Praeger.

Adam, D. (2005, February 16). U.S. soldiers to receive ecstasy to fight combat trauma. *The Guardian*, p. 7.

American Psychiatric Association. (2000). *Diagnostic and statistical manual of mental disorders* (text revision). Washington, DC: American Psychiatric Association.

Angyal, A. (1965). *Neurosis and treatment.* New York: John Wiley.

Applegate, R. (1976). *Kill or get killed* (Rev. ed.). Boulder, CO: Paladin Press.

Armstrong, K., Best, S., & Domenici, P. (2006). *Courage after fire: Coping strategies for troops returning from Iraq and Afghanistan and their families.* Berkeley, CA: Ulysses Press.

Assagioli, R. (1965). *Psychosynthesis: A manual of techniques.* New York: Hobbs, Dorman.

Atkinson, M. (2005, October 24). When we were psychos. *In These Times,* p. 35.

Aurobindo. (1997). *The complete works of Sri Aurobindo. Essays on the Gita* (Vol. 19). Pondicherry, India: Sri Aurobindo Ashram Press.

Babbin, J. (2004, October 25–31). Making a difference: Troops say Iraq not easy but worth it. *Washington Times,* pp. 13–15.

Baldwin, S.A., Daniel, C., Williams, D.C., & Houts, C.H. (2004, Summer). The creation, expansion, and embodiment of posttraumatic stress disorder: A case study in historical critical psychopathology. *The Scientific Review of Mental Health Practice, 3*(1).

Bandura, A. (1997). *Self-efficacy: The exercise of control.* New York: W.H. Freeman.

Barabasz, A., & Watkins, J.G. (2005). *Hypnotherapeutic techniques 2E.* New York: Brunner & Routledge.

Barath, A. (2003). Cultural art therapy in the treatment of war trauma in children and youth: Projects in the former Yugoslavia. In S. Krippner & T.M. McIntyre (Eds.), *The psychological impact of war trauma on civilians: An international perspective* (pp. 155–170). Westport, CT: Praeger.

Barrett, D., & Behbehani, J. (2003). Post-traumatic nightmares in Kuwait following the Iraqi invasion. In S. Krippner & T.M. McIntyre (Eds.), *The psychological impact of war trauma on civilians: An international perspective* (pp. 135–141). Westport, CT: Praeger.

Bartholomew, R.E., & Radford, B. (2007, January/February). Mass hysteria at Starpoint High. *Skeptical Inquirer*, pp. 55–58.

Baum, D. (2004, July 12). The price of valor. *The New Yorker*, pp. 44–52.

Beaumont, P. (2004, January 25). Stress epidemic strikes American forces in Iraq. *Guardian Unlimited*. Retrieved April 12, 2006, from http://observer.guardian.co.uk/international/story/0,6903,1130771.00.html.01/26/2004

Beck, A.T., & Emery, G. (1985). *Anxiety disorder and phobias: A cognitive perspective*. New York: Basic Books.

Beck, A.T., Rush, A.J., Shaw, B.F., & Emery, G. (1979). *Cognitive therapy of depression*. New York: Guilford.

Blacker, M., & Fairweather, A. (2006, November 10). Forgotten—except on Veteran's Day. *San Francisco Chronicle*, p. B11.

Blanck, G., & Blanck, R. (1974). *Ego psychology: Theory and practice*. New York: Columbia.

Blanck, G., & Blanck, R. (1986). *Ego psychology II: Psychoanalytic developmental psychology*. New York: Columbia.

Bolton, P. (2003). Assessing depression among survivors of the Rwanda genocide. In S. Krippner & T.M. McIntyre (Eds.), *The psychological impact of war trauma on civilians: An international perspective* (pp. 67–77). Westport, CT: Praeger.

Boorstein, S. (1997). *Clinical studies in transpersonal psychotherapy*. Albany: State University of New York Press.

Boot, M. (2006, December). From Saigon to Desert Storm: How the U.S. military reinvented itself after Vietnam. *American Heritage*, pp. 28–37.

Borkovec, T.D., Alcaine, O., & Behar, E. (2004). Avoidance theory of worry and generalized anxiety disorder. In R.G. Heimberg, C.L. Turk, & D.S. Mennin (Eds.), *Generalized anxiety disorder: Advances in research and practice* (pp. 77–108). New York: Guilford Press.

Boss, M. (1979). *Existential foundations of medicine and psychology* (S. Conway & A. Cleaves, Trans.). Northvale, NJ: Aaronson.

Brown, C.R., Rose, S., & Andrews, B. (2002). A brief screening instrument for posttraumatic stress disorder. *British Journal of Psychiatry, 181,* 158–162.

Brown, D., & Fromm, E. (1987). *Hypnosis and behavioral medicine*. Hillside, NJ: Erlbaum.

Brown, M. (1993). *Growing whole*. New York: Harper-Collins.

Brown, P. (1994). Toward a psychobiological model of dissociation and posttraumatic stress disorder. In S.J. Lynn & J. Rhue (Eds.), *Dissociation: Clinical and theoretical perspectives* (pp. 94–122). New York: Guilford.

Bryant, R.A., & Guthrie, R.M. (2005). Maladaptive appraisals as a risk factor for posttraumatic stress. *Psychological Science, 16,* 749–752.

Buber, M. (1958). *I and thou.* New York: Scribner.

Buber, M. (1984). *The dialogical principle.* Heidelberg, Germany: Verlag Lumbert Schneider.

Bugental, J.F.T. (1987). *The art of the psychotherapist.* New York: W.W. Norton.

Bupp, N. (2006, October/November). A talk with Mihaly Csikszentmihalyi—the father of "flow." *Free Inquiry,* pp. 39–40.

Burstow, B. (2005). A critique of posttraumatic stress disorder and the *DSM. Journal of Humanistic Psychology, 45,* 429–445.

Buss, D.M. (2004). *Evolutionary psychology: The new science of mind* (2nd ed.). New York: Pearson.

Bustos, E. (1990). Dealing with the unbearable. In P. Suedfeld (Ed.), *Psychology and torture* (pp. 143–163). New York: Hemisphere.

Cain, D.J. (2001). Defining characteristics, history, and evolution of humanistic psychotherapies. In D.J. Cain (Ed.), *Humanistic psychotherapies: Handbook of research and practice* (pp. 3–54). Washington, DC: American Psychological Association.

Caldwell, A.B. (2001). What do the MMPI scales fundamentally measure? Some hypotheses. *Journal of Personality Assessment, 76,* 1–17.

Campbell, J. (1968). *The hero with a thousand faces* (2nd ed.). Princeton, NJ: Princeton University Press.

Campbell, J. (1971). *The portable lung.* New York: Viking.

Campbell, J. (1972). *Myths to live by.* New York: Viking.

Cancelmo, J., Millan, F., & Vazquez, C.I. (1990). Culture and symptomology: The role of personal meaning in diagnosing and treatment. *American Journal of Psychoanalysis, 50*(2), 137–149.

Carbonell, J. (2004). Active ingredient study: Preliminary findings. In V.R. Volkman (Ed.), *Beyond therapy: Conversations on traumatic incident reduction* (pp. 111–120). Ann Arbor, MI: Loving Healing Press.

Cardozo, B.L., Bilukha, O.O., Crawford, G.A.G., Shaikh, I., Wolfe, M.I., Gerber, M.L., & Anderson, M. (2004). Mental health, social functioning, and disability in postwar Afghanistan. *Journal of the American Medical Association, 292,* 575–584.

Carey, L. (Ed.). (2006). *Expressive and creative arts methods for trauma survivors.* Philadelphia: Jessica Kingsley.

Carr, C. (2002). *The lessons of terror: A history of warfare against civilians, why it has always failed and why it will fail again.* New York: Random House.

Carson, R.C., Butcher, N.J., & Mineka, S. (2000). *Abnormal psychology and modern life.* Boston: Allyn and Bacon.

Chandrakirti. (2002). *Introduction to the Middle Way* (J. Khyenshe, Trans.). Boston: Shambhala.

Chaudhuri, H. (1965). *Integral yoga.* London: George Allen & Unwin.

Chirot, D., & Seligman, M.E.P. (Eds.). (2001). *Ethnopolitical warfare: Causes, consequences, and possible solutions.* Washington, DC: American Psychological Association.

Clarke, K.M. (1996). Change processes in a creation of meaning event. *Journal of Consulting and Clinical Psychology, 64,* 465–470.

Clason, G.S. (1955). *Richest man in Babylon* (reprint). New York: Hawthorne.

Clayton, C. J., Barlow, S.H., & Ballif-Spanvill, B. (1998). Principles of group violence with focus on terrorism. In H.V. Hall & L.C. Whitaker (Eds.), *Collective violence* (pp. 277–311). Boca Raton, FL: CRC Press.

Coalson, B. (2006). *Nightmares: Treatment of survivors with PTSD.* Unpublished paper, Saybrook Graduate School and Research Center, San Francisco.

Commons, M.L., Richard, F.A., & Armon, C. (1984). *Beyond formal operations.* Westport, CT: Praeger.

Conner, K.M., Davidson, J., & Lee, L. (2003). Spirituality, resilience, and anger in survivors of violent trauma: A community survey. *Journal of Traumatic Studies, 16*(5), 487–494.

Cook, B. (2005, November 21). Lasting damage. *In These Times,* p. 12.

Corey, G. (2004). *Theory and practice of counseling and psychotherapy* (7th ed.). Boston: Wadsworth.

Corliss, R. (2006, October 23). On duty, honor, and celebrity. *TIME,* p. 82.

Cortright, B. (1997). *Psychotherapy and spirit.* Albany: State University of New York Press.

Cozolino, L. (2002). *The neuroscience of psychotherapy.* New York: W.W. Norton.

Curtis, A.J. (2000). *Health psychology.* Oxford, UK: Routledge.

Dahl, C.I. (1989). Some problems of cross-cultural psychotherapy with refugees seeking treatment. *American Journal of Psychoanalysis, 49* (1), 19–32.

Daly, R.J., & Sand, E.A. (1987). *Psychological treatment of mental disease.* New York: Springer.

Daniels, V., & Horowitz, L.I. (1976). *Being and caring.* San Francisco: San Francisco Books.

Davis, R., & Zoroya, G. (May 8, 2007). Study suggests link between child abuse, troop deployment. *USA Today,* p. 4A.

Dawkins, R. (1982). *The extended phenotype.* Oxford, UK: W.H. Freeman.

Decker, L.R. (2007). Combat trauma: Treatment from a mystical/spiritual perspective. *Journal of Humanistic Psychology, 47,* 30–53.

DeJong, J.T.V.M., Komproe, I.H., & van Ommeren, M. (2003). Common mental disorders in postconflict settings. *Lancet, 361,* 2126–2130.

DeMeo, J. (1998). *Saharasia.* Ashland, OR: Natural Energy Works.

Donnelly, S.B. (2006, December 11). Iraq: The war without honors. *TIME,* p. 52.

Dorsey, D. (2005). *EMDR and the neurobiology and treatment of trauma.* Retrieved January 1, 2005, from Santa Barbara Graduate Institute's Preventing and Healing Stress Related Depression, Anxiety and Childhood Behavior Web site: http://www.traumaresources.org/article_dorsey1.htm

Drummet, A.R., Coleman, M., & Cable, S. (2003). Military families under stress: Implications for family life education. *Family Relations 52,* 279–287.

Earle-Warfel, E. (2005). *The application of chaos theory to the development of a dynamical perspective of posttraumatic stress disorder.* Unpublished paper, Saybrook Graduate School and Research Center, San Francisco.

Ehrenreich, B. (1997). *Blood rites: Origins and history of the passions of war.* New York: Henry Holt.

Eisenberg, D. (2005, February 28). From AWOL to exile. *TIME,* pp. 36–37.

Eisenberger, N.I., Lieberman, M.D., & Williams, K.D. (2003). Does rejection hurt? An fMRI study of social exclusion. *Science, 302,* 290–292.

Elliot, R., & Greenberg, L.S. (2001). Process-experiential psychotherapy. In D.J. Cain (Ed.), *Humanistic psychotherapies: Handbook of research and practice* (pp. 279–306). Washington, DC: American Psychological Association.

Ellis, A. (2001). *Overcoming destructive beliefs, feelings, and behaviors.* Amherst, NY: Prometheus Books.

Ellis, A., & Grieger, R. (1977). *Handbook of rational-emotive therapy.* New York: Springer.

Feinstein, D. (2007, in press). Energy psychology: Method, theory evidence. *Journal of Clinical Psychology.*

Feinstein, D., Craig, G., & Eden, D. (2005). *The promise of EP.* New York: Jeremy P. Tarcher/Penguin.

Feinstein, D., & Krippner, S. (1988). *Personal mythology.* Los Angeles: Tarcher.

Feinstein, D., & Krippner, S. (2006). *The mythic path.* Santa Rosa, CA: Elite Books.

Felmingham, K.L., Kemp, A.H., Williams, L.M., Das, P., Hughes, G., Peduto, A., & Bryant, R.A. (Forthcoming). Anterior cingulate and amygdala changes after cognitive behaviour therapy in PTSD. *Psychological Science.*

Ferguson, R.B. (2000). The causes and origins of primitive warfare. *Anthropological Quarterly, 73,* 159–164.

Fingarette, H. (1963). *The self in transformation.* New York: Basic.

Firman, J. (1996). *Self and self-realization.* Palo Alto, CA: Psychosynthesis.

Flick, N.C. (2005). *One bullet away: The making of a marine officer.* New York: Houghton-Mifflin.

Foa, E.B., Keane, T.M., & Friedman, M.J. (Eds.). (2000). *Effective treatments for PTSD.* New York: Guilford Press.

Frankl, V. (1956). *Man's search for meaning: An introduction to logotherapy.* Boston: Beacon Press.

Frederick, C., & McNeal, S. (1998). *Inner strengths: Contemporary psychotherapy and hypnosis for ego-strengthening.*

Freeman, S. (2005, May). Heirs of war. *AARP Bulletin,* pp. 21–23.

Freud, S. (1933). *New introductory lectures on psychoanalysis* (W.J.H. Sprott, Trans.). New York: W.W. Norton.

Friedman, M.J. (1994). Posttraumatic stress disorder. In R.J. Corsini (Ed.), *Encyclopedia of psychology: Vol. 3* (2nd ed., pp. 102–104). New York: John Wiley & Sons.

Frosch, D. (2004, December 15). A soldier's heart. *San Francisco Bay Guardian,* pp. 16–20.

Fullerton, C.S., & Ursano, R.J. (Eds.). (1997). *Posttraumatic stress disorder: Acute and long-term responses to trauma and disaster.* Washington, DC: American Psychiatric Press.

Galvin, F., & Hartmann, E. (1990). Nightmares: Terrors of the night. In S. Krippner (Ed.), *Dreamtime and dreamwork: Decoding the language of the night* (pp. 233–243). Los Angeles: Jeremy P. Tarcher.

Gerbode, F.A. (2004). Critical issues in trauma resolution. In V.R. Volkman (Ed.), *Beyond therapy: Conversations on traumatic incident reduction* (pp. 1–14). Ann Arbor, MI: Loving Healing Press.

Gergen, K.J. (1985). The social constructionist movement in modern psychology. *American Psychologist, 40,* 266–275.

Germer, C.K., Siegel, R.D., & Fulton, P.R. (Eds.). (2005). *Mindfulness and psychotherapy.* New York: Guilford Press.

Gettelman, E. (2007, January/February). Garry Trudeau: War on the funny pages. *Mother Jones,* pp. 74–75.

Gilligan, C. (1982). *In a different voice.* Cambridge, MA: Harvard University Press.

Giorgi, A., Barton, A., & Maes, C. (Eds.). (1983). *Duquesne studies in phenomenological psychology: Vol. IV.* Pittsburgh, PA: Duquesne University Press.

Gist, R., & Devilly, G.J. (2002). Post-trauma debriefing: The road too frequently traveled. *Lancet, 360,* 741–742.

Glasser, R.J. (2005, July). A war of disabilities. *Harper's Magazine,* pp. 59–62.

Goldman, R. (2007, April 6). Erasing the pain of the past. ABC News. Retrieved from http://abcnews.go.com/Health/story?id=2964509&page=1

Goldstein, J.S. (2001). *War and gender.* Cambridge, UK: Cambridge University Press.

Goleman, D. (1995). *Emotional intelligences.* New York: Bantam.

Good, G., Schopp, L.H., Thomson, D., Hathaway, S., Sanford-Martens, T., Mazurek, M., & Mintz, L.M. (1996). Masculine roles and rehabilitation outcomes among men recovering from serious injuries. *Psychology of Men and Masculinity, 7,* 165–176.

Goodman, D. (2004, November/December). Breaking ranks. *Mother Jones,* pp. 48–55.

Gottfried, J.L. (2004). *The mild traumatic brain injury workbook: Your program for regaining cognitive functioning and overcoming emotional pain.* Oakland, CA: New Harbinger.

Greenberg, J.R., & Mitchell, S.A. (1983). *Object relations in psychoanalysis theory.* Cambridge, MA: Harvard University Press.

Greening, T. (1997). Posttraumatic stress disorder: An existential-humanistic perspective. In S. Krippner & S. Powers (Eds.), *Broken images, broken selves: Dissociative narratives in clinical practice* (pp. 125–135). Washington, DC: Brunner/Mazel.

Greer, M. (2005, April). A new kind of war. *Monitor on Psychology,* pp. 38–40.

Grof, S. (1975). *LSD Psychotherapy.* Albany: State University of New York Press.

Grof, S. (1985). *Beyond the brain.* Albany: State University of New York Press.

Grof, S. (1988). *The adventure of self-discovery.* Albany: State University of New York Press.

Grof, S. (1998). *The cosmic game.* Albany: State University of New York Press.

Guha-Sapir, D., & van Panhuis, W.G. (2003). The importance of conflict-related mortality in civilian populations. *Lancet, 361,* 2126–2128.

Guthmann, E. (2007, January 5). The horror, the horror of Iraq, in poetry. *San Francisco Chronicle,* p. E1, E10.

Halliday, G. (1987). Direct psychological therapies for nightmares: A review. *Clinical Psychology Review, 7,* 501–523.

Hamod, S. (2005, March). *33 things you should know about the Middle East and America.* Retrieved March 6, 2005, from http://www.SmirkingChimp.com

Hampson, R., & Solvig, E. (2006, June 15). Combat stress takes toll. *USA Today,* pp. 1A, 7A.

Hartmann, E. (1999). *Dreams and nightmares: The new theory on the origin and meaning of dreams.* New York: Plenum.

Hayes, C. (2006, September). The good war on terror. *In These Times,* pp. 24–28.

Hayes, S.C., Strosahl, K.D., & Wilson, K.G. (1999). *Acceptance and commitment therapy.* New York: Guildford.

Hedges, C. (2002). *War is a force that gives us meaning.* New York: Random House.

Hefling, K. (2005, December 30). Army seeks to save war-torn marriages. *The San Juan Star,* p. 12.

Heidegger, M. (1962). *Being and time.* New York: Harper & Row.

Herman, J. (1997). *Trauma and recovery.* New York: Basic Books.

Hill, N. (1937). *Think and grow rich.* San Diego, CA: Aventine Press.

Hiro, D. (2007, January 1). The way forward. *Washington Spectator,* pp. 1–3.

Hoge, C.W., Auchterlonie, M.S., & Milliken, M.D. (2006). Mental health problems, use of mental health services, and attrition from military service after returning from deployment to Iraq or Afghanistan. *Journal of the American Medical Association, 295,* 1023–1032.

Hoge, C.W., Castro, C.A., Messer, S.C., & McGurk, D. (2004). Combat duty in Iraq and Afghanistan, mental health problems, and barriers to care. *New England Journal of Medicine, 351,* 13–22.

Hoge, C.W., Lesikar, S.E., Guevara, R., Lange, J., Brundage, J.F., Engle, C.C., Messer, S.C., & Orman, D.T. (2002). Mental disorders among U.S. Military personnel in the 1990s: Association with high levels of health care utilization and early military attrition. *American Journal of Psychiatry, 159,* 1576–1583.

Hook, M. (2005). *Ethics in victim services.* Baltimore: Sidran.

Horowitz, M.J. (1998). *Cognitive psychodynamics.* New York: Wiley.

Houppert, D. (2005. November 15). Little-known benefits for veterans and their families. *Bottomline on the News,* p. 6.

Hudgins, K. (2002). *Experiential treatment for PTSD: The therapeutic spiral model.* New York: Springer.

Hunter, N. (2004). *Understanding dissociative disorders: A guide for family physicians and healthcare professionals.* Williston, VT: Crown House.

Huntington, C.W., & WangChen, G.N. (1989). *The emptiness of emptiness.* Delhi: Motilal Banarsidass.

In search of "new blood": Vets want latest soldiers involved. (2006, November 6). National News, *Washington Times,* p. 19.

In the Capital. (2007, February). *Church & State,* p. 3.

Jaffe, G. (2005, October 10). Trauma takes toll on U.S. battlefield hero. *Wall Street Journal,* p. A8.

James, W. (1972). *The varieties of religious experience.* New York: Collier. (Original work published 1902.)

Janoff-Bulman, R. (1992). *Shattered assumptions: Toward a new psychology of trauma.* New York: Macmillan.

Jong, J.D. (2002). *Trauma, war, and violence.* New York: Plenum.

Kamalipour, Y.R. (1999). *Images of the U.S. around the world.* Albany: State University of New York Press.

Kaufman, W.D. (2006, Summer). Return to Pisa. *World War II Chronicles,* pp. 19–22.

Kegan, R. (1994). *In over our heads.* Cambridge, MA: Harvard University Press.

Kennedy, A. (2004, November, 2004). ACA Foundation releasing revised edition of trauma guidebook. *Counseling Today,* pp. 24, 26, 42.

Kimerling, R., Ouimette, P., & Wolfe, J. (Eds.). (2002). *Gender and PTSD.* New York: Guilford.

Kirk, S., & Kutchins, H. (1997). *Making us crazy: DSM: The psychiatric bible and the creation of mental illness.* New York: The Free Press.

Kleinman, A. (1989, February 26). When you're the one with AIDS, it's a different fight. *Los Angeles Times Book Review,* p. 8.

Knudsen, J.C. (1991). Therapeutic strategies for refugee coping. *Journal of Refugee Studies, 4,* 21–38.

Koole, S.L., Greenberg, J., & Pyszczynski, T. (2006). Introducing science to the psychology of the soul: Experimental existential psychology. *Current Directions in Psychological Science, 15,* 212–216.

Kramer, M. (2007). *The dream experience: A systematic exploration.* New York: Routledge.

Krippner, S. (1972). Marijuana and Vietnam: Twin dilemmas for American youth. In R.S. Parker (Ed.), *The emotional stress of war, violence, and peace* (pp. 176–225). Pittsburgh, PA: Stanwix House.

Krippner, S. (1997a). Dissociation in many times and places. In S. Krippner & S. Powers (Eds.), *Broken images, broken selves: Dissociative narratives in clinical practice* (pp. 3–40). Washington, DC: Brunner/Mazel.

Krippner, S. (1997b). The varieties of dissociative experience. In S. Krippner & S. Powers (Eds.), *Broken images, broken selves: Dissociative narratives in clinical practice* (pp. 336–361). Washington, DC: Brunner/Mazel.

Krippner, S. (2005). Spirituality across cultures, religions, and ethnicities. In R.H. Cox, B. Ervin-Cox, & L. Hoffman (Eds.), *Spirituality & psychological health* (pp. 204–240). Colorado Springs: Colorado School of Professional Psychology Press.

Krippner, S., & Colodzin, B. (1989). Multi-cultural methods of treating Vietnam veterans with posttraumatic stress disorder. *International Journal of Psychosomatics, 36,* 79–85.

Krippner, S., & McIntyre, T.M. (Eds.). (2003). Overview: In the wake of war. In S. Krippner & T.M. McIntyre (Eds.), *The psychological impact of war trauma on civilians: An international perspective* (pp. 1–14). Westport, CT: Praeger.

Krippner, S., & Paulson, D.S. (2006). Post-traumatic stress disorder among U.S. combat veterans. In T.G. Plante (Ed.), *Mental disorders of the new millennium: Vol. 2* (pp. 1–23). Westport, CT: Praeger.

Krippner, S., & Winkler, M. (1996). The "need to believe." In G. Stein (Ed.), *The encyclopedia of the paranormal* (pp. 441–454). Amherst, NY: Prometheus Books.

Lansing, K., Amen, D.G., Hanks, C., & Rudy, L. (2005). High-resolution brain SPECT imaging and eye movement desensitization and reprocessing in police officers with PTSD. *The Journal of Neuropsychiatry and Clinical Neurosciences, 17* (4), 526–532.

LeShan, L. (1992). *The psychology of war.* Chicago: Noble Press.

Levin, A. (2007, May). Combat stress should be considered preventable, manageable. *Psychiatric News, 42,* 2–26. Retrieved from http://pn.psychiatryonline.org/cgi/short/42/9/2?rss=1

Leyva, M. (2003). *Married to the military: A survival guide for military wives, girlfriends, and women in uniform.* New York: Fireside/Simon & Schuster.

Lewis-Fernandez, R., & Kleinman, A. (1995). Culture, personality, and psychopathology. *Journal of Abnormal Psychiatry, 103,* 67–71.

Lifton, R.J. (1979). *The broken connection.* New York: Simon and Schuster.

Livingston, K. (2006, October/November). God, Aristotle, and the new science of happiness. *Free Inquiry,* pp. 32–38.

MacNair, R. (2002). *Perpetration-induced traumatic stress: The psychological consequences of killing.* Westport, CT: Praeger.

Maldonado, J.R., & Spiegel, D. (1994). The treatment of post-traumatic stress disorder. In S.J. Lynn & J. Rhue (Eds.), *Dissociation: Clinical and theoretical perspectives* (pp. 215–241). New York: Guilford Press.

Mandino, O. (1974). *The greatest salesman in the world.* New York: Bantam Books.

Maslow, A.H. (1971). *The farther reaches of human nature.* New York: Viking Press.

Matsakis, A. (2007). *Back from the front.* Baltimore: Sidran Books.

May, R. (1981). *Freedom and destiny.* New York: W.W. Norton.

McIntyre, T.M., & Ventura, M. (2003). Children of war: Psychosocial sequelae of trauma in Angolan adolescents. In S. Krippner & T.M. McIntyre (Eds.), *The psychological impact of war trauma on civilians: An international perspective* (pp. 40–53). Westport, CT: Praeger.

Mendelson, R.M. (1987). *The synthesis of self: Vol. II.* New York: Plenum Press.

Mental Health Advisory Team IV. (2006). *Final report.* Washington, DC: Office of the Surgeon General, United States Army Medical Command.

Metzner, R. (1988). *Opening to inner light.* Los Angeles: Tarcher.

Military comes under fire for neglecting mental health care. (2006, June). News and briefs, *Counseling Today*, p. 3.

Miller, G. (2006). Widening the attack on combat-related mental health problems. *Science, 313,* 908–909.

Miller, M.W., & Keane, T.M. (2004). Posttraumatic stress disorder in adults. In *The concise Corsini encyclopedia of psychology and behavioral science* (pp. 716–719). New York: John Wiley & Sons.

Mol, S.S.L., Arntz, A., Metsemakers, J.F.M., Dinant, G.J., Vilters-Van Montfort, P.A.P., & Knottnerus, J.A. (2005). Symptoms of post-traumatic stress disorder alter non-traumatic events: Evidence from an open population study. *British Journal of Psychiatry, 186,* 494–499.

Moore, B.A., & Reger, G.M. (2006, February/March). Combating stress in Iraq. *Scientific American Mind,* pp. 30–37.

Moss, D. (1999). Biofeedback, mind body medicine, and higher limits of human nature. In D. Moss (Ed.), *Humanistic and transpersonal psychology* (pp. 145–161). Westport, CT: Greenwood.

Munk, M. (2007, January 5). *Purge the surge: It's a trap for the Democrats.* Retrieved January 7, 2007, from http://www.ufppc.org/content/view/5523/

Munsey, C. (2006, April). Soldier support. *Monitor on Psychology,* pp. 36–38.

Murti, T.R.V. (1956). *The central philosophy of Buddhism.* New Delhi: Munshiram Mahoharlal.

Napper, E. (1989). *Dependent arising and emptiness.* Boston: Wisdom.

Nelson, R. (2004). Suicide rates rise among soldiers in Iraq. *Lancet, 363,* 300.

Norcross, J.C., & Goldfried, M.R. (2005). *Handbook of psychotherapy integration* (2nd ed.). New York: Oxford University Press.

Norman, E.M. (1999). *We band of angels: The untold story of American nurses trapped on Bataan by the Japanese.* New York: Random House.

Nutt, D., Davidson, J.R.T., & Zahra, J. (Eds.). (2000). *Post-traumatic stress disorder: Management and treatment.* Malden, MA: Blackwell Science.

Palmer, J. (2007, March 26). Nation under strain: Violence takes severe mental toll on Iraqis. *Washington Times,* p. 19.

Pappas, J.D. (2003). Poisoned dissociative containers: Dissociative defenses in female victims of war rapes. In S. Krippner & T.M. McIntyre (Eds.), *The psychological impact of war trauma on civilians: An international perspective* (pp. 277–283). Westport, CT: Praeger.

Paulson, D.S. (1991). Myth, male initiation, and the Vietnam veteran. *Voices: Journal of the American Academy of Psychotherapy, 27,* 156–165.

Paulson, D.S. (1993, Winter). Authentic integral living: The search for the real self. *Voices,* 58–65.

Paulson, D.S. (1994). *Walking the point: Male initiation and the Vietnam experience.* Plantation, FL: Distinctive.

Paulson, D.S. (1995). The shadow of war. In S. Hansel, A. Steldle, G. Zaczek, & R. Zaczek (Eds.), *Heart: Survivor's views of trauma* (pp. 189–191). Lutherville, MD: Sidran Press.

Paulson, D.S. (1997). Participation in combat perceived as a male rite of passage. In S. Krippner & H. Kalweit (Eds.), *Yearbook of cross cultural medicine and psychotherapy* (pp. 51–65). Berlin: Verlag for Wissenschaft und Bildung.

Paulson, D.S. (1998). An approach to dealing with post-traumatic disorders in Vietnam veterans. *The American Academy of Experts in Traumatic Stress, 27*(1&2), 156–165.

Paulson, D.S. (1999a). Courage to be oneself. *Voices: Journal of the American Academy of Psychotherapists, 35*(3), 56–58.

Paulson, D.S. (1999b). Is where we are going where we want to be? *Journal of Esoteric Psychology, 8*(1), 1–15.

Paulson, D.S. (2001). The hard issues of life. *Pastoral Psychology, 49*(5), 385–394.

Paulson, D.S. (2003a). War and refugee suffering. In S. Krippner & T.M. McIntyre (Eds.), *The psychological effects of war trauma on civilians: An international perspective* (pp. 111–122). Westport, CT: Praeger.

Paulson, D.S. (2003b). *Applied statistical designs for the researcher.* New York: Marcel-Dekker.

Paulson, D.S. (2004). *Walking the point: Male initiation and the Vietnam experience.* (2nd ed.). New York: Paraview Press.

Paulson, D.S. (2006). *Handbook of regression and modeling: Applications for the clinical and pharmaceutical industries.* New York: Taylor & Francis.

Pennbaker, J.W., & Beall, K.S. (1986). Confronting a traumatic event. *Journal of Abnormal Psychology, 95,* 274–281.

Peters, R. (1990). *Living with dreams.* Bergvlei, South Africa: Random Century Group.

Peterson, C., & Seligman, M.E.P. (2004). *Character strengths and virtues.* New York: Oxford University Press.

Peterson, J.V., & Nisenholz, B. (1999). *Orientation to counseling* (4th ed.). Boston: Allyn & Bacon.

Pine, D.S. (2000). Anxiety disorders: Clinical features. In B.J. Saddock, & V.A. Sadock (Eds.), *Comprehensive textbook of psychiatry: Vol. 1* (7th ed.). Philadelphia: Lippincott, Williams, & Wilkins.

Pitman, R.K., Altman, B., Greenwald, E., Longpre, R.E., Macklin, R.L., Poire, R.E., & Steketee, G.S. (1991). Psychiatric complications during flooding therapy for posttraumatic stress disorder. *Journal of Clinical Psychiatry, 43,* 849–858.

Pizarro, J., Silver, R.C., & Prause, J.A. (2006). Physical and mental health costs of traumatic war experiences among Civil War veterans. *Archives of General Psychiatry, 63,* 193–200.

Pole, N., Cumberbatch, E., Taylor, W.M., Metzler, T.J., Marmar, C.R., & Neylan, T.C. (2005). Comparisons between high and low peritraumatic dissociation in cardiovascular and emotional activity while remembering trauma. *Journal of Trauma and Dissociation, 6,* 51–67.

Putnam, R.K. (2006). Combat effects on mental health. *Archives of General Psychiatry, 63,* 127.

Radhakrishnan, S. (1948). *The Bhagavadgītā.* London: George Allen & Unwin.

Rauch, S.L., Shin, L.M., Whalen, P.J., & Pitman, R.K. (1998). Neuroimaging and the neuroanatomy of post-traumatic stress disorder. *CNS Spectrums, 3*(2), 30–41.

Regan, T. (2005, October 18). Returning US soldiers face financial, medical difficulties: Critics say government is "turning its back" on veterans because of need for money in Iraq. *Christian Science Monitor* [Electronic Version]. Retrieved October 19, 2005, from http://www.csmonitor.com/2005/1018/dailyUpdate.html

Reitman, J. (2005, March 10). Surviving Fallujah. *Rolling Stone,* pp. 84–88.

Researchers identify "male warrior effect." (2006, September 8). *Reuters Know Now.* Retrieved September 15, 2006, from www.Reuters.com

Restak, R. (2003). *The new brain: How the modern age is rewiring your mind.* Emmaus, PA: Rodale/St. Martins Press.

Richards, P.S., & Bergin, A.E. (1997). *A spiritual strategy for counseling and psychotherapy.* Washington, DC: American Psychological Association.

Roberts, A.R., & Yeager, K.R. (Eds.). (2004). *Evidence-based practice manual: Research and outcome measures in health and human services.* New York: Oxford University Press.

Roemer, L., & Orsillo, S.M. (2002). Expanding our conceptualization of and treatment for generalized anxiety disorder: Integrating mindfulness/acceptance-based approaches with existing cognitive-behavioral models. *Clinical Psychology: Science and Practice, 9*(1), 54–68.

Rogers, C.R., Gendlin, G.T., Kiesler, D.V., & Truax, C.B. (1967). *The therapeutic relationship and its impact: A study of psychotherapy with schizophrenics.* Madison: University of Wisconsin Press.

Roland, A.L. (2002). *Radical therapy.* Novato, CA: Origin Press.

Roland, A.L. (2006, October 15). *Healing traumatic memories.* Retrieved October 17, 2006, from http://blogs.salon.com/0002256

Roland, A.L. (2007, February 5). *Troops return to painful wait for needed help.* Retrieved February 6, 2007, from http://blogs.salon.com/0002255/2007/02/06.html

Rossi, E.L., & Cheek, D.B. (1988). *Mind/body therapy: Method of ideodynamic healing in hypnosis.* New York: W.W. Norton.

Rothschild, B. (2003). *The body remembers casebook: Unifying methods and models in the treatment of trauma and PTSD.* New York: W.W. Norton.

Rotter, J.C., & Bovega, M.E. (1999). Counseling military families. *Family Journal, 7*(4), 379–382.

Runte, J.W., Bass, D., & Yep, D. (Eds.). (2004). *Terrorism, trauma, and tragedies: A counselor's guide to preparing and responding* (2nd ed.). Washington, DC: American Counseling Association Foundation.

Scaer, R. (2005). *The trauma spectrum: Hidden wounds and human resiliency.* New York: W.W. Norton.

Scarborough, R. (2007, January 1). Death toll of female soldiers is "troubling." *Washington Time,* pp. 1, 25.

Schickel, R. (2006, October 23). Clint's double take. *TIME,* pp. 101–102.

Schneider, K.J., & May, R. (1995). *The psychology of existence.* New York: McGraw-Hill.

Schwartz, S. (2004, November 15). Final letters home. *Schwartz Report,* pp. 1–3.

Seeman, J. (2001). Looking back, looking ahead: A synthesis. In D.J. Cain (Ed.), *Humanistic psychotherapies: Handbook of research and practice* (pp. 617–636). Washington, DC: American Psychological Association.

Seligman, M.E.P. (2002). *Authentic happiness.* New York: Free Press.

Seligman, M.E.P. (2005). Progress in positive psychology: Empirical validation of Interventions. *American Psychologist, 60,* 410–421.

Seligman, M.E.P., & Csikszentmihalyi, M. (2000). Positive psychology: An introduction. *American Psychologist, 55,* 5–14.

Selye, H. (1974). *Stress without distress.* New York: New American Library.

Serlin, I. (2006). Psychological effects of the new media coverage of the Iraq war. In P.R. Kimmel & C.E. Stout (Eds.), *Collateral damage: How the U.S. war on terrorism is harming American mental health* (pp. 145–153). Westport, CT: Praeger.

Serlin, I., & Cannon, J.T. (2004). A humanistic approach to the psychology of trauma. In D. Knafo (Ed.), *Living with terror, working with trauma* (pp. 313–530). New York: Jason Aaronson.

Shapiro, D.H., & Astin, J.A. (1998). *Control therapy: An integrated approach to psychotherapy, health, & healing.* New York: Wiley.

Shapiro, F. (1993). Eye movement desensitization and reprocessing (EMDR) in 1992. *Journal of Traumatic Stress, 6,* 417–421.

Shapiro, J. (2005, June 2). A woman guard member's struggle with PTSD. Retrieved June 12, 2006, from http://www.npr.org/templates/story/story.php?storyId=4676372

Shay, J. (2002). *Odysseus in America: Combat trauma and the trials of coming home.* New York: Scribner.

Sheikh, J.I., & Nguyen, C.T.M.H. (2000). Psychopharmacology: Anxiety drugs. In B.J. Sadock & V.A. Sadock (Eds.), *Comprehensive book of psychiatry* (7th ed., pp. 3084–3096). Philadelphia: Lippincott, Williams & Williams.

Smith, S. (2006, October 31). Film shines light again on shy hero. *Rocky Mountain News,* p. 19A.

Snyder, C.R., & Lopez, S.J. (Eds.). (2002). *Handbook of positive psychology.* New York: Oxford University Press.

Solomon, J.L. (2004). Modes of thought and meaning making: The aftermath of trauma. *Journal of Humanistic Psychology, 44,* 299–319.

Solomon, S., Greenberg, J., & Pyszczynski, T. (2003). Why war? Fear is the mother of violence. In S. Krippner & T.M. McIntyre (Eds.), *The psychological impact of war trauma on civilians: An international perspective* (pp. 299–309). Westport, CT: Praeger.

Sommers, C.H., & Satel, S. (2006). *One nation under therapy: How the helping culture is eroding self-reliance.* New York: St. Martin's Press.

Stein, R. (2006, November 10). Ex-soldier goes home but finds himself back in the game. *San Francisco Chronicle,* p. E5.

Stolorow, R.D., Brandcroft, B.T., & Atwood, G.E. (1987). *Psychoanalytic treatment: An intersubjective approach.* Hillsdale, NJ: Analytic Press.

Sue, D.W., & Sue, D. (1999). *Counseling the culturally different: Theory and practice.* New York: John Wiley & Sons.

Swingle, P.G., Pulos, L., & Swingle, M.K. (2004). Neurophysiological indicators of EFT treatment of post-traumatic stress. *Subtle Energies & Energy Medicine, 15,* 75–86.

Szasz, T. (1991). The uses of naming and the origin of the myth of mental illness. *American Psychologist, 16,* 59–65.

Taylor, C. (1989). *Sources of the self.* Cambridge, MA: Harvard University Press.

Taylor, J. (1992). *Where people fly and water runs uphill.* New York: Warner Books.

Tedeschi, R.G., & Calhoun, L.G. (1995). *Trauma and transformation.* Thousand Oaks, CA: Sage.

Teyber, E. (2000). *Interpersonal process in psychotherapy: A relational approach.* New York: Wadsworth.

The Holy Bible (Revised Standard Version). (1952). New York: Thomas Nelson and Sons.

Tick, E. (2005). *War and the soul: Healing our nation's veterans from post-traumatic stress disorder.* Wheaton, IL: Quest.

Truax, C.B., & Mitchell, K.M. (1971). Research on certain therapist interpersonal skills in relation to process and outcome. In A.E. Bergin & S.L. Garfield (Eds.), *Handbook of psychotherapy and behavior change* (pp. 299–344). New York: John Wiley & Sons.

Tuhus, M. (2007, February). Getting vets their benefits back. *In These Times,* pp. 9–10.

Turner, B. (2005). *Here, bullet.* Farmington, ME: Alice James.

van der Kolk, B.A. (1994). The body keeps the score: Memory and the evolving psychobiology of posttraumatic stress. *Harvard Review of Psychiatry, 1,* 253–265.

van der Veer, G. (1998). *Counseling and therapy with refugees and victims of trauma* (2nd ed.). West Sussex, England: Wiley.

Vaughan, F. (1995). *Shadows of the sacred.* Wheaton, IL: Theosophical Publishing House.

Vaughan, F. (2000). Personal communications. Mill Valley, CA.

Volkman, V.R. (2004). *Beyond trauma: Conversations on traumatic incidence reduction.* Ann Arbor, MI: L.H. Press.

Waller, D. (2006, September 4). How VA hospitals became the best. *TIME,* pp. 36–37.

Walsh, R.A., & McElwain, B. (2001). Existential psychotherapies. In D.J. Cain (Ed.), *Humanistic psychotherapies: Handbook of research and practice* (pp. 253–278). Washington, DC: American Psychological Association.

Wampold, B.E. (2001). *The great psychotherapy debate: Models, methods, findings.* Mahwah, NJ: Erlbaum Associates.

Washburn, M. (1994). *Transpersonal psychology in psychoanalytic perspectives.* Albany: State University of New York Press.

Washburn, M. (1995). *The ego and the dynamic ground.* Albany: State University of New York Press.

Watkins, J.G. (1987). *The practice of clinical hypnosis: Hypnotherapeutic techniques* (Vol. 1). New York: Irvington.

Webel, C. (2005). *Terror, terrorism, and the human condition.* New York: Pallgrave/Macmillan.

West, B. (2005). *No true glory: Frontline account of the battle for Fallujah.* New York: Bantam.

Whitaker, L.C. (2000). *Understanding and preventing violence: The psychology of human destructiveness.* Boca Raton, FL: CRC Press.

Whitmore, D. (1991). *Psychosynthesis counseling in action.* Newbury Park, CA: Sage.

Wiesel, E. (1996). *All rivers run to the sea: Memoirs.* New York: Schocken.

Wilber, K. (1995). *Sex, ecology, spirituality.* Boston: Shambhala.

Willis, R.J. (1994). *Transcendence in relationship: Existentialism and psychotherapy.* Norwood, NJ: Ablex.

Wilson, C. (1985). *A criminal history of mankind.* London: Grafton.

Winerman, L. (2006, October). Taking the pain away. *Monitor on Psychology,* pp. 35–36.

Wisneski, L.A., & Anderson, L. (2005). *The scientific basis of integrative medicine.* Boca Raton, FL: CRC Press.

Wolpe, J. (1982). *Behavioral therapy* (4th ed.). New York: Allyn & Bacon.

World Health Organization. (1993). *The International Classification of Diseases and Related Health Problems.* Geneva, Switzerland: World Health Organization.

Wright, E. (2004). *Generation kill.* New York: G.P. Putnam.

Young, A. (1995). *The harmony of illusions: Inventing post-traumatic stress disorder.* Princeton, NJ: Princeton University Press.

Zoroya, G. (2006a). Troubled troops in no-win flight. *USA Today,* p. 1A.

Zoroya, G. (2006b). Young vets' joblessness falls, but still high. *USA Today,* p. 3A.

Index

About the Authors

DARYL S. PAULSON is a psychologist, a Fellow of the American Academy of Traumatic Stress, and a veteran of the U.S. Marines who served in Vietnam. He has worked extensively with veterans affected by PTSD. Dr. Paulson is President and CEO of BioScience Laboratories, Inc. He has advanced degrees in microbiology, statistics, counseling, and psychology. Dr. Paulson is the author of numerous articles and nine books, among which are *Biostatistics and Microbiology: A Survival Manual* (forthcoming), *Handbook of Regression and Modeling* (2006), *Applied Statistical Designs for the Researcher* (2003), and *Competitive Business, Caring Business: An Integral Perspective for the 21st Century* (2002). He consults for the Department of Defense on Homeland Security issues and, in 2006, was named Statistical Advisor of the Year. He also teaches philosophy and psychology courses in a number of Adult Education programs and online and distance learning programs, such as through the University of Tomorrow.

STANLEY KRIPPNER is Professor of Psychology at Saybrook Graduate School and Research Center. He is the editor of *The Psychological Impact of War Trauma on Civilians* (Praeger, 2003). He is a member of the Advisory or Editorial Boards for several journals including *The American Journal of Clinical Hypnosis, The Anthropology of Consciousness,* and the *Journal of Humanistic Psychology.* His many awards include the American Psychological Association's Award for Distinguished Contributions to the International Advancement of Psychology.